MY THIRTY YEARS AS AN
FBI UNDERCOVER AGENT

GHOST

MICHAEL R. McGOWAN
AND RALPH PEZZULLO

ST. MARTIN'S PRESS ※ NEW YORK

AUTHOR'S NOTE: This is a true story, though some names have been changed, including the true names of law enforcement.

DISCLAIMER: This book contains no classified information. All FBI information contained within is considered unclassified. All FBI cases cited have been fully adjudicated through the judicial court process, are considered a matter of public record, and are available to the general public through court or public record searches.

www.stmartins.com

Library of Congress Cataloging-in-Publication Data

Names: McGowan, Michael (Michael R.), author. | Pezzullo, Ralph, author.
Title: Ghost : my thirty years as an FBI undercover agent / Michael McGowan and Ralph Pezzullo.
Description: First edition. | New York : St. Martin's Press, [2018]
Identifiers: LCCN 2018017178 | ISBN 9781250136657 (hardcover) | ISBN 9781250136664 (ebook)
Subjects: LCSH: McGowan, Michael (Michael R.) | United States. Federal Bureau of Investigation—Officials and employees—Biography. | Undercover operations—United States—History. | LCGFT: Autobiographies.
Classification: LCC HV8144.F43 M39 2018 | DDC 363.25092 [B]—dc23
LC record available at https://lccn.loc.gov/2018017178

Our books may be purchased in bulk for promotional, educational, or business use. Please contact your local bookseller or the Macmillan Corporate and Premium Sales Department at 1-800-221-7945, extension 5442, or by email at MacmillanSpecialMarkets@macmillan.com.

First Edition: October 2018

10 9 8 7 6 5 4 3 2 1

To my incredible wife . . . you are . . . and for . . .
everything . . . thank you . . .

To my challenging but wonderful children . . . rub some
dirt on it. . . . Part II . . . thanks for making me bonkers. . . .

To thousands of past, present, and future FBI street
Agents . . . hope this helps . . . and I hope you laughed a
little bit . . . thank you for allowing me into your special
club . . . it was the highest honor and privilege ever to walk
among you . . . the toughest, smartest, and funniest club in
the world . . . hang tough . . . be safe . . . and Godspeed. . . .

CONTENTS

1

STUNNED

April 10, 1994, started no differently than dozens of days before it. My internal clock roused me before dawn in the bedroom of our modest three-bedroom home in Swedesboro, New Jersey, and my brain immediately started reminding me of the things I had to accomplish that day at work—evidence tapes to review, transcriptions of phone surveillance logs to check. The life of an FBI Special Agent assigned to a Drug Squad was always busy with cases to investigate, paperwork to fill out, and trials to prepare for.

Today wasn't going to be any different. Or so I assumed. What stood out that morning as I lay in bed under the queen-sized comforter next to my beautiful wife, Samantha, was the fact that at this point in my young career as an FBI Agent and father, my life seemed damn near perfect.

Professionally things couldn't have gone better if I'd written the script myself. I had what I considered to be the best job in the world, protecting Americans and our way of life from those who would do us harm. I'd served as an FBI Special Agent for seven years and as a uniformed policeman for several years before that. During my first major undercover operation, my dedicated colleagues and I spent two years penetrating an international drug smuggling operation, which ended on the night of October 15, 1992, when we seized forty-six kilograms of high-grade Pakistani heroin, valued at $180 million. It was the largest heroin seizure ever in Philadelphia history, and still ranks as one of the top ten heroin seizures of all time.

It had been an enormous coup. And the kicker was that we obtained the heroin without paying one cent of U.S. taxpayer money. That's right. We had convinced the bad guys to front us the drugs. In other words, the bad guys expected us to pay them back, which we did in a sense, but not with money—with arrests halfway around the world in Pakistan.

In the blink of an eye, I'd gone from an unproven new FBI Agent to "Golden Boy." High-level management types, who didn't know my name or those of my colleagues before, were now heaping praise and awards on us. A year and a half later as the case moved toward trial, we still couldn't do any wrong.

In terms of my personal life, I'd had the luck and good sense to marry an incredible woman, who was strong, kind, and who shared the same blue-collar values that I had: work hard, take care of your family and loved ones, create a better life and a wider range of opportunities for your children.

When I kissed Sam and slipped out of bed, she sighed as if to say, I love you. Be safe. I had total confidence that while I went to play cops and robbers in the big city of Philadelphia, she would attend to the needs of our three children with boundless energy, spirit, and love.

With the lights off, I padded down the hallway in bare feet to look in on them. First, our two sons, Russell and Michael, ages eight and six. Their small bedroom formed a picture of every-day American life Norman Rockwell might have painted. Beds pressed together and sleeping so that their heads were inches apart, baseball gloves and other sports gear on the floor, a half-finished Lego construction tilting in the corner, shelves crammed with plastic guns, dirty clothes, coloring books, and Ninja Turtle figurines.

Around a corner, I peeked in the little bedroom of our three-year-old bundle of joy, Paige. Her fat cherub cheeks magically taking in and exhaling little breaths of air; a soft black and white blanket tossed haphazardly across her chubby legs. Was it my imagination or did she wink at me when I gave her a quick peck on the cheek and brushed the golden curls away from her eyes?

Silently I moved to our tiny, cold bathroom and slipped on my gym clothes—running gear and Everlast Boxing T-shirt cut at the sleeves to show off my guns. FBI American Eagle backpack in hand, I crept downstairs, collected my car keys, and passed the dark shadows of the wooden rocker in front of the TV, the expensive new couch we would be paying off forever, and the toys on the floor. It might have struck some people as suburban chaos, but I wouldn't have changed a thing.

Outside, still hours before dawn, I noticed in the moonlight that the lawn needed cutting and the front flowerbox with red geraniums had to be rehung, and mentally added them to next weekend's chores, which would have to be worked around baseball practices, karate lessons, other kids' activities, and Sam's weekend job as a bartender. It's the way she had worked her way through college. Now we needed the cash to supplement my modest salary. Nobody got rich working as an FBI Special Agent, nor did I get overtime for the long hours.

I wasn't complaining. Nor did Sam. Life was good. We'd recently purchased our first house on a cul-de-sac in a nice development surrounded by young families like ours—a schoolteacher across the street, a construction worker next door—our kids were happy and healthy, we were both gainfully employed, and my career trajectory was pointing up.

Feeling good, I fired up the fire-red Pontiac Trans Am in the driveway—a recent government seizure from some flashy drug dealer. It wasn't ideal for surveillance, but got me places fast, when needed. I checked to see that my formal FBI duds—business suit and tie—hung from a hanger in back. Then I went through my FBI backpack. Inside were two handguns—a duty-issued 9mm Glock and my Smith & Wesson 6906—handcuffs, and flashlights. In tan manila folders were FD-302s (interview summaries), court orders and applications, rough-draft transcripts of phone calls, and handwritten interview notes, which would be needed in various upcoming criminal trials. My badge and credentials were stuffed in a front pocket for easy access. They afforded me powerful legal and law enforcement powers and significant personal and professional responsibility.

In a separate plastic bag I carried my normal work clothes. Since I was assigned to a Drug Squad they consisted of a comfortable pair of jeans, an oversized Phillies baseball shirt long enough to conceal my firearm in public, and a pair of black running shoes. Working drugs, I needed to dress to blend in on the street with shoes that allowed me to run like hell if chasing a suspect. I also worked SWAT, which explained the long gun locked in the trunk.

At 4:45 AM, traffic was light on 295 heading north. KYW 1060 all-news radio reported that the downtown Coventry Market Deli was closing after fifteen years, and that the Phillies had downed the Reds 2–1 on a Pete Incaviglia homer in the ninth inning.

My head was elsewhere, on the massive amount of prep work I had to complete for the upcoming trial. I mentally organized the order of witnesses, the FBI diagrams needed, and considered the legal tricks and maneuvers defense counsel would likely deploy. Rumor had it that the Pakistani defendants might be pleading guilty. That could make much of what I was planning unnecessary, but I was determined to be prepared nonetheless.

As I crossed the Ben Franklin Bridge from New Jersey to Pennsylvania, a light mist started to fall turning the bricks of Center City dark red. If that was an omen of what was to come, I didn't read it.

A few minutes before 5:15, I turned past the concrete barricades in front of the William J. Green, Jr. Federal Building, and stopped at the entrance to the parking lot. I had to show my FBI credentials to the bored, grumpy security guard, before he pushed the button that raised the security barrier so I could enter the basement and park in my assigned spot.

Up on the sixth floor, I punched my FBI access code into the cipher lock and display and entered the main FBI reception area. There was no one to greet me from behind the desk, nor would there be for another three hours. Official FBI business hours started at 8:15 AM and ended at 5 PM on the dot.

Beyond the inner area, concealed behind bulletproof glass, hung triangulated photos of President Bill Clinton, Attorney General Janet Reno, and FBI Director Louis Freeh. To the right sat a memorial plaque dedicated to Agents killed in the line of duty.

A sober reminder of the dangers we faced, as I passed the main conference room—empty except for fifty precisely lined chairs,

U.S. and Commonwealth of Pennsylvania flags, and a wooden podium. Down the first hallway on my left sat the Organized Crime Squad #1, where old-timers with noses red with burst blood vessels chain-smoked at their desks as they tracked down mobsters whose names ended with vowels. Across from them was the Drug Squad #2, full of hard chargers who competed with my Squad (Drug Squad #3) for drug arrests, stats, and bragging rights. We were a competitive bunch.

On my way to my desk in Drug Squad #3, I passed some early arrivers like Pete Jerome, who bleated the FBI's equivalent of a morning greeting, "Look what the dog dragged in. You look like shit."

"Thanks, Jerome. Same to you."

If you didn't have thick skin, you didn't belong here. "Survival of the fittest" was the modus operandi. Those who couldn't trade rapid-fire insults were obliterated without mercy.

In the southwest corner past a long row of gunmetal filing cabinets stood four rows of five desks. Kind of like a classroom in grammar school, except we referred to this as the bullpen. Mine was the last desk in the last row, farthest away from the supervisor's office. Just the way I liked it. Out of sight, out of mind.

My desk was arranged my way, too—everything in its place, a place for everything. Neat and symptomatically OCD. I slung my backpack over the back of my chair and started checking my desk phone messages. Then I removed my daily handwritten to-do list from my pocket. Today's called for arranging Urdu-speaking language translators for the defendants in the upcoming trial, making sure the witnesses, especially the foreign law enforcement officers who helped us, had plenty of time to travel to the United States.

After roughly twenty minutes prioritizing the day's tasks, my

Squad mates started drifting in. Some looked sleep-deprived, some pissed off, others seemed lost in thought. Ours was a rainbow coalition of black, white, and brown, male and female, young and old, skinny and fat. We got along fine, despite the rough verbal jousting, which usually dealt with premature hair loss, recent weight gain, clothing choices, and choice of spouse or partner.

This morning's started up as usual with senior Agent Will Thompson circling his favorite target, Matt Boggs, who looked like the live embodiment of *MAD* magazine cartoon character Alfred E. Neuman, down to the space between his upper front teeth.

"Hey, Matt, you get a haircut?" Thompson asked.

Boggs obviously had and it was a doozy—a brutal Prince Valiant job sitting atop his larger than normal-sized head.

"Yeah, I got it yesterday," Matt answered, seemingly relieved that it was a simple question.

"You actually pay someone to cut your hair like that?" asked Special Agent Green jumping in.

"Yeah, five bucks," Boggs answered. "What do you think?"

A perfect setup for Thompson, who quickly quipped, "I hope they let you keep the bowl."

Green and Thompson laughed, and Boggs's face turned red.

Now it was Special Agent Tanguay's turn. With his Clark Gable mustache and gigantic belly, he turned to me and grunted, "Hey, Mike. You still planning to run in the marathon?"

"What's it to you, Fat Boy?" I asked without looking up.

"Run or walk?"

"Run, wise guy," I answered.

"Whoever you hire to carry you better have a strong back."

This was Tanguay's lame way of commenting on my un-runner-like physique, which could be best described as stout or stocky—

short of stature with ample upper body strength from lifting weights. Because of my size, I would be competing in the Boston Marathon's Clydesdale Division for males 180 pounds and up.

As part of my training, I rode down the elevator at 6 AM to the small gym and locker room in the basement and changed into my running gear. A half-dozen male Agents in less than sweet-smelling shorts, sweats, and T-shirts, grunted hellos. As a way to encourage us, our employer allotted forty-five minutes (classified as 66E Time) each day during working hours for physical training.

I laced up my gray New Balance 990s and exited the building. As I turned left on Market Street and hit my stride, the sun started to light up the overcast sky. I wasn't a natural or speedy runner, but once I started something I didn't quit. In fact, I'd completed my first marathon, the 26.2-mile Marine Corps Marathon, four years earlier with a respectable time of four hours, twenty-nine minutes.

My goal this morning was a briskly paced five miles along the Delaware River. As I passed the Liberty Bell and Independence Hall, I thought about the primary targets in the heroin case, Mohammed Salim Malik and his nephew, Shahid Hafeez Khawaja. Soon I'd be facing them in court.

I made a quick note to self: *Buy a couple new Brooks Brothers suits so you look sharp.* I thought of them as a reward for making the big case that had taken us to Canada, Europe, and Hong Kong. Second note to self: *Hide the credit card bill when it arrives at home.*

Seagulls barked overhead. To my left and right, I glimpsed the facades of upscale restaurants, brick colonial townhouses, small neighborhood bars, and tugboats moored at the shore.

I'd first laid eyes on heroin kingpin Malik in January 1994

when the Pakistani government put him and his nephew on a plane and they arrived at Philadelphia International Airport in shackles escorted by U.S. Marshals. I stood waiting to slap hand-cuffs on them and read them their Miranda rights, per the FBI custom whereby the Agent who makes the case gets the honor of taking the defendants into custody.

I'd met the much younger Khawaja before—a goofy kid who loved strip joints. We'd spent many hours watching him ogle half-naked women, while I was trying to get him to focus on the details of the deal. He looked shocked and scared when he stepped off the airplane, which was kind of what I had expected. It was his uncle Malik who surprised me.

He was a tiny man with a regal bearing and a gentle, calm manner. Not the fearsome Pakistani drug warrior who sat at number-five on the DEA's most wanted list that I had expected.

But looks were deceiving. As kindly as Malik appeared, the thousands of kilograms of heroin he'd sold around the world weren't agreeable at all—not to countless individuals and fami-lies whose lives it affected. The forty-six kilograms of heroin we had seized from him had been measured at 90 percent purity. If consumed, even by a longtime junkie, it would induce immedi-ate cardiac arrest. Cut three, four, or five times before it reached the street by middlemen and criminals it would inevitably inflict damage on college kids from good families, guys in the military, fathers with promising careers, and, even, mothers pushing baby carriages.

I'd seen the damage heroin could do as a uniformed cop working the streets of Burlington, Vermont. One night, I was sitting in the station house at the end of my shift, when I heard car tires screech at the rear of the station where we gassed up our cars. The occupants of the speeding car pushed someone out, and tore off. I arrived to see a young well-dressed man lying on street, convulsing. When he slipped into unconsciousness, I tried to resuscitate him by using mouth to mouth.

While I was working on the kid, my colleagues called an ambulance. Unfortunately, the young man died on the way to the hospital. I found out later that he was a student attending a nearby college and came from a good family. As a father myself, I couldn't imagine their loss.

After my run, I showered and dressed for street-work with my baby S&W stuck in the back waistband of my jeans.

Upstairs, the Squad area was full and the verbal insults were flying. Seconds later our supervisor, Al Packard—aka "The Colonel"—strode in wearing a starched white shirt, blue-and-red striped tie, and military-style crew cut. He shot us all the evil eye as if to say: Get your asses back to work. We did.

No one fucked with The Colonel. Not only was he a real Lt. Colonel in the Marine Reserves and physically imposing with massive forearms, he was also an excellent boss, who deflected the administrative bullshit so we could do our jobs.

Sony headphones over my ears, I began to attend to the non-glamorous task of painstakingly listening word for word to a criminal conversation, and comparing it to typed transcripts to make sure that the pages were a true and accurate representation of the words captured on tape. It was tedious, dull, and boring, and not the kind of FBI activity depicted in movies or TV shows, but absolutely critical to the success of our upcoming federal criminal prosecution.

After a couple of hours hunched over an outdated tape recorder, I took a break and walked around the office to kibitz with some of my buddies and check the SWAT training schedule to make sure I knew where and when I had to be over the next couple of weeks.

Seeing that it was getting close to lunchtime, I headed up to the Evidence Room Vault, which occupied more than half of the entire eighth floor. Since seized in October 1992, the forty-six kilograms sat among boxes of other FBI evidence including seized drugs, guns, knives, suitcases, computers, backpacks, and phones.

I told the vault support employee on duty that I wanted to review, mark, and prepare the drug evidence for transport to court. She asked me to sign in and write down the case file number.

As I entered the caged vault, I noticed a man in a white shirt and tie standing with another support person. He wasn't someone I recognized from our Division, and had FBIHQ written all over him. Strange, but none of my business.

While I started looking for the Pakistani heroin, two more support people entered the vault, walked over to the stranger without acknowledging me, and whispered something in his ear. Their behavior struck me as odd and alerting. An unpleasant feeling started to spread through my body.

The stranger turned to me and asked in an aggressive manner, "What are you looking for?"

I didn't know him from Adam and he hadn't bothered to introduce himself. So I responded with my usual curt, "Who the fuck are you?"

He replied simply, "You need to go see your SAC"—meaning the Special Agent in Charge, or Big Boss, or top guy in the entire office.

It had the effect of a slap to the face. Staggered and pissed off, I asked myself: *Why is a complete stranger telling me to leave the evidence vault and go see the Big Boss?* Then I noticed that one of the boxes he was examining had my case file number written on it.

What the hell is going on? I asked myself. *Why is he looking at the evidence in my case?*

Alarms sounded in my head. Rather than standing there and arguing, I returned to the Squad area to look for The Colonel, but he wasn't there. My mind racing a thousand miles an hour, I went down to Mahogany Row, where all Executive Management sat, and proceeded directly to the SAC's office, skipping two levels in the chain of command, my supervisor and the ASAC (Assistant Special Agent in Charge).

Our SAC was an outstanding leader who made a point of showing up at your desk on a regular basis and asking you what was going on with your various cases. He made it clear that if you worked hard, you had nothing to fear. On the other hand, if you were lazy, he would make your life miserable.

He and I had an excellent working relationship. So upon entering his office, I started ranting that there was some guy from HQ up in the evidence vault dicking around with my evidence. I reminded the SAC that I had an important trial coming up and didn't need some pencil pusher auditing some bullshit compliance issue when I had more important things to do.

The SAC looked me dead in the eye and said, "Mike, the trial is the least of your worries."

My heart skipped a beat.

"What?" I asked. "What are you talking about?"

He stared at me with steely eyes of a medieval executioner, causing a chill to course through my body. I'd never seen this side of him before.

"Mike," he started, "we have reason to believe that drug evidence is missing from the evidence vault. It's a very serious matter. An internal FBI investigation is underway. I want you to return to your Squad area now. You're not to discuss this matter with anyone including your wife, unless and until directed by me. You understand?"

I could barely get the words out. "Yes, sir."

"Dismissed."

I felt like I was going to either faint or throw up. I had no idea what had happened, but the SAC had made it clear that there was a huge problem and somehow I had ended up in the middle of it.

I literally couldn't think straight. Fragments of thoughts passed through my head and somehow, I don't remember how, I was back in the Squad area. But since I couldn't talk to anyone, I didn't want to be there. So I hurried outside.

All the while I kept telling myself to calm down and try to think straight, but it was impossible. My blood pressure had shot so high it felt like my head was about to explode.

Am I a suspect? I asked myself. *Does the SAC really think that after all the work I did to make the case, I stole the Pakistani heroin?*

To my rational mind that didn't seem possible.

But his words kept repeating in my head: The trial is the least of your worries.

Clearly, he does regard me as a suspect. Why?

Starting to panic, I got in my car and started driving aimlessly around the city. Nothing like this had ever happened to me before, and I didn't know what to do. I couldn't discuss the situation with other Agents, and I didn't want to upset my wife and kids. How could I go home and say, "Hi, honey. You know the case I worked on for two years around the clock? Well, the evidence was stolen, and the FBI thinks I did it?"

In the days that followed, the pressure grew. FBI internal investigators read me my Miranda rights and took my fingerprints. Incredibly, my own employer, the agency I had worked like a dog and risked my life for, was now accusing me of stealing almost $200 million in heroin and cocaine, and reselling it on the street like a common dope dealer.

How was this possible? Not only was my perfect life over, and the reputation I had worked so hard to establish in the toilet. If I couldn't find a way to prove my innocence, there was a strong possibility I'd end up in federal prison hanging with some of the asshole drug dealers I'd put away! I was in the fight of my life.

2

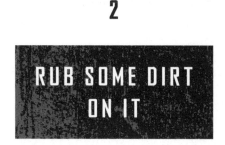

RUB SOME DIRT
ON IT

I grew up in a hardscrabble city in northeastern Massachusetts, the son of an Irish cop. Back in the nineteenth and early twentieth centuries, Haverhill had been a thriving industrial hive of shipbuilding, woolen mills, tanneries, and shoe-making. Crowned the "Queen Slipper City" of the world in the early 1900s, factories on the Merrimack River once produced one-tenth of all shoes sold in the United States.

When I lived there in the sixties, the Merrimack River was a heavily polluted body of rust-colored sludge unsuitable for fishing or swimming. Most of the industrial plants were closed. Haverhill had transformed into a tough-fisted decaying mill town with way too many boarded-up businesses and stores, and a seemingly equal number of neighborhood bars with names like Ray & Arlene's, The Huddle, and The Chit Chat Lounge where troubled and defeated people went to drown their sorrows. Haverhill was, and remains, the definition of blue-collar existence.

Our family lived in a predominantly blue-collar Irish neighborhood with some Greeks and Polish mixed in, surrounded by manual laborers, kitchen workers, firefighters, and cops. There were five kids with me in the middle and a sister and brother on either side. From my limited perspective, it was a normal childhood. We didn't have any extra money, and didn't think much of it, because all of our neighbors seemed to be in the same boat. To supplement Dad's income, Mom worked the midnight shift as a secretary at a local trucking company. We had no silver spoons.

As soon as we kids were old enough to work, we were expected to pitch in. You wanted a little spending money, you pumped gas, mowed lawns, or shoveled snow. My first salaried job was at thirteen when I washed dishes at a nursing home. After that I always had some kind of employment, even when I was in school or playing sports.

These were the days before cable, MTV, and surfing the web, and believe it or not, we survived on three channels of black-and-white. Because Dad was a cop, most of his friends were cops. In fact, police work seemed to run in our blood. My grandfather had been a policeman, and now my son continues the proud tradition that runs four generations strong.

In the early sixties, when I was still a little kid, everyone talked about the feared Boston Strangler who was killing innocent women. According to family lore, as my mother slept during the day I guarded her by sitting by her bed holding a baseball bat. I also patrolled the neighborhood to check that the doors were locked and recorded the numbers of strange license plates on the street.

When Dad arrived home from his shift, all of us in the family knew to avoid him until he removed his gun from its holster, set it on the top shelf in the kitchen cabinet, grabbed a bottle of whiskey from the same shelf and poured and downed two shots, one after the other. The whiskey usually had an immediate calming effect and made him pleasant, but on other occasions sent him down a dark path. We never knew which father would show up.

I didn't realize at first that he was a raging alcoholic. By junior high, I'd often come home and find Dad drunk and sprawled out on the sofa, reeking of stale whiskey. When he drank, he'd get physical, whacking us with his Garrison service belt, and slapping the back of our heads—which we dubbed "the clip." He directed most of his physical abuse at my mother. As a kid, I'd watch helplessly as he hit her. By high school, even though he was still bigger than I was, there were times when I pulled him off her, tears in her eyes and mine.

Mom never called the police, because Dad was the police, and the next day both he and she would act like nothing had happened. As hard as I've tried I still don't understand the demons he carried inside.

One beautiful summer day I was playing on the front stoop with my brothers and sisters when one of my alcoholic uncles came to visit. Dad wasn't home yet and my mother was asleep after working through the night. Soon after Dad returned home, we heard a loud argument erupt inside. Next thing I remember was the sound of shattering glass. I looked up to see my uncle crashing headfirst through the plateglass window and landing face-first at the bottom of the stoop. Bleeding like a cut pig and with glass shards sticking in his hair and skin, my uncle got up and staggered down the street.

We learned later that Dad had discovered him stealing money from our mother's purse. I didn't think a whole lot about it, because violent family incidents took place all the time. As I got older, I stopped inviting friends over and tried to hide this ugly truth.

Naturally, I adopted this method of settling arguments myself. So did other kids I knew. I suspect now that their home environments weren't so different from mine. Fistfights became our way of dealing with disputes about stealing someone's sandwich, an insult, or being the butt of a joke. No knives or weapons, just bare fists and bruised skin and pride.

If I returned home from a fight with a shiner, or bleeding from the nose, Dad's response was always the same, "Rub some dirt on it." That was the mantra he repeated whether you had a bone sticking out or had suffered a tough defeat on the baseball diamond. It was his way of saying: Life is tough, and there's no point bitching about it. Pick yourself up, brush yourself off, and take your best shot.

I remember one time returning home from a beer-induced brawl and my Dad looking at my swollen eye and asking, "Who gave you that?"

"Jimmy McDougal," I answered.

"Jimmy McDougal?" he responded with disgust in his voice. "He's a fucking golfer."

Dad didn't want to hear your problems. Most nights at dinnertime, Mom was asleep and he was working. So we kids made our own meals and did our homework. It was a rare occasion when the whole family sat down together for dinner and discussed the day's events.

Given the environment I grew up in, it seemed perfectly natural for me to take up drinking at an early age. By the time I started high school I was hanging on street corners with my buddies boozing, and handing bums a buck to go to the liquor store for us to buy Pabst Blue Ribbon beer or a pint of Southern Comfort. It didn't take me long to see where I was headed—drowning my troubles in the same bars Dad had when I was fifty years old.

I decided I wasn't going to let that happen, and knew that if I wanted out of Haverhill and out of the destructive cycle, I'd have to do it on my own. Dad made it clear that there would be no money to send us to college, probably because he was spending whatever extra there was on gambling and booze. I figured the only way I could escape was via sports, which I played incessantly at every park, field, and rink in the city.

Baseball became my primary outlet and passion. I discovered I had some physical skills passed on by my father who had been signed to a minor league with the New York Yankees in the late 1940s. I played ball whenever I could—sometimes from sunrise to sunset—and developed into a pretty good hitter. As a senior, I broke my high school's forty-year batting record and, unknowingly, started being noticed by professional scouts.

End of my senior year, a picture appeared in the local Haverhill paper of me being awarded a trophy while standing next to a scout from the New York Mets. Years later, I learned that the Mets had offered me a minor league contract, which my father turned down without ever telling me. He never explained why.

My plan at the end of senior year was to join the Marines under a buddy system that would allow me and a friend to remain together through basic training. My friend suggested that we hitchhike cross-country instead and figure out our futures along the way.

That summer of 1975, while I was debating which route to take, I worked as a playground instructor for neighborhood kids. One afternoon as I was supervising a whiffle ball match, I saw a police cruiser pull up to the park and my father get out. My first thought was that I was in some kind of trouble. Then I noticed he was carrying a letter.

The letter turned out to be from Rollins College in Winter Park, Florida, and it said that they were offering me a scholarship to play baseball. What? I read it a second time. The fact that I had never heard of Rollins College and hadn't applied, led me to believe that the letter was some kind of joke. But my father's serious expression revealed it wasn't.

He said, "This is the opportunity of a lifetime, son, and one you shouldn't pass up."

"Of course," I stammered back, feeling like I'd just been hit by lightning.

That letter came out of the blue and literally changed my life. To my dying day I'll always be grateful to Rollins College for offering me an opportunity to do the thing I loved most—play baseball— and attend college for almost free! All because I was pretty good at hitting a curveball. I felt like the luckiest kid on earth.

I left Haverhill at the end of the summer of 1975 with a steamer trunk packed with my scant belongings including my beloved Rawlings A2000 glove, freshly oiled and placed on top. I'd never been outside of New England and I'd never flown on a plane. I landed three hours later at Orlando International Airport with less than $20 in my pocket and with no idea how to get to the school.

Hours later, a graduate assistant showed up to drive me to Rollins College. As I looked out the window at the swaying palm trees and brilliant sunshine, the landscape was so foreign to me I might as well have been in Russia. After twenty minutes, we arrived at the town of Winter Park and entered an oasis of handsome buildings, trees, and manicured lawns on the banks of Lake Virginia.

"Welcome to Rollins College," the graduate assistant announced.

It was love at first sight.

Rollins, the graduate assistant explained, was a Division II powerhouse baseball school and also a place where wealthy families sent their beautiful daughters. Team upperclassmen arrived to greet me and show me the ropes—where my dorm was situated, when and where to get my meals, where the kegs were, and the best places to meet the beautiful girls.

They treated me like gold, and I quickly learned what it was like to be part of a team that worked toward a common goal—a skill that later became extremely useful in law enforcement. All the players on the team, whether African American, white, or Hispanic were brothers and we all had each other's backs.

During an exhibition game my freshman year, I remember an opposing runner spiking our second baseman, and me and the other twenty-five guys on our team jumping into the fray without considering the consequences.

As a young man away from home for the first time, I cut loose and quickly developed a rep for being a jokester. The order of my priorities became baseball, girls, beer, parties, and finally classes. Teammates nicknamed me "Scoop," not because of my prowess on the baseball field, but because of my ability to woo the ladies.

After practice, a group of us would usually stroll over to the local convenience store where we'd buy six-packs of Busch beer at ninety-nine cents a pop, and spend whatever we had left over on a cheap flavored wine called "Mad Dog" 20/20. One night with an ample amount of Busch and Mad Dog in my system, I wandered into the laundromat next door and challenged my friends to climb into one of the industrial-sized dryers and see how long they could tumble inside before getting sick or banging on the little round glass door and begging us to let them out.

This gave birth to a Rollins phenomenon known as the Industrial Dryer Races, which eventually attracted big crowds and all kinds of insane shenanigans. One brave and foolish friend stayed in the dryer so long, he had a permanent scar seared into his forearm.

On the baseball field, I had trouble locating fly balls in the high Florida sky. I also struggled at the plate, but eventually got on a solid hitting streak that had the coaches talking about promoting me to varsity. Toward the end of exhibition season, I slumped again, and was assigned to the lowly freshman squad.

Instead of working harder, I copped an attitude, acting like I was more interested in girls and staying up late and drinking than baseball. When I started showing up at practice late or hung over, the older guys on the team pulled me aside and told me to clean up my act. Then, I ripped up my ankle pushing off to make a catch.

Beginning of sophomore year I had to return to Massachusetts for major surgery and ending up wearing a cast from my foot to my hip for six months. I spent most of that time sitting on the beach in Florida drinking beer and stuffing beer tabs inside my cast. You should have seen the surprised looks on the faces on the doctors when they removed the cast and dozens of aluminum tabs spilled out.

During the grueling rehab process, I started to realize that my dreams of playing professional baseball weren't likely to come true. Sure, I could hit the hell out of a baseball and had been a phenom in cold New England, but Florida baseball involved a whole different level of competition. Now that I walked with a limp I probably wasn't ever going to become a five-tool player like some guys on our team. One of them named John Castino went on to become a professional baseball player for the Minnesota Twins and was named AL Rookie of the Year in 1979, my senior year.

As I started to consider the alternatives to baseball, I returned to my dorm from practice one afternoon in late October 1977 and received a message to call my brother. He informed me that Dad had suffered a major heart attack and died. It happened six months after his retirement from the Haverhill police force at age fifty-four.

Angrily, I smashed my hand into the wall. I was nineteen years old and suddenly without a father. I had no trust fund to fall back on, or wealthy relatives to help me out. I said to myself: *You're a big boy now. Rub some dirt on it and figure things out.*

Like most people, Dad had his good side and his bad. When he drank, he could be an abusive monster. But when sober, he was fun to be around and fatherly. It was a puzzling contradiction that I vowed I would never put my own family through, if I had one. God rest Dad's troubled soul.

Other cops in town had a code of taking care of their own and rallied around our family. Soon after my father's funeral, I remembered that my college offered a six-week work-study program during winter session for anyone interested in learning a profession. I asked one of the Haverhill cops if there was any way I could do an internship with them.

They graciously arranged a program that allowed me to remain in Haverhill over winter break. And they treated me like family, picking me up from our house at the beginning of their shift and returning me at the end. At first, I had to remain in the backseat when they responded to calls. But eventually they let me out to observe everything they did, and took the time to explain what, why, and how they were responding to particular situations.

Having grown up around cops, and accompanying Dad as he walked his beat starting when I was eight years old, I assumed I knew what cops did. Now a behavioral science major in college, I developed a real appreciation of the psychological complexities and nuances of police work. It wasn't just about knocking heads and keeping people in line. The cops I rode with spent most of their time dealing with the rejects of society—the mentally unstable, drunks, drug addicts, and homeless. And some of the officers I observed were among the most compassionate souls I'd ever met, giving people money out of their pockets and trying to help them out.

Also, I was shocked at the venom directed toward the police when they entered certain neighborhoods, and the restraint and good humor they showed when dealing with uncooperative people. I concluded that police work wasn't for the faint of heart. It was a nasty, difficult, thankless job, and I was hooked.

Junior year, when I returned to Rollins, I quit baseball to concentrate on my studies. My baseball coach, the infamous Boyd Coffie, bless his heart, arranged things at school so that I could keep my scholarship. Now focused on preparing for a career in law enforcement, I stopped acting like an immature idiot, buckled down, and started earning As.

It wasn't the major league dream I had imagined as a kid growing up in Haverhill. And it was a far grittier career than most kids pursued at prestigious Rollins College. But it was a future that intrigued me.

Like Dad used to say: Rub some dirt on it.

I did.

3

POLICE WORK

fter graduating from Rollins College in 1979, I returned to my home state of Massachusetts with the expectation of quickly getting a job on a local police force. Actually securing one turned out to be a lot harder than I thought.

Since Massachusetts was (and continues to be) a civil service state, all applicants for public service jobs have to take an exam. I scored in the ninety-ninth percentile, whereupon I was placed on a waiting list. Although I had a high score, there were two things working against me. First, military veterans who applied for public service jobs were given preference. Since it was '79 and the Vietnam War had ended four years earlier, there were a large number of vets who wanted to get into law enforcement—all of who were placed ahead of me on the list.

Second, the city of Boston had recently enacted a consent decree, which determined that for every Caucasian hired for a city job, they had to hire a minority applicant.

* * *

I stuck around Massachusetts for a while, doing odd jobs, and hoping to get called. After a year, I started looking for police work in other states.

It was during this time that I met my future wife, Sam, who was working her way through college as a bartender in Boston. After a year of me trying and failing miserably, she finally agreed to go out with me. For our first date, she didn't show up and later claimed she had "forgotten." I think she also mentioned the word "stalking" once or twice.

Most guys would have given up. But I persisted, and once we started dating, we quickly fell deeply in love with one another. Then, I was offered a job with a police department in Florida.

I was torn—excited to get started in police work, but unhappy to leave the woman I was planning to marry. Soon after I arrived in Florida, I ran into two other complications. One, I had a problem with my retina that had gone undetected and needed to be corrected with medication. And, two, unexpected family problems made it necessary that I live closer to Boston.

I was starting to wonder if I'd ever become a cop. Determined to be with Sam and land a police job, I kept searching and finally found one with the Burlington, Vermont, PD and received my badge on September 23, 1983.

Three months later, Sam and I were married in a small family wedding in Lynnfield, Massachusetts. With no money or time for a honeymoon, we moved into a tiny apartment in downtown Burlington. Sam found a job bartending and I started probationary field training with the Burlington PD.

Burlington in the early 1980s was a city in transition with an energetic young socialist mayor named Bernie Sanders. Sandwiched between the Green Mountains and Lake Champlain, Vermont's capital had once been the third largest lumber port in the nation. In the early twentieth century, it transitioned into a fuel depot for oil and gas shipped throughout New England. When I arrived in '83, the lakefront was badly polluted, the rail lines and oil storage facilities unused and rusting, and the city of fifty thousand was in decline.

In many ways, Burlington reminded me a lot of Haverhill and its population was a similar mix of blue-collar workers, the elderly, young professionals, and college students. The city's two largest employers were General Electric and the University of Vermont.

Sam and I were poor, but happy. While we were dating she told me she had a medical condition that made it impossible for her to have children. Six months after we moved to Burlington, Sam found out she was pregnant. We were ecstatic.

Meanwhile, I was a probationary rookie learning the ropes of being a cop. First thing I realized was that the dynamics of police interaction with the public is complicated. It's not like being a fireman, who is applauded when he or she arrives to rescue people, and save property. As a cop 80–90 percent of your contact with people is negative. You're called when someone has been assaulted, robbed, raped, or killed.

Because Burlington was predominantly a blue-collar town, we faced a constant stream of drunken-and-disorderlies, sexual assaults, stabbings, and incidents of domestic violence. On a daily basis, I was dealing with abused children, violent criminals, and the mentally disturbed, and dealing with things that most people in society never had to face.

My Field Training Officers (FTOs) taught me the critical requirement of a successful career in law enforcement—a sense of humor. Both of them had me laughing my ass off at the strange and crazy shit we saw every day.

Where they differed was in their approach to police work. My first FTO was a tough New Yorker, who locked everyone up and sorted out their stories later. The second, Hugh Edwards, aka "the Chaplain," had been an Army chaplain in Vietnam. His way of dealing with people was firm but compassionate. I adopted his methodology.

He taught me to be proactive and always be on the lookout for "bad guys" with outstanding arrest warrants, and to stop suspicious-looking cars. As we patrolled the downtown streets, the Chaplain would turn to me and ask, "Who's the guy in the plaid pants? Who's that guy drinking beer on the corner?"

Some days at the end of my shift my neck was tired from swiveling so much. The Chaplain would say, "The trick is to sniff out trouble before it happens."

His touch was deft. If we pulled up to a street corner where a group of questionable characters were hanging out, he'd roll down his window, and say, "We're watching you, gentlemen. Behave."

Then, he'd wink at one of them and ask, "Hey, Bobby, how's your mom doing? Next time you visit her in the hospital give her my best."

At the time Burlington was experiencing an epidemic of smashed windows and radios stolen from cars. My own Golf VW had been victimized, so I knew how it felt. We were aware that a particular gang was responsible for a lot of the break-ins and included a kid named Barry Glenn.

If we saw him outside his neighborhood, we figured there was a 98 percent chance he was committing a crime. So we'd bumper-lock him, which meant following him in our patrol car at five miles per hour, or getting out and walking beside him.

Sample conversation:

"Hey, Barry, you lost?"

"Go fuck yourself."

"That's no way to talk to a friend who is offering you a ride
    home."

"Yeah, right. . . . Feels more like you're threatening me."

"No, Barry why would you say that? We're offering to take
    you into custody now for something you're going to do
    later."

"Very funny."

We would ride his ass until he got so frustrated he went home.

After four months, I was assigned to a patrol car by myself. I
quickly learned that the way to earn the respect of your fellow
officers was to get to police distress calls in a hurry and call for
backup only when absolutely needed.

The Chaplain had told me, "Don't be one of those cops who
sits in the station talking shit. You shouldn't be in there for more
than five minutes. Put on your uniform and get to work. There's
no crime going on in the station house."

First thing I did was learn the city inside out. It was important
to know how to quickly get into a particular area, and the best
way to exit in an emergency. If I was patrolling six blocks of a
high-crime sector downtown, I had to memorize every store,
house, and apartment building.

I quickly realized that no matter how hard I worked, I was
merely sticking my finger in the dike of crime. We averaged
twenty to twenty-five calls for a ten-hour shift. If I answered a
domestic call, I might be two sentences into writing a report

when I'd get another call and have to rush off. If my calls backed up, my bosses would get on my ass.

I saw both horrible things and people at their finest. The biggest challenge was keeping up with the paperwork. It soon became obvious that given the pace and the physical nature of some aspects of the job, police work was a young man's game. No way I wanted to be an out-of-shape fifty-year-old officer climbing a fence chasing a suspect.

We did ten-hour shifts in fours and threes. That meant four days of ten hours each to make up a forty-hour workweek, and three days off. Most of us spent some of those three days off working special details to earn overtime, either directing traffic or looking for drunk drivers.

Our son Russell was born in February 1985, a healthy, cherubic boy who immediately became the center of our lives. Months before, shortly into a night shift, I had received a medical assist call from a nice residential neighborhood. Code 3 meant hurry to the scene with lights and siren. Code 1 was normal patrol. Since the dispatcher hadn't communicated a code, I drove to the scene at a leisurely pace.

On a medical assist, the fire department usually responded first, and we'd show up later. As I entered the neighborhood, I heard a call go out to the fire department. This time the dispatcher called it a Code 3. So I flipped on the siren and hit the gas, and arrived before the fire department and EMTs.

When I pulled up to the house, I saw that the front door was open and there was a woman standing in it screaming and waving her arms in distress.

I hurried up to her and asked, "What's the problem, ma'am?"

"My . . . oh my God. . . . Help! My . . . my baby . . . ! Oh, God. . . ." She was so upset, she was choking on the words.

I tried to get her to calm down, and tell me what was wrong, but she remained hysterical so I decided to search the house on my own.

The woman offered no resistance. What I saw when I entered was a nice starter home with everything in order.

"My baby!" the woman screamed behind me.

I got it. I was searching for a baby. I poked my head in a room toward the rear of the house and saw two cribs. There were infants in both of them of the same approximate age. One was moving around and acting like a normal baby. The second, who appeared to be a twin, lay still and was a shade of purple I'd never seen before.

My first thought was: *Oh, shit. . . .*

I reached down to find a pulse and the infant's skin felt like cold porcelain. A shiver went up my spine. I'd been a cop for less than two years at this point, and had never been on a call like this. The fire department and EMTs still hadn't arrived.

What do I do now?

As the mother appeared in the doorway behind me, screaming about trying to contact her husband at work, I scooped up the stricken infant in my hand. I remembered from the basic medical training I had learned at the police academy that when you do CPR on an infant you can't breathe in too hard or you risk bursting their delicate lungs.

So I started breathing into the baby's little mouth in gentle puffs. The mother continued to scream uncontrollably. It seemed as if the baby was responding, but I wasn't sure.

A hundred thoughts careened through my head as I puffed into the infant's mouth again. Then I remembered that there was a hospital emergency room four miles away. The medical personnel there would be better equipped to deal with the situation than me.

I ran past the mother with the baby in my arms and said, "I'm taking him to the hospital. Fletcher Allen, ma'am. I'll get back to you later."

She offered no resistance. I climbed behind the wheel with the baby in one hand, fired up the engine and siren with the other, and took off like a rocket. It was raining cats and dogs outside and the streets were slick. I said to myself, *Don't get into an accident and kill us both.*

As I steered through wet suburban streets, I tried massaging the infant's heart with my thumb. They were the longest four miles of my life.

Finally, I pulled to the curb and ran with the baby into the ER. Breathless, I handed him to a nurse. From the expression on her face and those of the other two hospital technicians standing with her, I could tell that the baby was lost.

Still clinging to the last vestiges of hope, I followed them down a corridor as they ran with it to an examination room. As I watched them massage the baby's heart, the enormity of what I was doing for a living hit me. Here was this wonderful family. It had been a normal night when they put their baby down to sleep. Then the unthinkable happened, and they were forced to rely on someone like me.

Somewhere amid the melee and shifting emotions, the mother and father arrived at the hospital, the infant was declared dead, and I had to inform them. My hands shook the whole time and I had to hold back the tears. The official cause of death was Sudden Infant Death Syndrome (SIDS).

After a few hours' sleep, I returned to work. The first thing my supervisor said when he saw me was, "Where's your paperwork on the medical assist call last night? You didn't submit a report."

As I typed it up, I relived every second of the experience—the mother's screams, the baby's ice-cold skin, the disappointment I had felt in not saving the baby.

I was in my midtwenties and a relative kid. Nobody counseled me or talked to me about the incident or the impact it had on me. It was part of the job, and taught me two things: One, always be prepared to the max, particularly when it comes to providing emergency medical assistance. And, two, life is precious!

For many years, the family who lost the baby sent me a Christmas card. Every time I opened one and saw a picture of the wife and husband with their son, along with their names and the name of the son who died, my heart broke again.

Less than a year after that incident, I'd become an FTO, too. Looking at the new recruits assigned to me, I'd think: *That was me a little while ago. Remember how scared and unsure you were, and how you couldn't really appreciate the responsibilities that come with the job?*

I tried to be both firm and sympathetic. Not like one FTO I knew who threw a trainee out of his car in a McDonald's parking lot and shouted, "You'll never be a cop, so go fill out an application," and then drove off.

I had mostly good trainees and a few who struggled. Winter of '85, I was training a kid named Morgan, who fell into the latter category. Guys at the precinct house constantly busted his balls about his name. "Hey, Morgan, how come you got a name that goes both ways. You trying to tell us something?"

He was earnest and kind with a master's degree in criminology. When we went on calls together, I talked to him about the importance of establishing control. I explained that as kids we're taught to be polite to strangers, but police work required something called "command presence."

For example, if you got a call to respond to a disturbance at a drunk's house and walked in and saw he had a beer in his hand, you didn't say, "Sir, please put that beer away so we can talk." Instead, you delivered something blunter and more direct like, "Put that beer bottle away before I knock it out of your fucking hand. Then tell me calmly what the hell is going on."

I said to Morgan, "When you walk into someone's house you've got to establish control in your own way."

"Yeah, I got it," he responded.

One night, two months into his training, we were nearing the end of our shift, when we got a call. "Disturbance on the fifth floor, 282 Buell."

Lots of cops go temporarily deaf at the end of their shifts. But I wasn't like that. Once we went over our ten-hour shift time, we started earning overtime. So what was the hurry?

The building in question was so close to the police station that you could actually see it from there. It had no elevator, so Morgan and I hoofed it to the fifth floor of the six-story building and knocked on the door. "Police. Let us in!"

We heard a lot of noise inside, but no one answered.

In police work, you only go into a house if you have no choice, because bad things can happen once you're inside. Optimally, you want the occupants to exit and talk to you in the hallway.

Back in the '80s, we carried PR-24 batons, which are L-shaped with a butt-like handle that becomes an extension of your arm. I banged on the door with the butt of the PR-24 for a full three minutes before someone turned down the music inside. Thirty seconds later a college-age woman answered the door. It looked like she'd been crying, but showed no signs of physical abuse.

I said, "Ma'am, we got a call about a disturbance."

As I spoke I looked past her to see if there was a threat behind her, and spotted a guy at the end of the apartment pacing back and forth.

"What's going on?" I asked.

"My boyfriend and I got into an argument," she answered casting her eyes to the floor.

"Well, you're going to have to keep it down. Is that your boyfriend back there?" I asked, pointing inside.

"Yeah."

I knew from experience that I had to be careful. Women in these situations often turned on the police and defended their boyfriends. That's why it was standard practice to respond to domestic calls with two officers.

I turned to Morgan and said, "You keep talking to her, while I go inside and check on him."

The second I crossed the threshold I felt the little hairs stand up on the back of my neck. It was a sixth sense that I was still learning to trust.

I stopped a few feet into the apartment and said, "Hey, buddy, the police are here. Can you come out and talk to me?"

"Sure," he responded politely.

There were a couple of beer bottles on the floor, but no signs of violence. Vermont state law at the time stated that if there was any sign of assault, we had to arrest at least one of the parties.

In this case they both seemed cooperative. The guy was in his midtwenties, wore a T-shirt and jeans, and seemed hopped up on something. I couldn't tell if he was drunk or high.

"What's up?" I asked him.

"We had an argument."

My job at that point was to de-escalate the situation by remaining calm.

"Look," I said, "we've got to figure this out. So step outside with me, so we can talk."

"About what, sir?" he asked.

In domestic arguments, we had to ascertain who was legally entitled to reside in the house or apartment. If the lease was in his name alone, the girlfriend would have to leave, even if she had been the victim.

I said, "First, I have to establish whose apartment this is."

We were still standing facing one another a few feet inside the apartment. I was wearing a thick leather jacket over my uniform.

"It's my apartment," he responded, "but she stays here. I think she signed the lease."

"That's confusing."

"Yes, I know, sir, but it's my apartment. Maybe her name is on the lease. I'm not sure."

As a policeman confronting a suspect I always had to assume there might be a confrontation at some point and size up how I would handle it. If the guy was a bodybuilder or a massive four hundred pounds, I had to be ready to draw my gun or hit him with my baton. This kid wasn't exactly skinny, but he wasn't muscular either. He appeared wiry and fit.

I said, "Follow me. Let's move outside."

I got him to follow me to the entrance. To my left was a door that led to an outside walkway area with plastic chairs. Meanwhile, Morgan moved with the woman farther inside.

From near the front door, I asked the boyfriend again, "Whose name is on the lease?"

"Mine is," he answered.

"So is mine," she shouted from inside.

Now the boyfriend got agitated and he and the girlfriend

started arguing back and forth about who was legally entitled to be there.

I said to her, "We need to figure out who is supposed to be here, because the other one has got to go."

The tension between them escalated. Meanwhile, the boyfriend and I still hadn't exited the apartment.

I said to him, "You're going to come out into the hallway with me, while my partner stays inside with her and we figure this out."

I couldn't tell what was going on inside his head. I knew he was hopped up on something. Maybe he took what I said to mean that even though it was his place, he was the one who was going to be kicked out.

All I know is that he took two steps toward the door, then screamed and sprung at me like a tiger on steroids. I hit him in the chest to try to stop him and felt his muscles flexing. Next thing I knew he had pushed me through the door that led to an outside walkway with a waist-high barrier on each end. Before I knew what was happening, the crazed boyfriend was going for my throat. I raised my hands to stop him.

Even though he had turned on me unexpectedly, I wasn't really concerned at this point, nor did I feel like fighting at the end of my shift. I was basically holding the guy and waiting for Morgan to come to my aid and help me take him down. In ninety-nine out of a hundred cases, as soon as someone grabs a cop, his partner is at his side in seconds. Our lives depend on one another, so we have to have the other's back.

But this case, Morgan remained in the apartment talking to the woman. He could see me and the boyfriend clearly, but didn't move.

Realizing I was on my own, and had to deal with a guy who had gone berserk, I tried to kick the boyfriend's legs out. Most people don't see it coming and go down immediately. But when I kicked this kid's legs, it felt like I was hitting an oak tree. His very taut muscles didn't budge.

Now it was getting serious. As we grappled in the cold air on the walkway, the boyfriend seemed to be growing bigger and stronger. We were about the same height, but I was thicker in the shoulders and torso from lifting weights. Like the Incredible Hulk, the boyfriend screamed again, lifted me off my feet, and threw me like a rag doll toward the edge. The hip-high metal railing stopped me. Otherwise, I would have fallen five stories into a rubble-filled alley.

My brain screamed at that point, *If you don't do something now, you're going to die!*

The boyfriend started trying to lift me and throw me over the railing. He had his hand on my chin and was trying to use his legs as leverage. Morgan still wasn't helping. Feeling a well of anger burst inside me, I waited for his legs to part, then rolled and kneed him in the balls as hard as I could.

The fight went out of him like air out of a punctured balloon, and he relaxed his grip. I immediately swung my body on top of him and cuffed the son of a bitch.

Now he was in agony and I was on my knees sucking wind. Looking up at the night sky, I kept telling myself I had a wife and kid at home and had just come within inches of losing my life. The maniac beneath me with his balls in his throat was so fucked up on God knows what, he probably would have gone over the ledge with me without even realizing what he was doing.

That's police work. One minute you're bored out of your skull, the next you're fighting for your life.

Morgan finally showed up. He looked at me standing over the handcuffed kid and started stuttering, "I . . . I w-w-wasn't sure . . . w-what was going on."

I growled, "Shut up and stop talking." Then I grabbed my radio and called for a second car. Guys at the station thought the message had been garbled because I almost never called for backup and had a partner with me. When I repeated that I needed help, they responded like the cavalry.

Later, when I walked back to the patrol car with the hand-cuffed boyfriend, I saw Morgan waiting in the passenger seat. "Look," he said, "I'm really sorry. I didn't know—"

I interrupted him with two words. "You're done."

It was the end of the workweek. I decided to take the next three days off and sit in bed, where I replayed the incident over and over in my head, and thanked God I was still alive.

I never told my wife. A couple of months earlier, I'd been jumped while on duty by some drunks in a bar and beat up pretty badly. When I returned home from that fight bleeding with two badly swollen eyes and a separated shoulder, and I told Sam what happened, she'd gotten extremely upset. We agreed at that point that for the sake of our marriage, I would never discuss what happened at work.

I stayed true to that promise.

Four days later, when I returned to work, Morgan had already submitted his resignation. Nice kid, but he wasn't suited for police work. Few people are.

4

QUANTICO

In February 1985, after less than two years as a uniform cop, I was promoted to detective. If that seems like a quick jump up the ladder, it was for several reasons. One, I had apparently distinguished myself as an aggressive and effective patrolman. Two, Burlington PD in the mid-'80s was short-handed, so competent cops were usually promoted quickly. And, three, I had someone helping me from above in the form of my former FTO, the Chaplain, who had been bumped up to detective a year ahead of me.

The Chaplain recommended me for assignment to the prosecutor's division of the State Attorney's Office. There, dressed in plain clothes, I learned how to assemble evidence so that it was airtight and overwhelming when presented in court. As I prepared witnesses and their testimony, I became fascinated with the whole subject of motivation. In other words, why did a particular suspect commit a specific crime? I figured that if I could think like them, I'd have a better chance making a case against them.

The understanding I developed came in handy a few months

later as I started investigating cases as a detective. If I had enjoyed being a patrolman, I liked investigating and solving crimes even more.

The cherry on the cake was the fact that I was often teamed up with the Chaplain. We complemented each other perfectly. He was an expert at getting people to talk, and I was the bricks and mortar guy, who built cases slowly and methodically piece by piece.

Together we solved robberies, sexual assaults, drug cases, and the brutal double homicide of two convenience store workers in November 1986—arresting the suspect in five days. We were so successful that one holier-than-thou prosecutor suggested that we must have been getting physical with our suspects because a high number of them were confessing to their crimes.

I was inclined to confront the prosecutor face-to-face and ask him to back up his claim with evidence. Before I could, the Chaplain addressed the situation with his trademark humor, filing the following fictional police report on Burlington PD Detective Bureau letterhead and submitting it to the prosecutor in question. (I'm Detective A):

COMPLAINT #86-19219
DATE: 7/7/86

On 7/7/86 I was present in the Detective Bureau when Detective A brought in two males and told me he had just seen them on Church Street with an amount of what he believed to be cocaine.

Detective A took one of the guys into an interview room and I took the other. Detective A told me to "go fuck with the other guy's head a little," so I went into the other interview room to try and fuck with the guy.

I went into the room and the first thing I said was don't lie to me or I'll smash my fucking gun across your face. Then I told him that if he touched my coffee I'd fucking kill him.

So I says to the guy "Whatyadoin' with that coke?" and he says to me "Hey."

I just kicked back in my chair, put my feet up and looked groovy as usual. I said to the subject "Subject, we can do this my way or we can do it another way." I think that kinda shook him up a bit, so he says to me, he says "You're the coolest guy I ever met. Like I said before I'll tell you everything you need to know, but don't let that motherfucker Detective A near me, he keeps hitting me." (The good cop/bad cop routine.)

So then ol' Detective A comes back in the room and asks if he can talk to me for a minute and I say "Sure." Outside the room Detective A asks what the guy told me and I said "Nothin," just like that "nothin."

And then Detective A says to me "Well then, make something the fuck up, saying something like 'Yeh, it's mine, what the fuck do you think pig fucker.'" Then Detective A runs into the interview room and cuffs the guy right in the back of the head, but there wasn't a whole lot of blood, just about a half a cup full.

As he's walking out of the interview room I hear Detective A say to the guy "Junior . . . I'm just doing my job" . . . and that's the greatest line I ever heard.

All of us in the detective's bureau laughed our asses off, and the pompous prosecutor never responded.

Back when I was a uniformed cop I had become friendly with several FBI Agents who were assisting us in a bank robbery investigation.

One day, one of them asked, "Hey, Mike, have you ever thought of joining the FBI?"

"Not really. No." Expecting to remain with the BPD for the rest of my career, it had never crossed my mind.

Next time I saw him he handed me an application. Attached

to it was a list of qualifications and the pay scale. When I saw that new FBI recruits made double what I earned as a police officer, I asked, "Where do I sign?"

Months later, on February 5, 1987, I received a letter on FBI letterhead that read, "You are hereby appointed a Special Agent with the Federal Bureau of Investigation."

I thought it was a joke a first. As I read it a second time, my hands started shaking. Toward the bottom it stated that my starting salary would be $24,732. At the time, it seemed like a million bucks. For the second time in my life, the contents of a sealed envelope was about to change the course of my life.

A few days later, I got a call on a Friday from an FBI Applicant Recruiter, who said, "There's a slot opening on Sunday. If you don't take it, it's going to someone else."

"You mean two days from now?"

"Two days from now, correct."

"What happens if I don't take it?"

"You go to the bottom of the list."

When I told Sam the news, she wasn't thrilled, and I couldn't blame her. Sure, we could use the extra money, but it was the middle of a tough New England winter and she was taking care of two-year-old Russell and was now pregnant with our second child. I quickly arranged for the Chaplain and another of my cop buddies to pack up our belongings and move Sam and Russell to her sister's house in Massachusetts, then flew to Washington, DC.

On February 9, 1987, I was sworn in as an FBI Special Agent trainee at the age of twenty-nine. The FBI Academy is housed on 547 acres within a Marine Corps base in Quantico, Virginia, and reminded me of a college campus. I shared a room with a guy who looked like an accountant, and in fact had been an accountant. We became fast friends.

Our class of fifty—Class #87-7—consisted of ten former cops, ten ex-military, and people from all walks of life, including a veterinarian and music teacher. All but three in our class were male, and we were a mix of white, African American, Asian, and Hispanic. One guy had previously been earning $250,000 a year in the financial sector. Rooming next to me was an ex-NYPD cop and Columbia University graduate who I'll call McDonald. He also happened to be built like a brick shithouse and looked like a movie star.

For some reason, he was always a nervous wreck, probably because of the insane amount of pressure he put on himself. I took it upon myself to try to lighten his mood, and remember telling him, "Godammit, McDonald, if I had half your shit, I'd be the Director in a week."

First day of class we all showed up in the best suits, white shirts, and ties. The women wore nice dresses. Everyone appeared scared shitless. I sat relaxed, waiting for someone to tell me that I was there due to some bureaucratic mistake and would soon be headed back to Burlington.

The instructor asked us all to introduce ourselves, relate a little about our backgrounds, and talk about why we had joined the FBI. Recruits stood and spoke with great seriousness about wanting to join the finest law enforcement agency in the world, and how their whole lives had been dedicated to this special moment.

When it was my turn, I said honestly, "I joined because I need the money." The instructor looked like someone had pissed on his shoes, while the two class counselors and the rest of the class cracked up. That moment set the tone for the rest of my Academy experience.

I was the blue-collar cop who worked hard, told it to you straight, and liked to crack jokes and play pranks to keep the class relaxed. It's not that I didn't take the training seriously. I did. At the same time, I liked having fun, and saw humor as an antidote to some of our stick-up-their-ass instructors. The truth was that a lot of the classroom work and physical fitness training we went through over the next four months were things I'd done before either in college, at the police academy, or as a cop.

During the four-month course I discovered I had a talent for mimicking people, and often entertained my classmates with impressions of our instructors minutes before they walked into the classroom. Encountering a classroom of snickering recruits, the instructors would look sternly in my direction, while I appeared angelic and nodded to McDonald sitting next to me.

I was also appointed de facto head of the "beverage committee." My duties involved summoning my fellow 87-7 recruits to an FBI barroom on campus known as The Boardroom, where we would quaff a few cold ones, crack jokes, and engage one another in conversation. That nighttime ritual helped the fifty of us from diverse backgrounds and walks of life meld into one cohesive unit.

The night before our formal graduation, friends and family members, and FBI instructors and officials gathered for a formal dinner and celebration. Sam and Russell flew in for the occasion. After awards were handed out and we heard from several guest speakers, classmates turned to me and urged me to take the mike. Fortified with a couple of beers, I walked to the dais and did an impromptu set of impersonations of classmates and instructors complete with walks, body language, and voices.

All I remember were the howls of laughter from the audience and the feeling that I was on a roll. Sam's mortification eased slightly when at the end my classmates gave me a standing ovation.

It was all in good fun, but not apparently to some Quantico bureaucrat who lambasted me the next day as I stood in line to be sworn in by the FBI Director. According to him, I had offended some very important people and had failed to conduct myself properly.

Fuck you for not being able to take a joke, I thought, but wisely kept my mouth shut.

An hour later, I received my official credentials and embarked on my FBI adventure. Luckily, I was assigned to one of the "Top Twelve"—meaning the FBI's twelve largest field offices, in my case, Philadelphia. Part of that had to do with my experience as a policeman. Other less experienced Agents were dispatched to smaller outposts. My accountant roommate was sent to Shreveport, Louisiana, and had to work his way up.

The downside of being assigned to one of the Top Twelve was that like all new Agents I was put on the Applicant Squad, which meant spending endless hours at a desk calling and interviewing people who had been listed as references on government employment applications. Bored out of my skull, I amused myself by observing the guys in the adjacent Squad who were members of the Bank Robbery/Fugitive Squad. They'd arrive in the morning, insult each other mercilessly, and then hit the streets looking for bad guys.

After several months of grunt work, I was moved to Public Corruption, where my first assignment was to investigate police malfeasance in connection with the infamous MOVE bombing of May 13, 1985, when during an armed standoff with members of the black liberation group MOVE, Philadelphia police dropped two bombs on a MOVE-occupied row house in West Philly. The resulting fire incinerated an entire block, killing 11 people and leaving more than 250 homeless. It was heady stuff for a former cop who had previously been serving warrants and arresting drunk drivers.

After that I was assigned to a police corruption case where I interviewed witnesses who claimed that Philadelphia narcotics cops had ripped them off. Most of the accusers turned out to be drug traffickers. As a former cop who had handled drug cases, I was skeptical of their testimony at first. But mounting evidence convinced me that members of the Narcotics Unit were guilty of serious wrongdoing.

It shattered some of my idealism about law enforcement but taught me how to build a complex RICO (Racketeer Influenced and Corrupt Organizations) case in federal court. After two lengthy trials, all but one of six former members of the Narcotics Unit were convicted or pled guilty, and sentenced to time in prison.

After a year on the Public Corruption Squad, I was given an opportunity to request a transfer. My first choice, the Bank Robbery/Fugitive Squad was staffed with heavy-hitting senior Agents and rarely accepted junior guys like me. Next in order of preference were the two Drug Squads in the Philadelphia office. One handled domestic drug trafficking, and the other Squad worked international, which in 1988 meant the Colombian drug cartels. I chose the latter: Squad 3—aka, the Colombian Drug Squad.

These were the early days of the FBI's involvement in investigating major international trafficking. Following the brutal drug wars of the early 1980s in Southern Florida, the FBI had been given concurrent jurisdiction with the DEA to work drug cases. The Squad I joined was relatively new and staffed with young, aggressive Agents.

I loved it from the get-go. No longer was I stuck behind a desk working the phones. Now I got to spend most of my time out on the streets, either doing surveillance, executing search warrants, or making arrests. The hours were long, stretching into most nights, and practically every weekend. But I didn't mind.

My partners were excellent—a very respected senior Agent, pulled me in immediately and mentored me, before leaving for his final assignment. When the senior Agent moved on I teamed up with his former partner, a young Agent I'll call Saul Johnson, aka "the Counselor," who had four years more experience than me and went on later to become the right-hand man of FBI Director Robert Mueller and the SAC of several major offices.

Johnson was a soft-spoken, studious former attorney who had the ability to remain calm in any situation and taught me to lead with my head. Our first major case was Operation Bacalao— Spanish for codfish, and named that because the suspects sometimes transported cocaine in refrigerated trucks.

Our main targets were the Aguilar family—a drug-trafficking organization led by husband (Julio Cesar) and his wife (Edith Guiterrez), and including his sister, brother-in-law, sister-in-law, and others. On the surface Julio and Edith appeared to be a normal middle-class couple from Colombia in their midthirties, residing and working in the United States on green cards. They lived in a modest Philadelphia row house, and drove an unflashy Nissan Pathfinder.

The Aguilars were being supplied with cocaine from Colombia through New York City. FBI New York was running a parallel drug investigation on the NYC supplier, a kindly fifty-year-old Colombian woman named Stella Mercado.

Initially I was put on physical surveillance, which involved sitting in a car for twelve hours at a stretch, following Julio Aguilar as he moved around town, and keeping track of what he was doing and with whom he was meeting. In the late '80s, U.S.

law enforcement often assumed women didn't play a major role in drug trafficking. So while we were following Julio around, his wife, Edith, was doing most of the real work.

We became aware of the extent of Edith's involvement once we obtained Title III approval to conduct electronic surveillance, and listen to the Aguilars' phones. This was my first Title III application, which turned out to be a time-consuming process that involved getting approval from a federal judge. While I collected the evidence and put it in sequence, the Counselor wrote the affidavits. Then the two of us met with a federal judge in his chambers, and answered his questions. It was by no means automatic that the application would be approved.

Once signed by a federal judge, the Title III had to be renewed every thirty days, which meant assembling new evidence and writing another affidavit. The Title III intercept turned out to be worth the trouble, because once we started listening to the Aguilar's phones, we quickly developed a clear and comprehensive picture of how their operation worked. Every month or so, Julio would call his supplier in Medellín, Colombia, and say something like, "We need a hundred pillows." Or he might fly to Colombia to deliver the message in person.

A week later a shipment of cocaine would arrive by boat or plane, usually in Miami, and we would track it from there to New York City and into the hands of Julio Aguilar's boss, the aforementioned Stella Mercado. Mercado would then make arrangements to truck the cocaine to Philadelphia, or sometimes sent it via couriers on Amtrak trains. She might call ahead and say, "Tomorrow we're going to be at First Street. Meet us there at three PM."

We would try to cover the meet and photograph or video the transfer. Once Julio and his family got their hands on the cocaine, they would have people on their staff cut it, bag it, and distribute it to hundreds of smaller dealers, couriers, and kids who would sell it on the streets.

Back in Burlington, I'd been a cop busting small-time dope dealers on street corners. I'd arrest some and watch others take their place the next day. Now as a federal Agent I was trying to build cases against the heads of the organization, so as to dismantle the entire criminal enterprise. The Aguilars, as harmless as they appeared, were major players in an international drug organization moving hundreds of millions of dollars' worth of cocaine a year, and destroying countless lives.

Since these were the early days working international narcotic cases we had little or no liaison with officials in Colombia, which meant we had no effective way of going after the big boss in Medellín. Our focus was Stella Mercado in New York and the Aguilar family itself.

In July 1989, after months of collecting evidence, Saul Johnson and I returned to federal court and obtained arrest warrants. In those days, FBI SWAT (which I later joined) conducted the raids and made the arrests. Most of the time they did this at between three and five in morning when the suspects were asleep.

The morning in question, Saul and I parked a few doors down from the Aguilars' house on North Front Street and observed Julio's Pathfinder parked in the driveway, and assumed that the suspects were inside. Then we made the call, "Let's hit the house."

We watched while SWAT moved in, smashed through the front door, and rushed in, weapons ready. Usually, arrests were over in a few minutes, but on this occasion, it was taking more time. We weren't allowed to enter until SWAT said, "Clear." So we waited nervously, hands in our pockets, wondering what the hell was going on.

After fifteen minutes, Saul went into the house. He exited minutes later and said, "They found Edith and the others. But where the fuck is Julio Cesar?"

"I don't know," I responded. "His car is here. He has to be here."

"Well, he isn't. We checked the house a number of times and can't find him."

Meanwhile, Edith Guiterrez was in custody and insisting that we take her to the station right away and book her so she could hire a lawyer to contest the charges.

Saul and I entered the residence—a standard row house with four floors—basement, main floor with living room and kitchen, bedrooms on the second and top floors. We started at the top and descended, searching under beds and inside closets. Julio Cesar happened to be on the heavy side, so there were only a limited number of spaces he could squeeze his big body into. We checked all of them, carefully. No sign of Julio.

We went through the house four more times, methodically. I was starting to panic, thinking, *It's my first big arrest and I screwed up.*

Maybe Julio Cesar had been tipped off and had fled. When I reached the basement the third time, I saw an old, grizzled SWAT officer named McQueen standing and measuring one of the walls with his hands.

He turned to me and said, "The dimensions are off."

"What?" I asked, thinking that maybe he had flipped his lid.

"See how this part of the wall sticks out?"

I looked at it again and realized he was right, but still wasn't sure what it meant. The SWAT officer put his ear to the drywall, smiled, then gestured to me to do the same. I heard someone breathing inside.

"Holy shit!"

"That's him," McQueen exclaimed. "Almost outsmarted us."

Speaking through the wall, I said, "Julio, you sneaky bastard, we know you're in there."

McQueen pointed to an opening above that Julio had slipped through. We waited for one of the SWAT guys to bring a sledge-hammer and bust through the wall. Then we slapped the cuffs on Julio Cesar.

According to the story that ran in *The Philadelphia Inquirer* on July 21, 1989, "Ten Colombia citizens and three Philadelphians have been named in a thirty-nine count cocaine-trafficking in-dictment released yesterday by the U.S. Attorney's Office."

All told, we ended up arresting more than forty suspects, in-cluding Stella Mercado in New York. Our search of the Aguilars' house didn't yield drugs, but we hadn't expected it to either as drugs were normally kept in separate stash houses. What we did seize were stacks of cash and ledgers that contained coded, hand-written records of all the Aguilars' drug transactions.

Even though we had an open-and-shut case, we now began the laborious job of assembling all the evidence, including surveil-lance logs, ledgers, and phone transcripts, and building a case brick by brick against each suspect to present to the judge and jury. The Aguilars and their associates were charged with mul-tiple serious federal drug offenses to include conspiracy and conspiracy with intent to distribute.

The Counselor and I had actually started working with the federal prosecutors for more than two years before the arrests. Now we coordinated with them on a daily basis for nearly an-other year before the cases went to trial, making sure every piece in the evidence chain fit tightly together, and leaving no room for a defense attorney to raise doubts.

In the end, most of the suspects pleaded guilty. Julio Cesar, Edith, and Stella were all sentenced to more than twenty years in federal prison.

Under federal forfeiture law, we had seized Julio Cesar's Nissan Pathfinder. After the case wrapped up, the government assigned the Pathfinder to me for my official use. Now, ironically, I was driving the same vehicle I had tailed for almost a year. It turned out to be a real nice car, which my kids aptly named "Julio's Ride."

5

FBI SWAT

In 1990, I'd been an FBI Special Agent for three years when a member of FBI PH SWAT walked over to my desk and handed me a schedule, a 10mm Glock, an old bulletproof vest, and other used gear, and said, "We're meeting at the Fort Dix range nine AM this Thursday. Be there."

I looked up at the FBI Special Agent affectionately known as "Stonehead"—because his head was shaped like that of a Cro-Magnon man—and said, "Thanks."

"Just keep your mouth shut and do whatever shit jobs we give you," Stonehead said as he left.

I felt honored. Being asked to join FBI SWAT was the military equivalent of becoming a Navy SEAL. They were the thirty hand-picked studs of the office and had a reputation for training hard, executing the toughest warrants, arresting the nastiest criminals, and having a good time.

Unlike today's FBI SWAT, where competitive tryouts would tax even Olympic-caliber athletes, selection in the '80s and '90s was based on experience and reputation. Practically every member of the team was either former police or military, was a hard-working street investigator who had handled major cases, wasn't shy around liquor, and knew when to keep their mouths shut. The selection process wasn't scientific, but somehow it worked.

The night before the meet, I was so excited I couldn't sleep. Being a punctuality freak, I showed up at the Fort Dix military base in central southern New Jersey, which housed a law enforcement complex for FBI SWAT's Philadelphia and Newark Divisions, at 8:35 AM only to find out I was the last guy there. As I parked my car, I noticed that in addition to their gear all the SWAT guys were carrying coolers. And some of the coolers were huge.

The senior team leader was the unofficial head of Bank Robbery/Fugitive Squad and a former Marine Captain named Chuck Manson, but universally known as "Jarhead." The first thing he said when he saw me was, "In SWAT if you're forty-five minutes early, you're late."

As I pulled on my gear, these colorful characters starting busting each other's balls.

"Hey, Jim, you go out last night?"

"Yeah, I was at the gym. Why?"

"Can you do me a favor and ask your wife something for me?"

"What?"

"Make sure she washes my underwear before she gives it back."

"Fuck you."

At Quantico I'd been trained to shoot .357 magnum revolvers at targets while standing still and dressed in civilian clothes. Now, in SWAT, we were sprinting up to moving targets in full gear, hitting the ground or taking cover, and firing 10mm Glocks and H&K MP5s to approximate real-life pressure situations. Between the bulky gear and the adrenaline coursing through my system, I couldn't hit the side of a barn.

Jarhead tortured me the entire time. "Hey, kid, you ever fire a gun before?"

"Yeah. Yeah."

Guys around me snickered and laughed.

"You point the end with the black hole and aim before you squeeze the trigger."

"Yeah. I know."

More laughter.

"You had your eyes tested recently? You forget to bring your glasses?"

Guys were howling, and I was dying from embarrassment. I was an above-average shooter, but most of the guys around me were lights-out. The more I shot, and we fired something like four hundred rounds, the better I got. Lunchtime came and the SWAT guys started reaching into the coolers and drinking beers as though they'd just returned from a week in the Sahara Desert. I enjoyed quaffing a few cold ones, too, but I'd never seen anything like this.

As they drank they started verbally abusing one another even worse than before. As the new man, I knew enough to keep my mouth shut and enjoy the entertainment. The onslaught was brutal and any sign of weakness made you a regular target. None of us escaped unscathed.

After lunch, we were taught how to use an electric power saw to cut through metal bars during federal prison riots, which were common in those days. The instructor fired up the nasty-looking device, its metal teeth screaming at a high pitch and gas-powered engine roaring. As soon as it made contact with metal bars, huge orange flames shot six feet into the air and black smoke began to billow out. The gnashing of metal on metal was unbearable, as was the smell.

One of the quietist guys on the team, who happened to be married to a female Agent known for her dominant ways, said, "That's Sally when I come home late with beer on my breath."

All thirty of us FBI SWAT members forgot the noise and smell and laughed our asses off.

At the end of the day, I watched guys stumble to their cars and head home three sheets to the wind with trunks filled with gear and weapons. I had consumed less alcohol than anyone, and I still probably shouldn't have taken the wheel of a government-owned vehicle. But this was the early '90s and the culture of drinking in the FBI was pervasive.

Amazingly, in my seven years assigned to Philadelphia FBI SWAT with twice-a-month training and prodigious beer consumption there was never a reported alcohol-related driving event. Don't ask me how.

When SWAT was called on a real mission we put all joking and drinking aside and focused intently on the task ahead, which almost always involved serious criminals and imminent danger. This usually happened three or four times a month. When the crack epidemic hit in the early '90s, the pace picked up to the point that we were raiding drug dens as often as twice a week.

Sometimes, as in the Aguilar case, SWAT raids were planned ahead of time and noted on a special bulletin board. In the case of a police shooting or similar emergency, I'd be at my desk working, when an announcement would come over the loudspeaker, "SWAT report immediately!" Five minutes later, I'd have retrieved my prepacked gear and would be flying out the door.

One afternoon, I had my nose in some paperwork when we got a call to help thwart a suspected kidnapping. A Chinese gang had grabbed some family members from a rival gang and we were tasked with trying to intercept the getaway car.

In the basement, I ran into The Colonel—a John Wayne look-alike, my immediate supervisor on the Colombian Drug Squad, and the SWAT coordinator—and two other members of SWAT. We piled into an FBI vehicle with The Colonel at the wheel and burned rubber. Within minutes we were speeding down a local highway and the speedometer was straining past a hundred miles per hour.

Buildings and vehicles flew by in a blur and I was about to piss my pants for two reasons. One, I happened to be seated in the front passenger seat—aka, the Death Seat—and, two, I'd gotten to know The Colonel pretty well at this point and as much as I respected and admired him I knew that he had several screws loose. He was currently on his fifth marriage.

I was about to mouth a few words of warning, when he turned and shot me a demented smile. It said something like: Isn't this fucking awesome? If the smile itself didn't freak me out, I was even more alarmed that he had taken his eyes off the road.

Is he trying to get us killed? I asked myself.

The answer that came back was "maybe."

I remember thinking that if we crashed, the car would explode on impact and our bodies would disintegrate. As we passed civilian cars at what felt like the speed of sound, I saw drivers drop their jaws in shock.

Over the radio, we were informed that FBI surveillance had the suspect's car in sight. The Colonel was determined to make the intercept, and ordered surveillance to back off, so we could do our thing. Felony car stops are a form of road ballet that have to be performed with great skill, precision, and timing. You not only had to prevent the stopped car from fleeing, you also had to stop civilian traffic, and you didn't want law enforcement arriving from opposite directions and getting caught in a crossfire.

We'd trained endless SWAT hours for scenarios like this, and now I saw a real car stop unfold before my eyes in a matter of seconds. The Colonel at the wheel zoomed up right behind the felony car, hit the siren and lights, and executed the stop in a sleepy town off the highway. With no shots fired, the victims were recovered and the suspects were in handcuffs. Amazing!

Seconds later twenty armed-to-the teeth FBI SWAT Agents arrived to secure the scene. Before the local police could unknot the massive traffic jam, I saw one family consisting of a mother, father, and two children in a station wagon with their faces pressed against the windows, looking at us petrified as if we were some strange ferocious animals in a zoo.

In my case SWAT turned out to be the perfect collateral duty. I worked cases during the day and spent a couple adrenaline-filled early mornings a month doing raids with a tight-knit group of guys who would do anything for one another. The camaraderie was incredible as you quickly learned to trust your life to the guys next to you.

In the beginning, I was just one of the guys. But as I earned my stripes, I became the primary breacher—known as Slot #1 in the stack—and would take down doors with a forty-pound battering ram or something called a Halligan bar—a combination metal claw, blade, and metal pick designed by a former deputy chief of the New York City Fire Department. The guy in Slot #2 carried a fifty-pound ballistic shield, and the team leader or assistant team leader occupied Slot #3. While every job in SWAT was important, Slots #1–#3 was where the action was. If there was going to be any shooting, it would most likely be directed to the first three guys in.

The object was to take the door down quickly, so guys could

get in and avoid the doorway or what we called the funnel of death. As in the Aguilar case, most raids took place in the early morning when suspects were asleep to maximize the element of surprise. Our watchwords were "speed," "surprise," and "overwhelming force."

By the mid-'90s I was executing warrants both with SWAT and as a Drug Squad Case Agent. One raid involved a family of drug traffickers named the Mendez brothers, who were suspected of having guns in their house. It was my case, so I chose the Squad guys needed and took charge of the raid.

I stood in Slot #2 with a shield. My job was to get in as soon as the door went down, and hurry up to a bedroom on the second floor to arrest the youngest brother and subject of the warrant, Nico Mendez (not his real name). A Philadelphia policeman who I had never met before was my partner that day.

We had about fifteen guys total, including several other PHPD policemen. It was pitch black when we assembled outside the house minutes before 5 AM. My big, muscular SWAT buddy Will Thompson stood in first position holding a sledgehammer. I gave the signal, and everyone readied their weapons.

I knocked and announced, "FBI! FBI!"

Seconds later Thompson whacked the door just below the lock. The doors on most row houses were made of wood and broke open easily. But this time when Thompson hit it, the door didn't budge. He pounded the door a second time. It still didn't give.

Meanwhile, I heard people moving around inside. Thompson continued pounding the door with the fifty-pound sledgehammer and was starting to exhaust himself. I was about to relieve him, when on the seventh or eighth try, the door wedged open far enough for me to squeeze a leg inside.

I twisted my body through the narrow opening even though I knew I was an easy target to anyone inside who wanted to take a shot.

Once in the house, I shouted, "FBI. FBI! Search warrant!"

With my gun ready, I tore up the steps with the PHPD officer fast on my heels. On the second floor, I hung a sharp left and hurried down a narrow hallway to the back bedroom where we knew Nico slept.

As I ran, I noticed that dawn was breaking outside. I was also aware of the potential danger I faced from anyone who decided to pop out of the rooms I passed. Downstairs, other Agents and cops had entered the house and were spreading to their designated positions.

I reached the bedroom and peeked in the open door. Squinting into the dark, I picked out a silhouette against the closed curtain and a naked woman on the bed.

She screamed at the top of her lungs, "Get the fuck out! This is private property! Get out!"

I glanced at her, then back at the silhouette, recognizing it as belonging to Mendez. In the blink of an eye, he started rolling toward me and into a closet along the right wall. The hairs on the back of my neck stood at attention.

My sixth sense told me that Mendez was going for some kind of weapon, probably a gun. Sure enough, a split second later, he reached into the closet, and pulled out a nasty-looking Mossberg shotgun.

I was in the room now. The light was murky at best. I had my pistol clutched in my hand and pointed center mass at Mendez's chest.

Time slowed. Despite the girlfriend's screams reverberating in my ears, I was laser focused on Mendez. Instead of firing, I sprung with every ounce of strength and slammed into him like an NFL linebacker as the black barrel bore started turning into my face. *Bang!* Both of us flew into the rear of the closet and hit the wall hard. I managed to land on top of him, knocking the air out of his lungs. With Mendez dazed, I quickly ripped the shotgun out of his hands, and banged him down to the floor so I could hand-cuff him. I wasn't gentle.

Now my heart was pounding so hard and so fast that I thought I was about to have a heart attack. I couldn't tell if it was because of the fear I'd felt, or the massive amount of adrenaline that had slammed into my system. FBI colleagues arrived to help me up and deal with the suspect. Others escorted me downstairs.

I'd come within nanoseconds of having my face obliterated with a shotgun. Outside I gulped fresh air, which helped me calm down. Concerned FBI guys came over to see if I was okay.

"Mike, you need us to take you to the hospital?" one of them asked.

"No, I'll be fine. I'm just a little shaken up."

The PHPD cop who had accompanied me to the bedroom came over and patted me on the shoulder in what I first thought was a gesture of sympathy. I was wrong. He was fucking pissed!

He asked, "What the fuck is wrong with you? You should have shot that son of a bitch. You know that? You fucked up. He would have shot you and he would have shot me, too!"

"I know," I responded.

"He nearly killed us both."

"You're right." I felt bad for letting a policeman down. I should have shot the bastard and had every legal right to do so. I don't know why I didn't.

Other cops and FBI Special Agents came out escorting a hand-cuffed Mendez.

"Guess what we found in the closet?" one of the Agents asked.

"What?" I asked back.

"A bag filled with cocaine."

"No shit."

"No shit," the FBI Special Agent echoed back. "When we pulled Nico up off the floor to take him in, he had no pants on. So I asked him, 'Hey, Nico, where's your jeans?' And the stupid motherfucker says, 'On the top shelf, under the motorcycle helmet.' So one of the cops reaches up to get the jeans and inside the motorcycle helmet he found a bag of coke."

You can't make this stuff up.

For days after, I remained shaken up, and kept asking myself over and over: *If I had been killed, what would have happened to my family?*

I took the next day off and took my sons Russell (four) and Michael (two) to the park. It was a beautiful spring day. As I pushed them on the swings, I thought, *Why the hell am I doing this? I'm making chump change and risking my life, for what?*

I already knew the answer. It was somewhat corny, but true: *There's real value to what I'm doing. I'm getting bad people off the streets, and protecting the public. I love my job. It's what generations of my family did before me. But this isn't playing cops and robbers with toy guns. It's real, and it means I've always got to be at the top of my game.*

If I knew all that before, now I felt it to the depth of my being. As I explained before, my wife and I had made a pact not to talk about what I did at work. But this time she could tell from my demeanor that something was wrong.

That night after she put the kids to bed, she turned to me and asked, "What happened yesterday?"

I lied. "Nothing."

"Then why did you stay home today?"

"It was beautiful outside so I decided to take the boys to the park."

She knew I was protecting her, and I knew she knew. That was the deal we'd struck and I was sticking to it.

In our case it worked. But it made me appreciate why spouses who have law enforcement husbands or wives reach a point where they say: If the job is more important than your family, I don't see how this marriage can continue.

There are other pressures beside the danger. When you're an FBI Agent you quickly realize that every move you make is scrutinized by your superiors and peers. They're watching to see if you're aggressive or passive, lazy or proactive, self-reliant or lean too much on others. Part of it is internal competition among a group with a lot of Type A personalities, and another part is the bureaucracy watching its ass.

I'd been on SWAT for five years and promoted to assistant team leader when I heard the call over the office PA, "Code Red, all SWAT to conference."

Normally FBI SWAT wasn't called unless there was some kind of federal jurisdiction. But in this case, the New Jersey State Police needed our help. Immediately my adrenaline started racing.

On April 20, 1995, three police officers were shot and two killed as they attempted to serve an arrest warrant on a transgender female named Leslie Nelson in the sleepy hamlet of Haddon Heights, New Jersey. Ms. Nelson had been a male named Glenn the first thirty-five years of her life and had spent the next two as a transgender female following a sex change operation. She also happened to have committed a felony ten years ago while still male.

The morning of the shooting, the three local police officers had gone to her parents' house in the small town of Haddon Heights, New Jersey, to question Ms. Nelson about allegations that she fondled her three-year-old niece and threatened her with a shotgun. Ms. Nelson had been cooperative during the course of the interrogation and revealed that she kept a loaded firearm in the house. That was a problem, because the law prohibited a felon from owning a gun.

So the police officers obtained an arrest warrant and returned to the house at 2 PM that afternoon. This time Ms. Nelson's elderly mother, Jean, let two of the officers in. When the officers reached the upstairs hallway, they encountered Leslie Nelson holding an AK-47 automatic rifle.

"Drop it! Drop it! Drop it!" a Camden County cop ordered.

Instead Ms. Nelson opened fired and hit the thirty-eight-year-old county officer with a hail of bullets. He died immediately. A Haddon Heights detective, who stood behind him, was struck in the chest, hand, arm, and leg. When Ms. Nelson's mother jumped between him and her daughter, Ms. Nelson stopped shooting and the detective managed to stumble out the front door and collapse on the lawn. He was later rescued by other cops and transported to a local hospital.

A third officer, and brother of the wounded detective was shot in the head and killed minutes later as he tried to evacuate families from houses across the street. It turned out that in addition to once being a man, Ms. Nelson was also an expert marksman.

By this point, Ms. Nelson's elderly parents had fled the house. She pushed the dead Camden County cop onto the front porch, and then donned a bulletproof vest and gas mask and barricaded herself on the top floor.

Other cops arrived, escorted neighborhood residents to a local church, and set up an armed perimeter. We arrived shortly thereafter geared up and ready to find more than one hundred police officers from twenty-seven different jurisdictions on the scene and in a state of chaos. This wasn't unexpected as crisis training for events of this nature were rudimentary at the time. Adding a horrible, ghoulish twist was the fact that the dead Camden County cop lay on the front porch where he couldn't be retrieved without exposing law enforcement to more automatic weapons fire.

Due to the large number of police officers from various jurisdictions and the strong emotions everyone was feeling over the fallen officers, it took longer than it should have to establish a Command Post with the New Jersey State Police in charge. We in FBI PH SWAT accepted that we would play a tactical support role.

We also understood that since the shooter was well-armed, had barricaded herself in her house, and wasn't responding to law enforcement, the standoff was likely to continue for a while. With guidance from the Command Post we worked out a schedule where we would rotate every twelve hours with the State Police and include an hour overlap to communicate new developments.

As anticipated, the standoff lasted through the first night and into the second day. As time dragged on and the media glare heightened, pressure to resolve the situation mounted. We were scheduled to take the midnight shift.

As an assistant FBI SWAT team leader, part of my job was to coordinate with the FBI supervisor in the Command Post. The supervisor had been one of my former bosses. He and I had never had a problem. But since supervisors and Agents generally traveled in separate social circles, I didn't know him well.

When I stopped by the Command Post before midnight to be briefed on recent developments, this supervisor had very little to say. But I sensed from the mood inside that something was about to break.

From the Command Post, I walked to our SWAT van and grabbed whatever I thought we might need during our shift, including extra tear gas canisters. From there I reported to the inside perimeter—fifteen yards from the front of house and partially hidden by large trees—to coordinate with my State Police counterpart.

The night was eerily quiet. Every so often we could see Ms. Nelson looking down at us from the second-floor window. An hour passed and my State Police counterpart didn't leave as I expected him to. Then I noticed increased radio traffic on State Police channels. When I tried to reach our FBI supervisor in the Command Post to find out what was going on, I discovered that our radios weren't working.

I turned to my New Jersey State Police counterpart and said, "I know something is about to happen. What the fuck is it?"

"We're getting ready to gas him out," he answered. "Time to earn our pay."

Minutes later, I heard the distinctive *whoosh-whoosh-whoosh* of a tear gas assault followed by the sound of shattering glass. The State Police attack continued for the next ten minutes, but didn't seem to be having the desired effect, because we continued to catch glimpses of Ms. Nelson wearing a gas mask through the second-story window.

At one point the State Police guy turned to me and asked, "You have any tear gas canisters on you? We're running out of gas."

Without hesitation, I answered, "Sure," and handed him the ones I had taken from the SWAT van.

The additional tear gas was fired and several hours later at around 4 AM, Leslie Nelson emerged from the house with her hands over her head and was quickly taken into custody.

The tragic ordeal was over. As State Police detectives and forensic experts examined the crime scene, I returned to my car. On the way, I passed one of our SWAT team leaders and mentioned that I had given the State Police some of our tear gas canisters.

Several days later, one of the senior guys in our office asked me about the tear gas. I answered in a wise-ass way, "Yeah, I gave it to them, and I wish I'd given them more."

He laughed, and then said, "Well, there might be a problem."

"What kind of problem?"

I soon found out that the FBI supervisor in the Command Post was accusing me of violating FBI policy for handing over tear gas without permission, and recommending disciplinary action.

I hit the fucking roof and wanted to confront the supervisor directly. He did his best to avoid me, and some of my fellow Agents managed to calm me down.

For days later, I sat at my desk stewing and waiting to be called to the front office to be interviewed. Meanwhile, I learned that other SWAT members were being questioned about my actions the night of the raid. Unable to hold my anger any longer, I marched down Mahogany Row and entered the office of the ASAC in charge of FBI SWAT.

I barely knew the ASAC at that point. I sat in one of the leather chairs in his office and vented, trying to control my temper, and explaining in blunt language that I made the tactical decision to hand over the tear gas to the State Police without asking my supervisor's permission, one, because I couldn't reach him on the radio that wasn't working, two, because it was the right thing to do under the circumstances, and, three, because I wasn't going to wait for permission to help another cop.

At one point during my emotional dissertation, I saw the ASAC crack a smile, but otherwise he reserved comment until I finished. At the end he simply said, "Don't worry about it. Good job."

I was never disciplined and remained on FBI SWAT for ten exciting and fun-filled years. Many of my SWAT teammates remain friends for life. And I'll be forever grateful for the honor and privilege of serving, the thrills and chills, the crazy times and stories, and most of all, the laughs. Thanks.

But my distrust of FBI supervisors lingered. What struck me was how quickly they were willing to turn on one of their own.

6

EASTLOAD

The year 1990 proved to be a turning point in my career. During the Bacalao investigation of the previous year, I'd worked as second fiddle to the Counselor, who acted as what was known in FBI lingo as the Case Agent. Now it was time for me to become a Case Agent—the captain of the investigative ship and the person who makes all operational calls, and has final authority. I was chomping at the bit.

The opportunity came in the form of an announcement over the office PA in the spring of 1990.

"Any Agent on a Drug Squad, pick up on line two."

Calls like this arrived every hour of every day to our office. Most of them came from wackos offering conspiracy theories, or misleading tips, or complaining about aliens in UFOs flying over their homes. Sometimes I would suggest that they tilt their tin foil hat a little more to the left, or cover their windows with butter to prevent X-rays from entering. But I answered, nonetheless, hoping that one of the hundreds of calls would yield a significant lead.

On May 15, 1990, when I picked up, a Hispanic male with a heavy accent described a one-kilo drug deal that was going to take place in a drug-infested area of North Philadelphia known as the "Badlands" in an hour. The Badlands was ground zero for all drug activity in Philadelphia, and where 95 percent of our Squad's work was concentrated.

The man provided the full names and physical descriptions of the two drug traffickers involved, a specific address, and the fact that the car they used would be equipped with a secret compartment known as a "hide." Before I could ask a single question, he hung up.

Sensing this tip was real, I asked a clerk to check the names and address against a shared FBI/DEA database called NADDIS (Narcotics and Dangerous Drugs Information System). Seconds after she entered their names, photos and lists of drug offenses appeared on the screen. I stood up in the Squad room and announced, "I've got a live one. Whoever is ready, let's hit this quick!"

Five guys followed me out the door and into the basement, where we fired up a couple cars and raced to the Badlands. We arrived at the location at 2:05 PM. The guy on the phone had said that the two dealers would be there at approximately 2:10.

Sure enough, five minutes later the car he described pulled up to the exact address. Two Hispanic men in their midtwenties got out empty handed, and went into the house. One was the size of a moose.

I snapped pictures of the two men and the car, and then radioed the Squad and said, "Showtime, guys. We're going to have to stop the car."

It was a hot day with a lot of people out on the street. If we tried stopping and arresting the suspects in the Badlands, we ran the risk of having the neighborhood turn against us and creating a shit storm. More importantly, if we made the stop in the Badlands every dope dealer would know about it in five minutes, and any chance we had of "flipping" the suspects, or getting them to cooperate with law enforcement, would go down the drain.

I radioed for a marked PHPD unit to set up on Roosevelt Blvd. A few minutes later the two Hispanic guys emerged from the house, carrying a gym bag. The gym bag was a tell—most dope dealers carried their product in gym bags at the time.

We watched the two dicking around in the backseat for a while. Then they took off. They drove like old ladies, well below the speed limit and heeding every traffic sign—another giveaway. We followed at a distance, while I manned the radio and coordinated the police cars.

A mile or so out of the Badlands, I gave the order to make the stop. The marked unit lit them up, burped their siren, and we pulled up behind it. I wanted the marked unit to make the initial stop so that the dope dealers couldn't later argue in court that they thought the guys in the unmarked car were trying to rob them, and, therefore, opened fire first—which is exactly what happened to a couple of Squad #2 Agents years later, who were badly wounded in a ferocious firefight.

"FBI! Get out of the car with your hands over your heads."

The driver was a nice-looking young man with a Florida driver's license, who identified himself as Nestor Lopez. He appeared cooperative, but started sweating like a pig. We separated him from the passenger, the Moose, who was already eye-fucking the cops.

By this point in my career, I'd stopped hundreds of drivers and dealt with hundreds of dope dealers. In any pair, one was always the alpha male. In this case, it was Moose. I didn't speak Spanish, but I know enough to understand the Spanish words for motherfucker (*hijo de puta*), which was constantly coming out of Moose's mouth, I told one of our guys to cuff him and stick him in one of the cars.

According to the 1968 Supreme Court decision *Terry v. Ohio*, the Fourth Amendment prohibition against unreasonable searches and seizures is not violated when a police officer stops a suspect on the street without probable cause for arrest, if the police officer has a reasonable suspicion that the person has committed or is about to commit a crime and has a reasonable belief that the person may be armed and dangerous.

The fact that we had seen the suspects coming out of a known drug house and hiding a gym bag in their car gave us reasonable cause. Also, the decision by the Supreme Court in *Michigan v. Long* (1983) extended *Terry v. Ohio* to allow searches of car compartments during a stop with reasonable suspicion.

So we were well within our rights to search the car. I calmly explained the situation to Nestor, whose shirt was now soaked with sweat and seemed ready to crack.

His response was: "I don't know what you're talking about, man."

"My friend," I replied, "we saw you come out of the drug house carrying a gym bag and fucking around in the backseat with Godzilla over there. If you don't tell me where the gym bag is, I'm calling the dogs."

"I don't have no gym bag," Nestor contended.

I looked him straight in the eyes and said, "Forget about Moose. He's going to jail for being stupid. I thought you might be brighter, but now you're acting stupid, too. Do you understand the situation you're in, or not?"

In other words, I knew there was cocaine in that car and we

weren't going anywhere until we found it. But when I looked through the windows into the car, I couldn't see a gym bag on or under the backseat.

I turned to Nestor and said, "This is your last chance to do the right thing."

He continued playing dumb, saying, "I still don't know what you're talking about."

I called for the K-9 Unit. As soon as their van turned the corner and started toward us, Nestor said, "Okay, man, I'll show you where it is."

He was also in handcuffs at this point. Nestor said, "Give me my car keys."

"Do I look stupid?" I responded. "No way that's going to happen."

"You're not getting shit without the car keys, man."

I looked at him hard. "Where's the gym bag?"

"You're not going to find it," he responded.

I climbed into the car and searched every inch of the front and back. Then I popped the trunk. No bag. I asked some of the Squad guys to look. They searched under all the seats thoroughly using a flashlight. Still no gym bag.

WTF? I was starting to wonder if my mind was playing tricks on me.

Nestor saw the confusion on my face and said, "If you give me the keys, I'll get it."

"Alright," I responded, "but if you try to run, I'll shoot you in the back." I was kidding but I'm pretty sure he didn't know that.

I undid the cuffs and handed him the keys. Nestor got in the car, started the ignition, and punched a series of radio buttons. I heard electronic buzzing and clicking, and then something metal popped open. Nestor reached into a secret compartment between the backseat and trunk, and came out with the gym bag. Inside the bag was a kilo of cocaine. Sweet.

The Moose and Nestor were now legally completely hosed, and charged with possession with intent to distribute one kilo of cocaine. During the early 1990s when the War on Drugs was on full throttle, both men were facing serious federal jail time.

Back at the Squad, while processing Nestor, I learned he was a native of Cuba and had come to the United States through the famous Mariel boatlift of the early '80s. He worked in the automobile industry when not selling dope, and knew his way around auto garages.

Messing with Nestor's head, I said to him, "You're fucked, kid, which is a shame. Your life is over. By the time you get out of jail, you're going to be an old man. No woman is ever going to look at you again."

After a few minutes, he looked up at me and groaned, "I gotta talk to my wife."

"Fuck that, my man. You're not talking to anyone. You're under arrest."

"Look . . . I'll cooperate with you guys, but I have to talk to my wife first."

"Forget it."

Usually when someone who is willing to cooperate speaks to a family member, the whole neighborhood knows about it ten minutes later, which renders the potential informer useless.

I was in the mug room taking Nestor's mug shots, when a Squad mate poked his head in and whispered, "His wife is here."

"What?"

"His wife is sitting outside."

That was strange because we hadn't given Nestor a chance to

call her. The only thing that made sense was that Moose—who had been processed by another Agent—must have been allowed to call his wife, and Moose's wife called Nestor's wife.

Peering through the one-way window to the waiting room, I saw this well–dressed, gorgeous Hispanic woman sitting with her legs crossed. She looked like a modern-day Sofía Vergara. My first thought was: *What the hell's she doing with him?*

In those days, I often led with my mouth rather than my head. "What the fuck, Nestor. How'd you land her?" I asked.

"Who?"

"Your wife. She's here."

He looked surprised. Normally in a situation like this we didn't allow suspects to talk to members of their families. But after letting them both stew awhile, I decided to make an exception.

"My friend," I started, "I'm going to bring your wife back here, and I'm going to sit with the two of you and I don't want you speaking Spanish. Understand?"

I called in a Mormon Agent who was fluent in Spanish just in case, and sure enough as soon as Nestor's wife saw her husband, she started jabbering at him *en Español*.

The Mormon Agent turned to me and said, "She told him that she's leaving him if he doesn't cooperate. She wants him to do whatever you say."

That was music to my ears. Nestor later explained that another part of the reason he agreed to cooperate was I had treated him professionally and with respect from the time of the car stop. That was a practice I'd learned during my days as a cop. I dealt with suspects the same way I would want to be treated under the same circumstances. It was up to them what type of law enforcement relationship they wanted to have. If they chose to be difficult, I could also be *extremely* difficult, too—totally up to them.

People usually become informants for three reasons:

1. They face criminal charges (or are "jammed up," in FBI parlance) and are seeking favorable treatment in court.
2. They're interested in eliminating their competition in the criminal world.
3. They're mercenaries who do it for the money.

Types two and three are dangerous, because they can turn on you at any time. The best informers are people like Nestor, who are motivated to work with law enforcement in order to get their criminal charges reduced.

For someone to become an FBI informant they have to meet a strict set of legal criteria and be approved by the FBI brass. They generally rule out anyone who has ever been convicted of a violent crime. Since Nestor was a drug dealer with no violent offenses on his record, he was accepted. His wife turned out to be a classy, educated woman with a good job at a utility company.

She started cooperating with us from Day One. Nestor, meanwhile, cooled his heels in jail, but was entitled to a bail hearing every thirty days. Because the courts were filled with spies working for the various drug-trafficking organizations, we didn't want to risk going to court and asking for his release. Instead, every thirty days at Nestor's bail hearing his lawyer would argue to lower his bail. After three months, it dropped to a reasonable amount, which Nestor's wife promptly paid. Once released, Nestor immediately reported for FBI informant duty, and I knew exactly what I wanted to use him for.

In the late '80s/early '90s, hides were new to both dope dealers and law enforcement. In fact, before we had stopped Nestor's car, I'd never seen one before. It got me thinking: *Maybe we set up an Undercover Operation (UCO) where we offer cars with hides, and use them to catch bad guys.*

UCOs and Title III electronic surveillance were the two most complex, demanding, difficult, and effective investigative techniques in the FBI's arsenal. I'd been part of a Title III investigation in the Bacalao case, but had never done a UCO. This seemed like the perfect time to try.

Back in those days, the FBI was just starting to use computers. So I spent several days after Nestor's arrest calling FBI offices all over the country. I asked each one: "Do you know anyone in the FBI or law enforcement who has run an undercover operation like this?"

The Los Angeles Division happened to be my sixth call. Agents there described an FBI resident agency office in Santa Ana, California, that had initiated a similar and very successful undercover operation a year earlier. They called their's "Loadtrak." Like a good FBI Agent, I immediately "borrowed" their concept for the East Coast and dubbed ours "Eastload."

Then, I traveled out to Santa Ana to see how they had set theirs up. Agents in the Orange County municipality generously shared all the nuts and bolts of their UCO. They showed me the various hide cars and trucks, and introduced me to the mechanics who had built the sophisticated hides.

Now that I could show the existence of a very successful precedent in another FBI Division, it turned out to be relatively easy to get my plan approved. Again, like a good FBI Agent, I "borrowed" all of LA's paperwork, or "ponies" in FBI speak, and started to draft my first FBI UCO.

The process to get an undercover operation approved required extensive preparation, research, logic, hard work, and long hours. There were multiple layers of approvals to secure from our own

Division, FBIHQ, and the Department of Justice. The FBI wasn't about to invest significant time, effort, manpower, and money on some goofy idea. It took a couple of months and gave me writer's cramps, before we got the green light from Washington with a budget of more than $500,000 for hide buildouts and dope buys.

Next came something we called "backstopping"—or fabricating a story with false documents to support an undercover operation. In this case, we wanted to set up a business that rented out cars with hides to drug dealers and thereby catch a lot of bad guys. We scoured the local area for an appropriate facility and found a huge warehouse in an industrial complex across the Delaware River in New Jersey big enough to accommodate twenty cars with private offices in front. Video monitors, listening devices, and one-way glass had to be installed.

More importantly, we had to build a profile for the business by incorporating it and getting insurance, just like a real company. Everything had to look perfectly legit if scrutinized. To start our fleet, we picked out three government-seized cars, a van, and a truck and hired the same Santa Ana mechanics to build hides inside them. They had to be the best, because if I wanted to run a successful FBI UCO, every detail had to be done right.

As the Case Agent of the UCO, I would be managing everything from behind the scenes. I also needed people to help me with logistics and the enormous amount of FBI paperwork that would be generated. From our Squad, I selected a young African American FBI Special Agent named Hank Roberts, whom I had just finished training to be my #2, and another Squad Agent named Wayne Kent, to be the admin guy. (More on Kent later.)

Critical to the success of the operation would be the undercover guys who would actually interact with the drug dealers and sell our services. Nestor and his wife were going to be our front people. With street cred among traffickers around the Philadelphia area, they were perfect to spread the news about our business. Since they couldn't appear to be managing the entire business themselves, they were going to need assistants to help man the showroom and do other tasks.

Our "clientele" was likely to be largely Hispanic, so we wanted native-Spanish speakers. At the time, the only Agents in our office who spoke fluent Spanish happened to be white. While working the Bacalao case I had gotten to know a number of New Jersey State Troopers, who had helped us execute stops, arrests, and huge drug seizures on Route 95 between New York City and Philadelphia. I picked two excellent, aggressive Hispanic NJ State Troopers to be our undercovers. They jumped at the opportunity to get out of uniform into plain clothes with plenty of nice jewelry and watches courtesy of the FBI.

In November 1990, five months after stopping Nestor's car and after spending $250,000 of FBI money in start-up costs to create MRK Services, we were ready to launch Eastload. Given the financial investment from the FBI, the pressure to succeed was high.

Armed with a pocketful of freshly printed business cards, Nestor went out into the drug-trafficking community and spread the word about our services. They included the five vehicles with hides and the first brick-sized cell phones.

Nestor acted as our recruiter, vetter, and salesman, and handed out business cards to major dealers only. We didn't want this to be a walk-in-off-the-street kind of business. If you didn't have a business card from Nestor, you didn't get in.

He did his job so well that when we got ready to open our doors one morning at 9 AM, there was a line of people waiting to get in. Once in the showroom, drug traffickers checked out our vehicles and phones. Then just like in a legitimate car dealership one of the undercovers would saunter over and discuss price and terms.

A typical conversation went like this:

UNDERCOVER: "How many pairs of shoes do you have?"
(Undercovers never used the terms of *cocaine* or *kilos*.)
"Four hundred," a customer answered.
"Then you're going to need the van. Right this way."

Our sparkling white Econoline van had a hide that could accommodate five hundred kilos and rented for $500 a day. We never let a conveyance leave without having a positive identification on the renter as a predicated drug trafficker, and a valid legal reason to initiate an investigation. All our vehicles were equipped with trackers, and everything that went on in the showroom was video and audiotaped.

Within weeks, we became the Hertz of drug dealers in the Philadelphia/southern New Jersey/New York City area. Demand for our services was so high that we had to order five more vehicles. The vans and trucks were by far the most popular, and they were being used to move large loads.

Even with ten vehicles in our arsenal, we had to be extremely selective. There were only so many vans and trucks we could follow and arrests we could make. It got to the point where we were turning down eight out of ten requests for our products.

Additionally, we were running Title III intercepts on the cell phones we leased out. Swamped with paperwork and the logistics of tracking vehicles and phones, we started to narrow our focus to only the big suppliers. At the same time, we had to be strategic in order to hide our hand.

Say we followed a car to a stash house. Instead of hitting the car, we might raid the stash house days later and with legal warrants. Next time around, we might do the opposite. The point was to confuse the bad guys and wall off our New Jersey operation. We didn't want the dealers to suspect that the FBI was running the car and cell phone rental scheme, and they never did.

We learned that most major Colombian suppliers were located in New York City, and made them our priority. When local Philadelphia dealers used our vehicles to travel to New York City, we assumed they were carrying money. And when they returned to Philadelphia, we figured they were transporting dope. Sometimes we'd let the money go and seized the dope. Other times, working with the New York FBI or New Jersey Police, we seized the money.

Once we followed one of our vans to a drug house in the Badlands and watched guys fill the hide with hockey bags. When we stopped the van on the Jersey Turnpike, we discovered the hockey bags were packed with a half million dollars in cash—a good day's haul.

Sophisticated and experienced drug-trafficking organizations like the Colombians built losing dope in law enforcement seizures into their business model. They moved so damn much of it that forfeiting some was no big deal. But hitting their money really pissed them off. The recorded conversations at MRK were hilarious, with dopers complaining to our undercovers that they were having a run of bad luck, and us encouraging them to push harder to make up the losses, and when they did, whacking them again.

In the spring of 1991, Eastload became so successful that word about our rental operation had spread from the streets into far away federal prisons. A pint-sized Cuban dealer named Cristobal Paz, serving a ten-year sentence for distribution of cocaine at a federal prison in Kentucky, learned about us through a business associate in Philadelphia named Theodore Santiago.

Paz's sentence was about to expire and once out, he wanted to make fast money. We first heard Paz's name when he reached out to Nestor through Santiago and inquired about our hide cars and phones. When we ran Paz's name through NADDIS, it showed up in connection with more than twenty drug investigations. Come on down!!

Literally days after Paz's release from prison, he strutted into our showroom with Santiago like he was the real-life Scarface. As I listened the arrogant little fuck demanded one of our hide cars immediately. Trouble was we didn't have any available.

Paz puffed out his chest at one of our undercovers and asked, "Do you know who I am?"

Minutes later, he held up one of our brick-sized cell phones and said, "Give me two of these. You know the FBI can't record these."

He was mistaken. We not only had federal court authority to listen on the cell phone he rented from us for ninety days, we also subpoenaed his phone records from prison. They revealed that Paz was communicating with major Colombian suppliers in New York and talking with them about setting up windfall future deals.

A week or so after his first visit, Paz got the hide car he wanted and started moving dope. We followed the first car to his New York supplier. The second time he rented a hide car from us, we waited until he left and hit his stash house, which contained thirty-five kilos of cocaine he had just obtained from a Medellín kingpin in New York.

Hoping that Paz could lead us to bigger fish, we made the strategic decision not to immediately arrest him. Because of the seizure of the thirty-five kilos, he owed money to the kingpin in New York—a Colombian man named Jose Gonzalez-Rivera. We focused on Paz and Gonzalez-Rivera almost exclusively for months, tracking their daily movements and monitoring their communications and learned that Gonzalez-Rivera was dealing directly with the Pablo Escobar organization in Medellín.

Two years into Eastload and after a year of following Paz, we'd amassed an impressive amount of highly incriminating evidence against Paz, Gonzalez-Rivera, and their associates, and it was time to throw their asses in jail. On arrest day, we had the undercover troopers order five kilos of coke from Paz. The exchange took place on the Jersey side of the Benjamin Franklin Bridge— not far from the location of our showroom. The cops accepted four kilos to be paid for later, and rejected one kilo by claiming it was of inferior quality, or "shit." The whole transaction was videotaped.

When Paz drove away, I signaled a marked New Jersey State Police unit to pull him over and arrest him. Simultaneously, we grabbed Jose Gonzalez-Rivera and ten of their top associates in New York City, Philadelphia, New Jersey, Baltimore, and Washington, DC.

On February 7, 1992, the U.S. Attorney for the Eastern District of Pennsylvania returned a twenty-eight count indictment charging the twelve defendants with multiple federal drug offenses for conspiring to distribute in excess of 320 kilograms of cocaine valued at $6 million dollars. In the indictment, the U.S. attorney stated, "This is the first time in this district that we have brought an indictment against a Medellín, Colombia, cartel cell leader."

Both Gonzalez-Rivera and Paz were charged with a CCE—running a Continuing Criminal Enterprise, aka the federal "Kingpin" criminal statute, the heaviest federal drug hit possible. If convicted of the CCE count, they faced life in prison.

I loathed Paz at this point. To underline the point that he was being charged under the Kingpin statute, I put a paper Burger King hat on his head for his booking photo.

The little fucker was so pissed at the prospect of spending more time in prison after that he tried to chest-bump me as he got up from the chair. I read the CCE statute to him, emphasizing the life sentence potential, and I could see the gears turning in his head.

I remember thinking: *I hope this asshole doesn't have anything to offer, because I don't want anything else to do with him.*

The arrests of Paz and Gonzalez-Rivera were the culmination of an enormously time-consuming and exhausting UCO—two years of sixteen-hour days and seven-day weeks with many missed birthdays and holidays. In return, we'd arrested approximately fifty drug dealers and had taken a huge amount of dope off the streets.

Over those two years, I'd tried to be a good father to our growing family, which now included five-year-old Russell, Michael born in 1987, and Paige born in 1990. I'd even signed up to coach my son Russell's T-ball team. But because of my unpredictable work schedule, I sometimes ended up missing three or four games in a row.

Now I wanted to make it up to my wife and kids after basically being MIA for two years.

In meetings with Paz and his lawyer after his arrest but before his trial, Paz kept intimating that he possessed valuable information, which he was willing to share in exchange for favorable consideration in court. A big part of me didn't want anything further to do with him. I was also dealing with something like thirty other defendants, some of whom were offering to cooperate and kick-start new investigations.

Assistant U.S. Attorney Shane Thomas, who was handling the case and a good friend of mine, advised, "You're letting Paz get under your skin. It's better to hear him out."

"Alright," I answered. "Tell his attorney that in our next meeting, Paz either plays his card, or we're moving on."

A few days later, Paz, his attorney, Shane Thomas, and I met in Shane's office.

I looked Paz in the eye and said bluntly, "This is your last chance. Shit or get off the pot."

He leaned back, nodded confidently, and said in heavily accented English, "You know who I can give you on a silver platter?"

"Who?"

"Mohammed Salim Malik," he said with great importance.

I'd never heard the name before. "How do you spell that?"

Paz spelled it for me and I wrote it down.

"Seriously?" he asked. "You never heard his name before?"

"No. I don't know who the fuck he is."

"Go look him up, man. He's famous. He's one of DEA's most wanted."

The hairs stood up on the back of my neck, but I showed no reaction. "Let's hear what you've got on him first."

Paz explained that while he was serving time in federal prison in McCreary, Kentucky, he had met Mohammed Salim Malik, who was in for ten years for trafficking hashish to the United

States. The two dope dealers had discussed a wide-ranging international plan whereby Pakistani heroin would be traded for cocaine from Medellín, Colombia, with Malik and Paz serving as the intermediaries.

The scheme was brilliant in a diabolical way, as it would open huge markets for both the Colombians and Pakistanis in Europe and the Americas, respectively. And had the potential to be a huge, multimillion-dollar operation.

Paz explained that the two men had finalized the plan months before Malik finished serving his sentence. Malik had gotten out first and was now back in Pakistan and waiting to hear from Paz and put the proposal into action.

I walked away thinking, *If this is real, I've got to pursue it. But my wife won't be happy.* I was also concerned that a year had passed since Paz had been released from prison. Maybe Malik had lost interest in the scheme in the interim.

First thing I had to do was check to see if Malik really was as important as Paz claimed he was. When I looked him up on NADDIS, all these alarm bells went off instructing us to notify DEA immediately. Malik was a prized target and considered one of the top five heroin distributors in Pakistan.

Shane and I spoke to the DEA and they said they had open cases on Malik. But the reality was that he was walking around free in the city of Karachi, Paz was offering to cooperate with us, and the DEA and FBI shared jurisdiction in drug cases, including international investigations.

We responded to the DEA diplomatically, "Great. We're here to help. We're going to take a shot at him ourselves."

My gut told me that Malik could be a major win. Other Agents on our Squad were more skeptical, asking, "How are you going to get in touch with him?" And, "Why are you bothering?"

"I'm bothering," I answered, "because he's one of the top heroin distributors in the world, and he needs to be locked up—again."

I'd already been lucky once with the tip that led me to Nestor. I wasn't going to let the excuses of my exhaustion, or the added workload, or the possible consequences at home cause me to turn my back on this opportunity either.

It was time to saddle up again.

7

PAKISTANI GOLD

Again, we had to jump through hoops before FBIHQ and the Justice Department approved our new undercover operation in March 1992. It helped enormously that this time I had "made my bones" (FBI-speak) in the Bacalao and Eastload investigations. In other words, I had successfully investigated and prosecuted major cases from start to finish. My FBI boss assigned three other Special Agents to help me work the new Pakistani UCO.

From the get-go, we ran into difficulties, including the fact that handling Cristobal Paz as an informant was a logistical nightmare. Because of the seriousness of the charges against him, no federal judge was willing to release him into our long-term custody. So every time we needed Paz to communicate with Mohammed Salim Malik, we had to seek permission from the court to take him from prison.

During the time Paz was in our custody, it was our responsibility to guard him 24/7. We assigned two older guys in the office who didn't mind spending hours sitting in our undercover office to serve as his security team. Their duties included escorting Paz back and forth from prison to our off-site undercover office, feeding him, and dealing with his bullshit. Every time we picked him up, he arrived with another litany of requests and complaints. He wanted a steak sandwich, he needed a more comfortable bed, because the one in prison didn't meet his standards, he didn't like the way we were running the case.

Another challenge involved the time difference between southern New Jersey and Karachi—Karachi is ten hours ahead. From our undercover office located in an office park in southern New Jersey, Paz initiated contact with Malik via phone and fax. He explained to Malik that he had recently been released from prison and was anxious to get the drug exchange scheme moving. The Pakistani drug trafficker seemed interested.

My mother once told me, "If you want to do something right, do it yourself." At the start of the operation, I requested a fax machine that we could use exclusively for communications with Malik. When I tested the machine that the FBI supplied by sending a sample message to our office machine, the fax went out with an FBI header—not a good idea when running an undercover operation. I made it a practice to double- and triple-check everything.

Paz was born in Cuba, and like Nestor, had come to the United States in the summer of 1980 during the infamous Mariel boatlift when Cuban leader Fidel Castro permitted 125,000 Cubans to leave the country and head to Florida. A number of those released were mental patients and criminals—Paz among the latter. Over the dozen or so years Paz had resided in the United States, he had spent most of it in prison or engaged in some form of criminal activity.

Paz had never developed a proficiency in English. Meanwhile,

Malik's faxes were carefully worded and sounded as though they had been written by an English professor.

After a month or two of at least seventy electronic messages between southern New Jersey and Pakistan, the two drug traffickers started speaking directly over the phone. Now the language barrier between Paz, a native-Spanish speaker, and Malik, a native-Urdu speaker, became a more serious issue. The former worried that his English wasn't good enough to negotiate the complexities of an international drug swap.

He needed help. I requested and got a fourth Agent named Lee Ross, who looked about twelve years old and spoke fluent Spanish. Despite the fact that Lee was a new recruit and new recruits usually got the shit assignments, I immediately designated him Paz's "cousin," and used him as the English translator between Paz and Malik.

Malik claimed to be running a travel agency in Karachi. The two principals, fearful that the DEA was listening in on their communications, spoke in code, referring to heroin and cocaine as "friend," "marbles," or "carpets."

"I need rugs. Lots of rugs," Paz said during one conversation.

"How many?" Malik asked.

"Hundreds at a time. Good quality rugs."

"I can arrange that. The rugs are the best you can find—the highest quality rugs in all of Pakistan."

The Paz-Malik talks might have sounded casual, but were actually carefully worked out on our end. Two days before Paz was scheduled to come to our undercover office, I'd start writing the outlines of a script for him to follow. Over the weeks and months, I got pretty good at thinking and talking like a dope dealer.

At the end of one conversation with Malik, Paz would set up

the time of their next communication. Sometimes Malik would call unexpectedly. A special red phone in the office was dedicated exclusively to Malik. Everyone had instructions not to pick it up when it rang.

Several times, Lee Ross answered the red phone by mistake and would have to explain that his cousin Paz was out on other business. Once, the red phone rang when Paz was on another phone yacking with one of his relatives. I got his attention, pointed to the red phone, and indicated that he should answer it promptly.

Paz, being an arrogant little prick, responded with a dismissive wave of his hand and turned his back to me. He continued to gab with his relative and ignore the ringing phone.

My world turned red. I'd never laid a hand on an informant before, and never have since. But this time, after months of putting up with Paz's constant complaints about how stupid we were and how he was being treated unfairly, I grabbed him by the collar, lifted him out of his chair, and threw him across the room like a human Frisbee as the other Agents froze in shock.

A dazed Paz pulled himself up and proceeded to answer the phone. When the conversation with Malik ended, he turned to me and with indignation in his voice asked, "Are you fucking insane, man? You are a crazy man. . . . What the fuck . . . you could have killed me. You're out of your fucking mind."

I came right back at him, still boiling hot. "You ever blow me off again when I tell you to do something, you midget motherfucker, maybe I will kill you. When I tell you to answer the phone, answer the phone!" I was all ready for Round Two.

Paz backed away shouting, "You can't treat me like this. I quit! I'm afraid to talk to you. I want to talk to the judge."

"Listen to me, Paz, and listen clearly," I said getting in his face. "Next time the phone rings, you've got three seconds to pick it up before you piss me off. You haven't seen me pissed off yet. What just happened, is nothing."

Paz always answered the Malik phone promptly after that.

Starting in February 1992, we listened in on approximately 135 calls between Paz and Malik. At the beginning, the odds of the operation's success had been infinitesimal, but they slowly increased as we persevered through one obstacle after another and inched forward.

In a conversation in April, Malik said, "Listen to me carefully. . . . I have something really big. I'm waiting on a signal from you. I'm almost ready . . . and I can do any damn thing. . . ."

In a fax sent in June, he boasted, "Let me educate you about my product. . . . This product contains between 85 and 90 percent, which means you can cut it four to six times."

He wasn't talking about apples. Heroin of the purity he referred to was unheard of in the United States at the time and if injected would be lethal. The amounts he talked about were unprecedented as well. In the early '90s, an exchange involving one or two kilograms of heroin was considered a huge deal in the United States. Now, we were overhearing Malik and Paz discuss the importation of up to five hundred kilograms of heroin worth hundreds of millions of dollars.

The amounts Paz and Malik discussed were so staggering that the DEA suggested the entire scheme was "not credible." Between managing the undercover operation and stealing time to spend with my family, I studied Malik and his native Pakistan. I learned that Pakistan was part of the "Golden Crescent," and shared a long border with the country of Afghanistan—the source of 90 percent of the world's heroin—and that the majority of Afghan heroin passed through Pakistan before it was distributed to Iran, Russia, Europe, and North America. So the quantities

Malik was talking about weren't outside the realm of possibility.

The initial trade had remained the same one they had outlined in prison—an exchange of a hundred kilos of cocaine for fifty kilos of heroin. Heroin was more expensive. One day Malik upped the ante.

He said to Paz over the phone, "I need 150 pair of shoes of your best merchandize."

"Then how many marbles will you send to me?" Paz asked.

"Fifty."

"No way," Paz answered. "If we do it that way you're screwing me on the deal."

Like most drug traffickers, Paz couldn't add two and two together, but was phenomenally skilled at negotiating dope deals. The purity of the drugs proved to be a complicating factor. Five kilos of heroin at 90 percent purity was more valuable than ten kilos at 20 percent.

Both Malik and Paz also struggled to solve the dilemma of how the exchange would take place. Once one of them sent their drugs, what would prevent the second guy from screwing him?

On the FBI side, we also faced a conundrum. Legal restrictions prevented us from sending illegal drugs to Malik in Pakistan. Nor could we front the millions of dollars required to purchase heroin from him. In 1992, one kilo of heroin had a street value of about $200,000, and Malik was offering to send a first shipment of fifty kilos. All we needed to legally charge him was a few ounces.

Faced with both problems, we came up with a solution, which was to ask Malik to send us a sample so we could test its purity and use it to establish a network for his product in the United States. The problem was that at the time it was practically unheard of for drug traffickers to front their product because of the possibility of being ripped off. In the scenario we came up with, we were counting on Malik to realize that the possible rewards outweighed the risk.

As Case Agent, I directed everything through Paz and Lee. The mental concentration, the daily pressure, and the fear of making a minor mistake that would compromise everything we had worked toward weighed heavily. After the more taxing exchanges, I would be so mentally exhausted that I would lay on the hard concrete office floor and immediately fall asleep.

It took months of daily phones calls to convince Malik to accept our plan. Now the remaining problem was the purity. In April 1992, I instructed Paz to try to set up a face-to-face meeting. During their next phone conversation, Paz said to Malik, "We have to get in the same room. This phone stuff isn't working."

"I agree," Malik responded. "Why don't you come here, so we can talk in person?"

Since Paz was spending his nights in a prison cell in New Jersey, there was no way he was going to Pakistan. Malik, on the other hand, had no interest in returning to the country that had locked him away for ten years. I suggested another friendly country—Canada. A month later, Malik offered to send his thirty-eight-year-old nephew Shahid Hafeez Khawaja in his place. The meeting was to take place in Montreal, Canada, which Malik thought of as outside the purview of U.S. law. What he didn't know was that Canadian and U.S. law enforcement officials had a long history of cooperation in criminal investigations.

This case didn't prove be an exception. Canadian authorities quickly offered to help us in any way. The next problem we encountered was that we couldn't take Paz out of the country. We recruited my old informant Nestor instead, and Paz told Malik that he was tied up with local business and was sending a trusted lieutenant to negotiate on his behalf.

I accompanied Nestor and Lee to Montreal in mid-May 1992, but as the Case Agent remained out of sight. Together with members of the Ontario Provincial Police (OPP) I watched as Nestor greeted Shahid at the Intercontinental Hotel in downtown Montreal. Shahid wasn't what I had expected, and looked more like a goofy computer salesman than a drug trafficker. He spoke excellent English with a slight lisp.

The first actual sit-down was scheduled for that evening at a local strip club. I slipped into the seedy club ahead of time and found the manager.

With dance music blaring in the background, I said to him, "I have a business associate named Khawaja coming in later and I want you to take good care of him." Then I greased his palm with a little green.

The manager nodded and replied, "You got it, pal."

In the company of two plainclothes OPP guys, I watched from a side table as Khawaja arrived in the company of Nestor and Lee. The moment Khawaja spied the naked dancers twirling and grinding on the stage, his eyes almost popped out of his head.

It struck me as both funny and sad. Here was a young married man with pockets full of money who had apparently never seen a nude woman before. He sat completely mesmerized by the dancers as beads of sweat dripped from his face onto his open-collared shirt. Getting him to discuss the possible dope deal wasn't going to be easy.

The Canadian cops and I drank beer, and tried to look inconspicuous. At this point in my career, I'd done very little undercover work, and was looking around the joint at the various customers trying to figure out who was who—traveling sales-man, undercover cop, criminal. As someone who'd always been interested in peoples' behavior, I found the clientele fascinating.

My intense curiosity caught the attention of a couple of hard-assed customers who walked over to me and asked roughly, "What the fuck are you looking at?"

"Sorry," I answered. "I was daydreaming."

Time to focus and blend. As the hours dragged on and Kha-waja kept spending money on girls and dances, I started to worry that he'd get rolled. I also wondered how I was going to explain the hundreds of dollars we were spending in the strip club to my FBI bosses.

The next day I got Nestor to convince Khawaja to accompany him to New Jersey, so he could meet Paz in person and settle business. As in the Eastload case, Nestor played his role perfectly. But when we tried to get him back into the United States, we ran into an unexpected snafu. Because of legal issues with Nestor's original travel documents from Cuba, he was banned from re-entering the United States.

So we sent Khawaja ahead to New Jersey to relax while we finished some other drug business in Montreal, and asked FBIHQ to petition the State Department and other U.S. government agencies to quickly resolve Nestor's travel problem so he could return to the States and not raise any suspicion. After three in-tense days of FBI lobbying, other government agencies refused to budge. By day five I started to worry that the whole under-cover was going up in smoke. We had to calm down Malik, who couldn't understand why we were spending time on a different drug deal.

The UCO seemed to be coming apart. One afternoon, as I was commiserating with my Canadian cop friends over drinks in their police station—yes, they had a fully stocked bar in their station that worked on the honor system—they offered to help. I assumed they knew a way to cut through the bureaucratic red tape. Instead with beer suds dripping from their mustaches they drunkenly offered to load Nestor in the trunk of one of their cars and sneak him across the border. They even suggested perforating the trunk with strategically placed bullet holes so Nestor wouldn't have trouble breathing. I got the sense this wasn't the first time our Canadian friends had pulled this stunt.

"You can't be serious?" I asked with a grin.

"We're dead serious," one of the Canadian cops replied.

After laughing my ass off, I wondered how my FBI superiors would react if they found out. Not well, I decided. The next day U.S. bureaucratic common sense finally kicked in, and Nestor was granted legal permission to return to the United States.

At our New Jersey office we produced Paz for a cameo appearance. Khawaja then called his uncle and told him what great guys we were, and asked us to take him to Atlantic City to ogle more naked dancers. He spent two days there partying. He was so distracted that we had to ask Malik to talk sense into his nephew so he could settle down long enough to work out the terms of a deal.

After months of tense negotiations, Malik finally agreed to front us 50 kilograms of heroin, which we would supposedly distribute and sell in the United States and use to convince our clients that we were supplying the best heroin in the world. All profits would be split fifty-fifty. If we were successful, Malik agreed to ship an additional 450 kilograms of heroin to be paid for cash on delivery (COD).

Even after securing a verbal agreement with Malik, no one in the FBI or DEA thought we could pull it off. I had one high-level FBI official tell me to "stop chasing the heroin fairy." Since that edict was issued from somebody who sat behind a desk every day, I didn't pay too much attention.

We spent the next few months painstakingly building credible backstopping legends for our purported shipping and receiving companies, and negotiating the nitty-gritty of the deal. The pace of phone calls between our New Jersey office and Karachi picked up further.

Finally in August 1992, Malik informed us that he was sending a load of heroin in steamer trunks to JFK Airport in New York. Our excitement spiked. We were finally going to get a chance to prove the skeptics wrong.

Three of us drove up to JFK and arrived after midnight. We'd already arranged for the steamer trunks to be moved to a secure room. As Case Agent, I was given the honor of opening the first of three very bulky trunks. Recognizing Malik's handwriting on the U.S. Customs forms, visions of bricks of heroin flashed in my head.

My heart beating fast, I opened the lid of the first trunk and saw what looked like stacks of Pakistani Yellow Pages books inside. I figured the heroin had to be hidden in hollowed-out sections of the books—a common trafficking ploy. Instead when I picked up one of the phone books and opened it all I found were pages and pages of Pakistani names and phone numbers.

"Fuck!"

I frantically leafed through the other phone books. Nothing but pages.

One of my colleagues uttered some words of encouragement. "The dope has got to be in one of the other trunks."

We ripped through the others. Same thing. Pakistani Yellow Pages, but no drugs. My heart sunk and my mood darkened to the point of devastation.

The three of us rode back to Philadelphia in total silence, as my mind imagined the heaps of abuse I was about to get from my superiors. We'd spent a lot of FBI time and money and delivered nothing.

The investigative leash squeezing tight around my neck, I asked myself, *Is Malik deliberately fucking with us? Why? Does he want to do this deal, or not?* My head spun in circles.

The following day, our guys fetched Paz from prison. When I told him about the phone books, he seemed as stunned as I was.

Surprisingly, Malik was unapologetic and businesslike when Paz spoke to him on the phone. He asked, "Did you receive the trunks?"

"Yes, we did," Paz answered. "But—"

"Where?"

"JFK Airport."

"Good. Read me the labels."

"What labels?" Paz asked.

"The labels that were on the trunks."

"You mean the shipping labels?"

"No, the labels put on by the U.S. Customs inspectors."

As they spoke, it slowly dawned on me that Malik wasn't playing games. He'd sent the load of phone books to test if a shipment from a new business address in Pakistan would pass through U.S. Customs and arrive safely at our undercover office. As an experienced international trafficker, Malik knew that any first-time delivery from a source of supply country such as Pakistan would be red-flagged and probably searched by U.S. Customs. He was being smart, not stupid, and intentionally didn't tell us that he was sending a test shipment so that we didn't do anything unusual.

My FBI bosses and Squad mates didn't see it that way. From

their perspective, we'd spent six months of time, energy, and FBI money for several trunk loads of Pakistani phone books. We quickly became the laughingstock of our local office and FBIHQ.

In typical FBI fashion, the comments from the Drug Squads were brutal.

"Hey, Mike. Nice work on nabbing those Pakistani Yellow Pages—how many years they going to get?"

"Yeah, next time I need to look up a car repair place in Karachi I know who to ask."

The many jokes made at my expense rattled my waning confidence. The person in the Squad most supportive was my immediate boss, The Colonel, who pulled me aside and told me to keep my head down and keep working the case.

Determined to rally the team, I told them that every day we remained in the hunt was a good day. Malik was still talking to us and didn't seem suspicious. By this point, I had listened to hours of conversations, and felt I could detect even the subtlest change in his tone and manner.

We inched forward. Finally, on October 12, Malik informed us that six pieces of luggage would be departing Karachi, Pakistan, for Philadelphia on Swiss Air flight #395 the following day. Three of the pieces would contain jogging suits and the other three pieces of luggage would hold the "requirements" that had been discussed.

All of us remained low-key this time. When I told my bosses the news, they seemed unimpressed.

The shipment was scheduled to land on October 15, 1992, at Philadelphia International Airport. If we seized it as law enforcement, we risked tipping off Malik and his associates. So we arranged to receive the boxes in our current role as UCAs (Undercover Agents).

Once we confirmed with Customs officials that the "six pieces of luggage" had arrived for our covert company, we had them moved to a private and secure area. We arrived at the airport around 3 AM when very few people were around.

My heart rate rising, I led the way into the secure backroom and saw the luggage—three suitcases and three large boxes wrapped in layers of thick plastic and burlap. Recognizing Malik's handwriting on the Customs forms, my mind raced to dozens of possible outcomes, some good, some awful.

We set the suitcases aside, and then as professional courtesy as the Case Agent, I was given the privilege to open the first box. Lee handed me a box cutter and I struggled and cut through the thick plastic and burlap. Holding my breath, I reached inside the first box and removed . . . a handful of cotton bathrobes.

"Not again!" It felt like my heart had stopped beating. A huge cloud of doom filled the quiet room.

Issuing a stream of curses, I threw a handful of robes to the floor in disgust. Then I reached my arm deeper into the box. Under another layer of robes, I felt something hard and rectangular. Holding my breath, I moved my hand to the right and grazed another brick-like object, then another, and another.

"Pay dirt, guys!" I shouted. "I think we got something!"

Time seemed to stand still as we tore through the boxes and removed one brick after another. Each brick we assumed held one kilogram of heroin and was worth about $200,000 in the United States. As they kept coming, we beamed at one another like kids on Christmas morning. I was smiling so much, I must have looked like a complete idiot.

"Can you believe this, Mike?" one of the guys asked.

"We've hit the fucking heroin lottery!"

We eventually counted forty-six bricks containing a total of

44.6 kilos of heroin, or slightly less than a hundred pounds. Lab tests later determined that they averaged 85 percent purity, which was unheard of at the time. Cutting it three or four times would triple or quadruple its street value.

The DEA later placed a street value of $180 million on it, and we had gotten the heroin without spending a dime of government money. It seemed unbelievable.

Then it dawned on me that we'd better lock the heroin away quickly. So we packed the bricks in the trunk of our car and raced back to our FBI office, arriving at 6 AM. The secure evidence vault wasn't going to open until the start of regular FBI working hours, 8:15 AM.

We piled the bricks on a long metal dolly and waited in the Squad #3 work area. The only way I could think of to secure the heroin before the vault opened was to climb on top of the bricks and sit on them.

I was half asleep when the first person entered the office. It was the leader of the other Drug Squad—Squad #2—a tough, competent Supervisory Special Agent with twenty-five-plus years of experience. When he saw us sitting on the bricks of heroin wrapped in plastic, he froze as though struck by lightning.

"Is that what I think it is?" he stammered.

"Yup."

"Coke or heroin?"

"It's heroin. Forty-six kilos."

"Holy shit!"

More Special Agents arrived. Word of the seizure spread like wildfire through the office. Someone called FBIHQ in Washington and news of the haul circulated there as well.

People I barely knew surrounded me, patted me on the back, and congratulated me. I'd become the most popular guy in the office in an instant. The only thing I wanted to do was lock the heroin into the evidence room, and go home to see my wife and kids, who I'd practically ignored for the past year, and sleep.

Weeks later, as the excitement of the seizure continued, I learned that the Assistant Director of the Criminal Investigation Division—the number-three official in the FBI hierarchy—was on his way from Washington to hold a press conference. It dawned on me that only days earlier, this official and most of the other people congratulating me, didn't know my name. Suddenly, a mere five years into my career, I'd become the FBI's "Golden Boy"—FBI-speak for an Agent who can do no wrong.

It felt good, but there was still a lot of investigative work to do. In order to make arrests we had to attach bodies to the drugs. Fortunately, the internet was in its infancy as was twenty-four-hour cable TV news channels. So news of the seizure didn't reach Malik and Khawaja in Pakistan. Our goal now was to lock them up.

The lure was the millions of dollars in cash owed to Malik from the supposed sale of the heroin in the United States. During a conversation between Malik and Paz on October 27, Malik proposed that Paz travel to Hong Kong to deliver the first payment of $2 million to his nephew Khawaja. Through Paz, we tried to convince Malik to travel to Hong Kong with his nephew.

In '92, Hong Kong was still a British colony and subject to U.S.-UK extradition agreements. Since the transfer of sovereignty to the Chinese People's Republic was scheduled to take place in a few years, our liaisons were both British police who spoke Chinese and People's Republic of China police who spoke some English.

Other than the Canadian cops, I'd never really worked with foreign law enforcement counterparts before, and didn't know what to expect when Lee, another Agent, and I arrived in densely populated Hong Kong. I soon learned that cops are cops no matter where they work. Both the British and Chinese police were very warm hosts, complete ballbusters (in foreign languages), and wined and dined us nonstop, as we continued to try to convince Malik to leave Karachi with Khawaja and meet us in Hong Kong.

Since my tastes in food are pretty basic, I avoided the more exotic dishes. At one buffet dinner, I thought I was eating a chicken dish, only to learn that it was really pigeon. No thanks.

During another evening escapade that involved the consumption of copious adult beverages, a group of very happy UK and Chinese officers helped me into a car and took off like maniacs into the countryside. They seemed to be enjoying themselves enormously. I, meanwhile, had no idea where we were going or what they were up to.

After forty minutes of winding through the dark countryside, we pulled up to a decrepit saloon/club in the middle of nowhere where my foreign hosts were greeted like regulars. One of the Chinese cops introduced me to a woman of about seventy with two missing front teeth. She bowed and I nodded politely as the cop and woman jabbered back and forth in Chinese. Before I knew what was happening, the elderly woman took me firmly by the hand and was leading me to a backroom.

That's when a British cop stopped me and explained that the old woman was a very experienced prostitute who was prepared to grant me three carnal wishes.

"Thanks," I said, turning back, "but I'm fine."

One of the Chinese policemen told me that I didn't know what I was missing and that the old woman's missing front teeth only enhanced her "skills."

"That's okay. I don't mean to insult her or her skills. But I think I'll pass."

Minutes later another prostitute joined us at our table and asked for my business card to keep as "a memory." A strange request, I thought, in our current setting and one I politely declined. It's not that I'm a prude; I just didn't think it was smart to leave an FBI calling card as a memento in a whorehouse—although I did see many business cards from customers from all over the world, including Dallas, Texas.

As we left my police hosts explained that we had driven into Communist China. They found great amusement at my shocked reaction. Now I was really glad that I hadn't accepted the three carnal wishes from the elderly woman. Imagine the reaction if I had and the news got back to FBIHQ.

Let's see if we got this right. . . . While on official business you took a detour into Communist China to have sexual relations with a toothless, seventy-year-old woman?

Lee, the third FBI Agent, and I remained in Hong Kong for a week, hoping that Malik would join us and we could arrest him. But the canny drug trafficker didn't budge. Nor did he respond positively to other entreaties to meet in London or other locations around the world.

Finally, in January 1993, four months after the heroin seizure, Malik and Khawaja were arrested by Pakistani law enforcement. During the last recorded call between Paz and Malik, we directed Malik to a location in Karachi where the Pakistani authorities were waiting for him.

Because of the extradition process, I knew it could take months before we had Malik and Khawaja in U.S. custody. Still, I was enormously pleased. My team and I had arrested one of the world's leading heroin traffickers and had seized an enormous amount of heroin valued at $180 million at no cost. In fact, it had been the largest heroin seizure in Philadelphia history, and the eighth largest in the world at that time.

After only five years in, I was feeling very good about my choice to join the FBI. Little did I know that a little more than one year later, my promising FBI career would suddenly become a real-life nightmare, all because of the prized, seized heroin.

8

BETRAYAL

In January 1994, I slapped the handcuffs on Malik and Khawaja when they were extradited to the United States, and successfully concluded the UCO that had drawn the two Pakistani drug traffickers out of the shadows. Now began the long, tedious process of preparing the case for trial with my buddy Assistant U.S. Attorney Shane Thomas. January 1994 was also the last time I drove Paz back to jail, and said good-bye to the informant with a curt, "Next time I see you will be in court." As usual, he scowled and started ranting about the terrible way he was being treated.

Without a doubt, Paz had played a critical part in the UCO that had nabbed the Pakistani drug traffickers. He'd also been a royal pain in the ass all the way through. He'd cooperated with us for only one reason—to save his skinny ass—because he was facing a life sentence for trafficking 320 kilos of cocaine soon after he had been released from federal prison on another drug-trafficking charge, and was looking for a break from the judge. True to our word, we filed a Section 5K1.1 form with the court in accordance with the U.S. Sentencing Guidelines. It stated that Paz had provided substantial assistance in the investigation of another person.

This allowed the judge to reduce Paz's overall sentence, which in Paz's case had a mandatory minimum of no less than twenty years and a maximum of life.

On the day of his sentencing in early '94, I sat with AUSA Thomas waiting for the judge to arrive. I observed a pretty Hispanic woman entering the nearly empty courtroom in the company of two well-dressed children and sitting in the back row.

"That's Paz's wife," whispered Thomas.

"Good-looking woman," I responded. "What she's doing with the garment bag?"

"Beats me."

We watched the marshal walk over to her and overheard him say, "Ma'am, you can't come into the court with this."

"No," Paz's wife replied, "I'm the defendant's wife. This is his suit."

The marshal unzipped the bag. Inside was a very fashionable suit, shirt, and tie. The suit alone looked like it cost $1,000. It signaled to me that in Paz's sick mind, he thought he was going to be released that day.

Thomas shook his head and whispered, "Arrogant little fuck."

"Typical Paz," I responded.

Minutes later Paz entered the court as cocky as ever in the company of two armed marshals and wearing an orange prison jumpsuit. After surveying the room, he winked at his wife, waved a big hello to his children, and smirked toward the government table to remind us that he was the smartest guy in the room.

Speaking through a court translator, he introduced his wife and children. Then, puffing his chest out like a self-proclaimed hero, he explained to the judge how because of his hard work and ingenuity the FBI had made an important international case. True to form, he expressed no remorse over the crime he had committed, nor did he display a drop of humility. At the end, he seemed to be waiting for the occupants of the courtroom to jump to their feet and applaud.

Instead the sentencing judge—a known ballbuster—looked at him stone-faced. I thought I detected smoke emanating from his ears. Following court practice, the judge announced Paz's sentence in months—234. I quickly did the math in my head. It came out to nineteen and a half years, six months below the maximum minimum sentence.

I saw Paz's attorney lean toward his client and relay the bad news, and Paz's face turn a deep shade of red. He puffed out his cheeks like a blowfish and stared at the judge in disbelief.

I disliked Paz immensely, but felt a little bad for him. On reflection, the judge's sentence was totally justified. Paz hadn't learned a thing from his first stint in federal prison and had immediately returned to drug trafficking when released. That was the last time I ever saw him.

At the start of 1994, I was feeling good about my life and career. Having just wrapped up a major international heroin case, I was now considered one of the more successful Case Agents in the Philadelphia office. I was having a blast on SWAT. Waiting for me at home every night was a wonderful wife and three healthy kids. Then my perfect world exploded.

A few months later in April, as I was preparing for Khawaja's and Malik's trials, I learned that the 44.6 kilos of the seized Pakistani heroin had been stolen from the FBI evidence vault and replaced with baking powder. In addition, 11 kilos of cocaine from the Eastload investigation had also gone missing. The combined value of the two missing drug loads exceeded $200 million, and I was considered the chief suspect.

In the blink of an eye, I went from FBI "Golden Boy" to "Public Enemy #1." The whole thing was incomprehensible, and the pressure almost unbearable—as though my head had been placed in a vise and was slowly being squeezed tighter with every second that passed.

The SAC had instructed me not to tell anyone—including my Squad mates and wife. I was scared to death and didn't have anyone to turn to for advice. I briefly thought of hiring an attorney, but decided against it, one, because I knew I was innocent; and, two, because I couldn't afford one.

Adding to my distress was the fact that nearly everyone in the office knew about the heroin theft and thought I was guilty. Most of my Squad mates and friends on SWAT stood by me, but Executive Management in particular treated me like I was scum. I understood that since I had access to the evidence vault and as the Case Agent was officially authorized to review and handle the heroin evidence at any time, it made logical sense to consider me a suspect. What I couldn't understand was how quickly colleagues and FBI brass turned against me.

I expected that they more than anyone would respect my integrity and appreciate all the long hours I had put in and risks I had taken.

But the cold, hard reality was that they didn't. Nor did they make any effort to hide their negative judgments of my character—judgments that were clearly spelled out on their faces every time I encountered one of them in the office and heard their whispered asides when I walked into a room.

Because I couldn't explain my situation without risking being called on the carpet for insubordination, I kept my feelings to myself. The best I could do when someone looked at me funny was respond with a sharp, "What the fuck are you looking at?"

Probably the hardest thing I had to do was officially inform the federal prosecutor in the case and my close friend Shane Thomas about the heroin theft. Shane seemed suitably shocked. Then, I had to look him in the eye, tell him I was the main suspect, and swear to him that I didn't do it.

"Of course not, Mike," he answered. "That goes unsaid."

The next time I was summoned to the SAC's office, he informed me that the FBI was obligated to notify the U.S. Attorney's Office about the heroin theft, and they would pass that information on to both the court and the defendants. Malik's attorney had previously indicated that his client was going to plead guilty. Now his plea would likely change.

I felt mortified. It seemed that with every passing second all our hard work and my whole career was slipping further down the drain.

My mind raced every second of every day with fears of my future incarceration and how it would affect my family. Sleep was impossible and concentration on work was extremely difficult. Still, I had to report to the office every day where I endured more whispers, suspicious looks, and other forms of humiliation, and waited for the walls to close in on me and crush me to death.

I thought about going to The Colonel, and asking, "What the fuck am I supposed to do?"

But even that could have been construed as a form of insubordination. So I walked around like a zombie and waited to be arrested. My only solace was knowing that I didn't steal the heroin, which I told myself a hundred times a day, sometimes out loud, which drew more stares.

The only way I had to let off stream was to go to the gym and work out like a madman, which I did whenever I could. I briefly considered drinking to ease the anxiety, but decided against it because I was afraid I wouldn't be able to stop and didn't want to subject my family to the same torment my father had inflicted on me, my siblings, and my mother.

Rumors about me swirled around the office. A week after being informed about the investigation, one of the secretaries told me that the FBI was planning to search my house. They were going to do it when I wasn't there, but my wife and kids were home.

I thought of telling my wife: If the FBI knocks on the door, tell them to go fuck themselves.

I decided not to. Given her negative attitude toward the FBI and blunt style, I figured she would probably do that anyway, should it happen.

I spent more time at home, fixing shutters and doing the kinds of odd jobs around the house that I had ignored for years. My wife looked worried. Several times, she asked, "What's up?"

"Nothing," was my answer.

We both knew it was a lie, but I was sticking to the deal we had made while I was a cop.

One evening, I was home mowing the back lawn for the fifth time that week. Around 6:30 I walked inside and saw that my pager had gone off and was displaying the main number of the Philadelphia office.

I called and the operator put me through to the SAC.

"Boss," I said, "it's McGowan."

"McGowan, we need to interview you."

"Tomorrow morning?" I asked.

"No. Get your ass in here now."

I showered and dressed, and as I came down the steps, a voice in my head said: *Go kiss your wife and kids in case they lock you up.*

I found Russell, Michael, and Paige outside playing with their friends, hugged each of them, and told them I loved them. They looked at me funny and went right back to playing with their bikes and wrestling. I turned and saw Sam standing behind the screen door watching. With the huge lump in my throat I kissed her on the forehead, and we exchanged a look that acknowledged that whatever was about to happen could change our lives forever.

Then I got in my car and started driving like a wild man. Flying over the Ben Franklin Bridge into Pennsylvania, I looked at the speedometer and saw that I was pushing ninety. I said to myself, *You're going to get into an accident and then everyone is going to think you killed yourself because you were guilty. Is that what you want your children to remember?*

Upon reaching the office, the SAC sent me directly to the interview room. I'd heard before that two guys from Executive Management were running the initial investigation. Because they were paper pushers and not seasoned street Agents, I feared they wouldn't know what they were doing. I didn't want to end up like other people who had been arrested and sent to jail for crimes they hadn't committed.

When I entered the interview room, I instead saw two seasoned street Agents, Bill Courtney and Steve Allen. I didn't know them personally, but was aware of their stellar reputations. Both had formerly served in the NYC office as Case Agents and had twenty years of experience.

I remember feeling relieved and saying to myself, *Thank God*.

The first thing they did was read me my Miranda rights. I'd done the same thing to hundreds of suspects myself. Now I felt all the anger and frustration I was holding rising up inside me.

I said, "Guys, I kind of know what it says."

"Do you understand your rights as they've been read to you? Are you willing to waive those rights now?" the investigators asked.

"Are you fucking kidding me?" I shot back as weeks of bottled up emotion spilled forth. "Yes, I understand my fucking rights. I'm an FBI Agent and this is absolute bullshit. I can't believe the FBI thinks I could have done this."

They asked if I wanted to consult a lawyer. I declined even though I probably shouldn't have. Fuck them—I didn't do anything wrong.

Then they asked me to sign my name and initial each paragraph of the Miranda Warnings. It felt like an out-of-body experience. I really was the main subject of a massive FBI investigation into a vile crime. Unbelievable!

I signed the document and threw it back across the table.

Courtney asked, "What Squad are you assigned to?"

"Squad #3. The Colombia Drug Squad. But you know that already."

"What's your current investigation?"

"Knock off the bullshit, guys," I responded. "I can't believe you really believe that I took that shit. You motherfuckers, I worked my ass off to get that heroin, and you think I stole it? Fuck you!"

Allen looked up and asked without emotion, "Are you done?"

"Fuck you!"

I was ready for a brawl, or what was known in law enforcement as a "confrontational interview." They proceeded to walk me through the case, step by step.

"When was the dope seized?"

"October 15, 1992."

"Did you secure it in the FBI evidence vault that day?"

"Yes, I did."

"Would your fingerprints be on it?"

"Fuck, yeah. I touched every single brick. That's kind of how it works when you're the Case Agent and you make the seizure."

"What do you think happened to the missing evidence?"

"How the fuck would I know?"

Even in my highly agitated state, I said to myself: *If these guys are real investigators, if they do their job the right way, maybe this will work out.*

After all, it wasn't a difficult crime to solve. Only someone with access to the FBI evidence vault could have stolen the heroin. That narrowed the list of suspects considerably.

Toward the end of the three-hour interview, one of the investigators asked, "Are you willing to take a polygraph test?"

"Fuck, yeah. Hook me up right now. I didn't fucking do it."

"Will you consent to another interview?"

"Fuck, yes. Any time."

"Will you need to have an attorney present?"

"No. How many times do I have to tell you motherfuckers I didn't do it? I didn't steal that shit. Are you done?"

Afterward, I felt somewhat relieved, and drove home with the car windows open and slept through the night for the first time in a week.

Next day when I arrived at work, I was summoned to the interview room again. Bill Courtney and Steve Allen sat waiting in freshly pressed suits and looking like a million bucks, and me feeling like dog shit.

Courtney said, "We need to take your prints. Major case prints."

I swallowed hard. "You want me to provide you with major case prints?"

"Yes. Will you consent voluntarily?"

"Yes."

Dark thoughts filtered through my head as they led me down a corridor to our mug room, where I had fingerprinted and photographed Malik, Khawaja, Paz, Gonzalez-Rivera, and other suspected criminals. Major case prints were usually taken only in serious felony offenses. With the door open so the entire office could see what they were doing, Courtney and Allen took my finger and palm prints one at a time. Squad members, clerks, and secretaries peered in the door to see what was going on.

Next I expected the investigators to slap handcuffs on me and arrest me. Instead they marched me back to the interview room and started grilling me again.

A dozen more days of interviews followed. Courtney and Allen kept going over and over the same sequence of events. Maybe they were trying to catch me in a lie. Or maybe they were starting to believe I was telling the truth.

"When did you seize the heroin?"

"October 15, 1992. You asked me that already. Why are you guys busting my balls?"

"You drove the heroin straight from the Philadelphia airport to this office to put it in the evidence vault?"

"That's correct. If I was planning to steal it, I would have done it that night and no one would have seen the heroin in the first place. But I didn't. I loaded it into the evidence vault. Other Agents were with me the entire time."

The interviews were long and mentally exhausting. One morning I was sitting at my desk in the Squad room, when I saw Jarhead approach. I considered the former Marine a close friend, mentor, and role model.

I steeled myself for more abuse from someone that everyone in the office looked up to. With the whole Squad watching, Jarhead leaned across my desk, looked me in the eye, and in a booming voice said, "I don't know what the fuck is going on here, and I don't know what's going to happen. But I know one thing for sure, Mike, you didn't have anything to do with this bullshit. So fuck them!"

He shook my hand and walked away. The moment was electric.

I was so moved, I started to well up inside, and will never forget his complete support.

At around the same time, word leaked out that a second Agent assigned to Drug Squad #3 and a close friend of mine named Will Thompson was also being investigated in connection to the heroin theft. It made no sense because he was even more of a straight arrow than I was. The two of us sometimes worked out together. I remembered that a month or so earlier, Thompson and I had snuck out early from work one day to play a round of golf.

While we were teeing off on the eighth hole, Thompson turned to me and said that he thought we were being followed. He'd formerly served on the FBI Surveillance Squad and knew the vehicles they drove and their techniques.

"You really think the FBI sent out a surveillance team to follow us because we're playing golf during business hours?" I asked.

"Sure seems that way, Mike."

At the time, I laughed and told Thompson he was being para-noid. Looking back on the incident, that's exactly what they had been doing. The FBI was following us because they considered us suspects. Years later, I became friends with one of the surveil-lance Agents who had been watching us that day, and he told me the first time he set eyes on me was through a pair of bin-oculars.

The interrogations by Courtney and Allen continued but grew shorter as they narrowed their questions to specific periods of time. During a meeting in mid-May 1994, Allen asked me when I had last examined the heroin evidence.

"Right after we seized it," I answered. "In the fall of '92."

"You sure?"

"Of course, I'm sure. There would be no other reason to check it until right before the trial."

"Was it April 27, 1993?" one of them asked.

"I don't think so. . . . But let me check my dates."

I asked to return to my desk to get my calendar book for 1993, where as an anal retentive, I recorded the details of every day's activities. The book showed that on April 27, 1993, I was out of the office with the entire Philadelphia FBI SWAT team at a train-ing facility ninety miles away.

Allen handed me a document and asked me to review it. It turned out to be the evidence vault sign-in sheet.

He said, "Take a look at the April 27, 1993, date and verify the entry next to your file number."

My eyes scanned halfway down the document and stopped at my file number, 281F-PH-75449. The signature beside it wasn't mine. I looked at the entry a second time and my heart stopped as I recognized the handwriting. I knew it because I'd seen it a hundred times. The handwriting belonged to Wayne Kent, one of the Agents assigned to the Eastload case, and someone who was not involved in the Malik heroin case.

In a split second all the pieces clicked into place.

"That's not my signature, it's Kent's," I said. "Wayne stole your fucking heroin." Then I handed the log back.

"You sure?" Allen asked.

"Yes, I'm sure. One hundred percent."

I was red-hot mad, not at the investigators, but at Kent, who had put me through this fucking nightmare. He was a second-tier Agent with a reputation for climbing on to good cases and letting others do the heavy lifting. During Eastload he grew his hair out and rode a motorcycle to create the impression that he was working undercover when he played no undercover role whatsoever. Instead, his duties included turning on the lights in the morning and putting on the coffee.

Kent was a burly guy from Kentucky and was married with a young stepdaughter. He and I had served on SWAT together and had never had a problem before. Now I wanted to wring his fucking neck.

A year earlier Kent had been diagnosed with Hodgkin's disease—a cancer of the lymphatic system. While he was being treated, The Colonel, against FBI policy but as a kind human gesture, had put him on restricted duty and had assigned him to listen to surveillance tapes in a room next to the evidence vault so he could continue to draw his full pay. That's where he had cooked up his evil plan.

Later evidence would show that he conceived it only after word leaked out that Malik was planning to plead guilty and not go to trial. Had that happened, the heroin would have been incinerated, per FBI policy. Kent took the calculated risk that no one would examine the heroin or the evidence room log before the drugs were destroyed.

When Kent entered the evidence vault on April 27, 1993, and entered my file number in the presence of a support employee, he did so specifically to point the finger at me. Access to the vault required passing through a cipher-locked door guarded and opened by a support employee and then unlocking an interior metal cage door using a key kept by the ASAC.

Kent must have memorized the combination to the cipher door and entered it sometime after April 27 and after office hours when no one was around. All of us knew that the key to the metal cage door, which the ASAC was supposed to keep closely guarded in a locked safe, actually sat in a coffee cup on his desk.

This was the same buffoon ASAC who had been pushing to have me arrested and my house searched.

Once inside the basketball court–sized vault, Kent cut the bottom of the bags, replaced the heroin with baking soda, and sealed the bags with special FBI heat-sealing equipment. He repeated the same process with the eleven kilos of cocaine from Eastload. The only Agent connected to both cases was me.

Then he went into the Drug Squad #2 when no one was around and wrote down the names and addresses of drug dealers in Boston, New York, and Philadelphia. Using the alias Salvatore, he mailed solicitations to these dealers offering "unlimited quantities" of high-grade heroin at half street value prices. Included in the solicitation were one-ounce packet samples of the drugs. Dealers were instructed to call a pager number for purchase instructions and send cash—$75,000 per kilogram—to private postal boxes in southern New Jersey registered under Will

Thompson's name. That's why Thompson had been investigated, too.

The FBI learned about the scheme in early March from drug dealers in Philadelphia and Boston, who had received the letters from "Salvatore" and suspected they were being set up. Kent's solicitations offered "Middle Eastern brown heroin," which matched the cache we had seized in October '92.

The irony was that Kent's scheme would have worked had the drug dealers not contacted the FBI. He had already sold $77,000 worth when they did.

Using a device called a "clone beeper," which extracts phone numbers from a telephone pager, investigators obtained a kilo of heroin from "Salvatore" without paying any money upfront. Coincidentally, Salvatore's drugs matched the color, purity, and consistency of the seized Pakistani heroin. Also, the drugs were sent in distinctive packaging used to protect a type of military binoculars purchased by FBI SWAT three years earlier. Finally, Kent's fingerprints were found on the tape that was used to reseal the heroin packages in the evidence room.

Shortly after my last interview with Courtney and Allen, word started to leak out that Kent was the real culprit in the heroin theft. Because the investigators were still building their case, Kent wasn't arrested right away, which created a strange and somewhat dangerous situation. We all knew that Kent was a SWAT firearms instructor and therefore armed to the teeth.

One day, a week or so after my last interview, a very senior Agent went out to the FBI firing range and saw Kent working the line. Fearful that Kent could snap and shoot everyone at the range from behind, the senior Agent immediately left, returned to our office and told the bosses there what he'd seen and refused to go back to the range until Kent was gone.

A few days later, Philadelphia Executive Management—the same guys who previously wanted to arrest me—summoned me to a conference room and said, "We're going to arrest Kent and need your help."

"Why?" I asked dumbfounded.

"Because you've worked with him on SWAT and Eastload, and we need your advice."

"You people are unreal," I answered.

A few days later, the SAC called me to his office and said, "We're arresting Kent on Friday. Don't come to work that day under any circumstances."

I couldn't believe what I had just heard. "Excuse me," I said.

"Don't come to work on Friday."

"I've never been told *not* to come to work," I responded. Apparently, they were afraid I would use the opportunity to punch Kent in the mouth.

Seven o'clock Friday evening, June 3, Kent was summoned to the interview room, confronted with the evidence, fired, and arrested. He confessed to stealing the drugs from the evidence vault and said that he had acted alone. Simultaneously, Agents in Kentucky raided the home of his grandparents. In the basement, they found twenty-eight kilograms of the missing Pakistani heroin, an electronic scale, and $65,000 in cash hidden in his grandmother's washing machine.

That same night, I told my wife what had happened. She was even more pissed than I was.

Her exact words: "I knew something was going on. From the way you were acting, I was worried you were going to do something crazy. To hell with the FBI. You should quit."

The following Monday morning, people started coming up to me in the office and acting like they were my best friends again.

To those who had turned against me, I said, "Fuck you. Leave me alone." To this day, I still refuse to speak to them.

In the afternoon, the SAC called me to his office. He said, "I hear you're still upset. What can I do to make things better?"

"Where do I go to get my reputation back?" I asked, still smoking hot. "You arrested Kent. How about making an announcement to the whole office that Thompson and I had nothing to do with the theft."

The next day, the SAC called everyone together. In front of three hundred people he made a statement about Kent's arrest but never mentioned Thompson or me by name, or that fact that we were completely innocent.

I went up to him afterward and expressed my disappointment in less than pleasant terms, whereupon he told me to return to my desk and cool down.

Fuck him.

Three weeks later, the SAC called and said, "Be here tomorrow morning at seven sharp. You and I have to report to the Director in DC."

"Good. I can't wait."

"Keep your mouth shut," he warned.

"I'll try."

The next morning as we rode the Amtrak train to DC together, the SAC started babbling about the Phillies and the weather. I turned to him and said, "Boss, let's stop pretending. We're never going to be the same again."

In June '94, Louis Freeh was the FBI Director, appointed by President Bill Clinton in September 1993. Earlier in his career he'd served as a Special Agent in New York and DC, an Assistant U.S. Attorney, and a federal judge. He still is the only FBI Special Agent to be named Director, and is highly respected within the agency. Ironically, my SAC had been Freeh's supervisor when he was a rookie Agent in New York.

It took a lot for me to be intimidated, but Director Freeh scared the shit out of me as I sat in his office and he went through the entire Pakistan drug case and theft, and asked me pointed questions regarding both. It was clear that he had studied it thoroughly. After forty minutes, he stood, looked me square in the eye and said, "Special Agent McGowan, on behalf of the FBI, I want to apologize to you personally."

"Thank you, sir."

"I understand that you're a little upset and I understand."

I couldn't help myself. I said, "I think it's a little more than upset, sir. They wanted to lock me up."

The Director's apology was classy and impressive. During the train ride back to Philadelphia, the SAC turned to me and asked, "Are you satisfied now?"

"Boss," I said, "you don't get it. You guys really fucked Thompson and me, and I'll never be the same. I'm a big boy, and I understand—the FBI monster always wins."

When I got back to my desk I wrote a letter of thanks to the two investigators, Courtney and Allen. It ended with the sentence: "Apparently in the FBI you're guilty until you can prove your innocence."

On February 14, 1995, eight months after his arrest, Wayne Kent pleaded guilty to theft of government property and trafficking in heroin and cocaine, and was sentenced to twenty-five years in federal prison without parole. His attorney had asked U.S. District Judge Clarence Newcomer to show leniency on the grounds of "diminished mental capacity" resulting from the pressure of undercover narcotics work and the fear of dying of cancer. Judge Newcomer didn't buy it.

"There are a lot of people out there who are dying," the judge responded, "but that's no justification for violating the law. These acts were done by someone who was in a position of the highest degree of trust. Now the defendant must pay the penalty."

I couldn't have agreed more. Fuck him and throw away the key.

9

REDEMPTION

Being accused of stealing $200 million worth of heroin and cocaine by the FBI had turned my whole life upside down. Now that my name was cleared, the sense of betrayal and emotional devastation I'd felt didn't just magically disappear.

I simply couldn't get over the fact that FBI management had turned on me in a second when I'd been an honest, hardworking Agent who busted his ass to make big cases. I now had a chip on my shoulder the size of Mount Rushmore. My options were to either walk away from the FBI, which I couldn't afford to do, or to rub it in the faces of the bastards who had humiliated me.

My Dad had taught me that when you're knocked down, you get back up and fight harder, and that's exactly what I planned to do. The truth was I enjoyed running undercover operations and had been successful. So I stopped interacting with most of the people in the office, and searched for a way to turn my resentment into something positive.

During the fall of '94, I came up with a plan that involved flipping Malik and using him to catch bigger fish in Pakistan, the same way I had used Nestor to bag Paz, and Paz to bag Malik. Since the FBI heroin theft had been widely reported, it would be easy enough to circulate the fabricated story that Malik had been released because of the missing evidence. Since the internet and digital news were in their infant stages in the mid-'90s, chances were remote that the real story would ever reach Pakistan.

The first person I pitched the idea to was my good friend, Assistant U.S. Attorney Shane Thomas.

Thomas—a complete gentleman—looked at me like I was trying to sell him week-old fish. "Are you fucking out of your mind, Mike?" he responded. "You just got out of this mess, now you want to jump back into it?"

I had expected that response, and calmly explained, "Why not capitalize on what really happened? The heroin evidence actually was stolen. Everybody and his sister knows that. Why not put out the word that Malik had to be released, and then use him?"

I could see the prosecutor's gears turning in Thomas's head. "I don't know," he said rubbing his forehead. "What do your FBI people say?"

"I haven't broached it to them. I want to get your blessing first."

"Alright," said Thomas. "Let me think about it."

He got back to me a week later. "You're nuts. But if you can get your people on board, I'll work with you on this."

I went to see The Colonel, who responded with similar reticence, "Jesus Christ, Mike. That case has caused enough misery already. No one here wants anything else to do with that nightmare."

"Why not make something good out of it?"

Like Thomas, he looked at me with disbelief and a little pity. Under normal circumstance, The Colonel would have had no problem telling me to work on something else. But since Kent's arrest, people in the office were treating me with kid gloves.

"Alright," The Colonel relented. "If you can get the prosecutors on board, you can give it a try."

I'd already gotten the go-ahead from Thomas. The next step was to ask the court to release Malik into our custody. A week later, Thomas and I made our pitch to an understandably skeptical Judge Bert Harvest. The judge listened with concern and spelled out the guidelines we would have to follow.

Next up was Malik and his defense attorney. The latter wasn't excited, but agreed to arrange a conference with his client.

At the time Malik was in his late sixties and not in good health. Before the heroin theft, he had indicated that he was going to plead guilty to the two charges against him: (1) "Conspiring to import approximately 500 kilograms from Pakistan to the United States," and (2) "aiding and abetting and willfully causing the importation into the United States from Pakistan of approximately 44.6 kilograms of a substance containing a detectable amount of heroin, a Schedule I narcotic drug controlled substance."

Following the theft, and after prosecutors informed his attorney about the missing evidence, Malik had withdrawn his guilty plea. Now that most of the missing evidence had been retrieved, we had sufficient evidence to convict him, and he knew it. Malik also understood that because of his previous federal trafficking conviction, if found guilty this time, he would probably die in a U.S. prison, and never see his homeland again.

Malik, his attorney, Thomas, and I met at the U.S. Attorney's Office under the guise of a status hearing on the evidence issue and did so to not raise the suspicions of the prisoners living with Malik. The polite, diminutive five-foot-two-inch Pakistani man in the orange prison jumpsuit was fluent in English and spoke it with a hint of a British accent. He was calm and focused, and far more intelligent than your average dope dealer.

I quickly laid out how the plan would work, his role and responsibilities and the possible future court consideration to his current case. If Malik agreed to cooperate, be would be released into FBI custody and put up in a suburban apartment where he would be guarded and electronically monitored 24/7. From that location, he would reach out to his drug contacts in Pakistan and tell them that he had been released from prison because the evidence in his case had been stolen. Malik could also explain that he still hadn't been legally cleared to return to Pakistan, which his lawyer told him could take many months. In the meantime, he needed to support himself by doing what he knew best—negotiating a drug deal.

Malik expressed his appreciation for the professional way we had treated him. He also applauded the way we had set up the undercover operation with Paz and said he had never suspected that U.S. law enforcement was behind it until Pakistani cops arrested him in his office in January 1993. For this and other reasons, he indicated that he was inclined to cooperate with Uncle Sam.

He also explained that as an international businessman who happened to be in the enterprise of trafficking drugs, he operated according to a simple business model based on the laws of supply and demand. The world's largest supply of heroin was located in the northwest tribal provinces of Pakistan and the biggest demand in the world came from the United States.

The DEA had already tagged Malik as one of the top five heroin traffickers in the world. I had no doubt that his contacts in the Pakistani supply network were deep. In the first international heroin case, we had been able to take advantage of the heroin-cocaine exchange plan Paz and Malik had concocted in prison. This one depended upon Malik's willingness and ability to exploit his contacts in Pakistan.

In our very first Assistant United States Attorney (AUSA) conference, I asked, "Who is your primary supplier in Pakistan?"

Malik named Ayub Afridi Khan, who was reported to be one of the biggest, if not *the* biggest, drug barons in the world. Khan, he explained, rarely ventured out of the Federally Administered Tribal Areas of Pakistan and lived in splendor in a highly secure compound surrounded by antiaircraft missiles in the remote and grim market town of Landi Kotal. There secret labs refined opium that had been smuggled from Afghanistan through the Khyber Pass into heroin, which was then shipped all over the world.

According to Malik, Khan's tribe, the Afridi, had controlled Khyber smuggling routes for much of recorded history. Hundreds of years ago, they trafficked gold. Now they were moving the modern-day equivalent—opium and heroin.

Having never heard of Pakistan's Federally Administered Tribal Areas, I literally had to look it up on a map. I learned that it was a mountainous and lawless semiautonomous tribal region located in the northwest area of the country and bordering Afghanistan. It had a population of approximately 2.5 million Pashtuns from various tribes.

I also found out that Ayub Afridi Khan was virtually untouchable in his native country because of his close ties to the Pakistani military, forged in the 1980s when he agreed to use his smuggling network to move CIA-supplied weapons to mujahideen rebels fighting the Soviets in Afghanistan.

In order to develop a case against Khan, we needed to identify another Pakistani drug trafficker or a relative who dealt with

Khan directly. Preferably one who spoke English. Malik said he had the perfect candidate—a Pakistani businessman and journalist named Farhat Rizvi, who frequently traveled to the United States and had even been a media guest at the White House. Rizvi and Malik had worked together before on other deals involving heroin supplied by Khan through a blood relative named Babu Khan.

I spent most of the rest of '94 securing official FBIHQ approval for the new UCO, recruiting other Agents, and getting the complex international operation on its feet.

By January 1995, Malik was living in a comfortable suburban apartment rigged with FBI cameras and listening devices, and guarded 24/7 by FBI personnel. We set up our UCO command center in the apartment next door. I sat beside Malik as he made his first call to Farhat Rizvi in Karachi.

The two men conversed in Urdu. After the call, Malik explained in English that Rizvi was willing to work with Malik again, but didn't understand how a Pakistani man who had been convicted once and subsequently extradited from Pakistan a second time on a serious drug change could be walking around free.

We had anticipated Rizvi's doubts and had a plan in place to address them. Malik explained that he couldn't leave the United States until his legal situation was resolved and invited Rizvi to visit him the next time he was in the United States.

Since the FBI had no Urdu-speaking Agents or linguists on its payroll at the time, we had to hire an Urdu language specialist to translate and transcribe their call and all subsequent conversations between Malik and Rizvi to ensure that Malik wasn't misleading us in any way. The process was tedious, time-consuming, expensive, and necessary according to FBI Informant Rule #1—never completely trust an informant.

Sometime in February, Rizvi informed Malik that he was arriving in the United States in early March. In anticipation of their
meeting, I outlined the structure of the drug-trafficking scheme
that we wanted Malik to sell to Rizvi. Then I arranged for Agents
to watch Rizvi as he arrived at JFK airport in New York, took the
train down to Philadelphia, and hailed a cab from the 30th Street
Station to our apartment.

Fifty-year-old Farhat Hasan Rizvi carried himself like a sophisticated international journalist. He arrived at Malik's apartment
dressed in a business suit and smelling like he hadn't bathed in
weeks. Because we wanted to create the impression that Malik
was a free man, we allowed him to leave the apartment in Rizvi's company and stroll around the grounds. I gave Malik clear
guidelines for how far he could go.

What Malik didn't know was that we had about a dozen Agents
discreetly following him to make sure he didn't run off, and a
couple of SWAT Agents ready just in case the two men tried to
flee by car. No way did I want to have to explain to Judge Harvest how we had lost him after the snafu over the heroin evidence.

Malik and Rizvi were deep in conversation when they returned
to the apartment. I watched through the video monitor, but
couldn't understand what they were saying. Judging from the
two men's body language it appeared as though Malik had taken
charge.

The meeting stretched to four hours. After Rizvi left, I sat with
Malik and debriefed him for another several hours. It became
apparent right away that he hadn't followed the outlines of my
plan.

I said, "Salim, what are you doing? I told you we had to do A,
B, and C in that order."

"Well," he responded with complete confidence. "My plan is better."

"According to your plan, we are expected to pay several million dollars up front, which is never going to happen. Salim, I need them to front the dope, just like you did."

We continued butting heads. Unlike Paz, once Malik understood my legal concerns, he helped me tweak the plan until it worked for the FBI and would, hopefully, make sense in Pakistan. When the debriefing ended, I completed the unglamorous, but necessary task of writing up a summary to share with the prosecutors, who were demanding to see it right away. Additionally, I sent the audiotapes of the meeting to the Urdu translator so I could learn exactly what the two men had said.

I was now spending so much time at the UCO apartment that I was practically living there. When I received the English transcripts several days later, it became more apparent that Malik was an expert at the mechanics of making drug deals, but didn't understand the evidentiary chain and legal protocols we had to establish in order to make a prosecutable case.

I thought we might actually pull this off, if we could find the right FBI undercover Agent to pose as Malik's business partner and use him to negotiate the nitty-gritty details of the drug deal. That way we wouldn't have to depend completely on Malik, who could screw us at any point. To play this role, I needed an undercover FBI Agent who could come across convincingly as a successful high-level businessman with international experience and flair.

While I was in the process of looking for someone, my SAC called and said, "I have the perfect guy."

Because I still had a bad taste in my mouth from the heroin

theft, I responded, "No, thanks. I'll figure it out. I don't need your help."

"Come on, Mike," he shot back, "stop being a dick. Let's bury the hatchet and move on."

"Whatever."

"Do me a favor and meet this guy just once. He's got a ton of experience and worked with me and Louis Freeh in New York. His name is Chris Brady. You won't be disappointed."

I hadn't found anyone else, so I agreed to meet.

One week later I drove to the airport to meet Brady who was flying in from Miami. Into the arrival area walked this guy who reminded me of the Hulk with a beard and massive shoulders.

"Chris?" I asked.

Out of his mouth came a high-pitched voice completely incongruent to his tough appearance. "Mike?"

He and I hit it off immediately. One the first things, he asked was, "What's this I hear about this heroin theft thing?"

After I relayed the story, he responded with a sharp, "Fuck that. Glad you locked his ass up."

As a street and undercover Agent with about ten years more experience than me, he seemed to have as much disdain for FBI management as I did. When I called around to colleagues later to get a fix on Brady's reputation, several of them responded with: "If you've got Brady, your case is made."

Brady was too humble to ever speak about his accomplishments, so I learned from others that he'd been a Vietnam War veteran and had previously worked for another U.S. government intelligence agency and was a consummate expert at running undercover operations.

I said to myself, *Keep your mouth shut, your eyes and ears open, and learn from this guy.* Brady became my mentor, confidant, and lifelong friend. Working with him was like having a personal tutor in FBI Undercover.

To my mind there was always one way to do something. Brady taught me differently. He'd tell me, "Mike, you're the Case Agent. You make the decisions, but here are your options." Then he'd outline three different approaches we could take.

My typical response was, "I never thought of the other two."

And his comeback, "Well, get your ass in gear."

While I was meeting Brady, Rizvi had traveled to Pakistan's Federally Administered Tribal Areas to meet with Babu Khan. Because Rizvi was afraid of discussing a potential drug deal on the phone, he was returning to the United States to talk in person. Malik directed him to Miami to meet "the businessman"— Brady—who would be buying the heroin and distributing it in the United States.

Among the many things I learned from Chris Brady was that the FBI had access to a yacht that was docked in the Miami area and could be used for UCOs.

He said, "We get this guy on the yacht, Mike, and it's done."

I had total faith in him at this point and instructed Malik to call Rizvi and explain that he was too ill to travel and give him the address of the marina where the meeting would take place. On the specified date and time, I watched as Rizvi got out of a Miami cab and started walking past the more modest boats docked there.

I called Malik in Philadelphia and said, "Rizvi's on the dock, but he needs to go to Berth twenty-six."

Minutes later, Rizvi answered his cell phone and started walking toward the bigger boats. His eyes widened as he stopped in front of an enormous yacht. Greeting him were well-dressed

Colombian and Cuban American FBI undercover Agents. They helped him on board and introduced him to Brady, who wore a $5,000 suit and carried himself like John Gotti.

Brady proceeded to play Rizvi like a fiddle as the two men discussed the importation of multi-kilogram loads of heroin (or "jackets") into the United States. Later that night, over dinner, Brady explained to me the importance of the luxurious setting and expensive suits.

"Mike," he said, "you have to understand that I'm supposed to be a successful international businessman. If I show up driving a Toyota or wearing cheap socks, the bad guys are going to suspect something is up. You can't half-ass it. It's gotta look real."

From that point on the Pakistani drug trafficker and journalist Rizvi was putty in our hands. Of course, as in any UCO, there were unforeseen complications. First, Afridi and Babu Khan back in Pakistan weren't buying our deal and were making all kinds of financial demands. Second, I had a new boss.

The Colonel had moved onto a job in DC. Replacing him was an Agent named Bill Morse, who had been on the other Drug Squad. He and I used to sit on opposite sides of a wall of file cabinets that separated the two Squads. Day after day I would hear him talk on the phone about mundane administrative matters—the epitome of a type of Agent we referred to as a "desk-rider," and terrified of risking his life on the streets.

To put it mildly, I wasn't thrilled when Morse was named supervisor of Squad #3. I was four months into the new UCO and regularly putting in sixteen-hour days when he called me at our undercover apartment.

He said, "Mike, this is Morse. I need you to come in."

"What for?" I asked.

"I need you to update me on the case."

"Fine. I can do that over the phone."

"No, I need you to come into the office."

"But I've got a ton of shit to do here. I'm sorry, but I don't have time."

"Be here Tuesday morning, eight AM," Morse ordered.

Great. It was our first conversation and we were already banging heads. Tuesday morning, I reported to the office and sat down opposite my new boss. He started peppering me with dumb questions about things he could have easily answered himself if he read the file.

I sat through forty minutes of his bullshit, then got to my feet and said, "Bill, I really don't have time for this. The SAC has signed off on the UCO. Other than coming in to sign my work sheet, I have shit to do."

Throughout the spring and summer of '95, all of us working the UCO were engaged in difficult, long-distance negotiations. Every month or so Rizvi would return to the States and relay the latest offer from Afridi and Babu Khan. In June, he handed Brady a four-gram sample of Pakistani heroin and offered to send five hundred jackets (kilos of heroin) to the United States by sea as an initial shipment. The problem was that the Khans wanted a $1 million deposit first.

Unlike in the Malik case, we weren't negotiating an exchange of drugs. Nor was the FBI going to send any money to the Khans for heroin. So we had to convince the Khans to front us kilos that Brady could use to establish a distribution network in the United States.

The Pakistanis were tough negotiators. Back and forth we went over prices and amounts as they weighed the risks against what we presented as a sure financial windfall. Rizvi served as conduit and messenger. Every time he visited the United States, the pace of negotiations moved quickly. But when Rizvi returned to Pakistan and made his way to Landi Kotal for a sit-down with Afridi and Babu Khan, we waited weeks.

Thinking ahead, Brady and I had serious doubts that the Khans would be willing to risk sending heroin directly to the United States. Yes, the United States represented the largest market in the world, but it was also the only country at the time actively seeking to lock up foreign drug suppliers, and the Khans knew that.

We developed an alternate plan to ship the heroin to Italy first, where Brady claimed to have organized crime connections who would then be responsible for smuggling it into the United States. I contacted the Italian State Police (*Polizia di Stato*) to solicit their help and ask if they had a port we could use. They suggested a place called Pescara—a small port on the Adriatic coast.

The last week of September '95, Brady and I traveled there with AUSA Shane Thomas to survey the port and coordinate with Italian police officials. We arrived at a picturesque, vibrant, and ancient coastal town at the mouth of the Atreno-Pescara river with beautiful wide beaches set against the backdrop of the Appennine Mountains. Its origins dated to before the Roman conquest.

The Italian cops couldn't have been more generous hosts. On the first afternoon, five of them took the three of us to lunch at a scenic seaside restaurant. One of the Italians went in to talk to the owner, while we waited. Soon we saw people streaming out of the establishment as they though were escaping a fire.

Then the charming Italian policeman appeared in the doorway and waved us in. He explained that the owner had cleared the restaurant so that we could enjoy what turned into a three-hour lunch by ourselves.

We left Italy a week later with all the logistics of the heroin shipment plan worked out. But it turned out it wasn't needed. Two months later when Rizvi arrived in Philadelphia to finalize the heroin deal, he explained that he, the Khans, and others had decided to transport 150 kilograms by air instead of by sea from Pakistan to Miami. The heroin would be sent via an associate of the Khans' and Rizvi's named Javed Ahmed, and the proceeds of the sale of the heroin were to be forwarded to Ahmed's company bank account in Karachi.

On January 18, 1996, Rizvi faxed us an invoice from Ahmed's company stating that twenty-five cartons of leather jackets, leather shoes, and onyx household goods would be arriving at Miami International Airport four days later on a Lufthansa cargo flight from Karachi. We weren't sure if we were receiving a dummy shipment to see if it passed through U.S. Customs—as Malik had done initially—or were actually getting sample drugs.

With great anticipation, I arrived in Miami and met Brady at the airport. With the help of about twenty local FBI Agents, we moved the wooden crates that had arrived from Pakistan to a parking lot at the rear of the Miami office. On January 25 at 8 AM, the temperature was already pushing past ninety.

As the Case Agent, I was again given the honor of opening the first crate. With my heart pounding, and the Miami Agents watching, Brady handed me a box cutter and a crowbar and I tore into the first crate. I reached in and started pulling out expensive leather jackets and shoes and throwing them to the pavement.

Brady tapped me on the shoulder and said, "Slow down, Mike. Slow down. You've got to check the pockets and inside the shoes."

Finding no heroin in the first crate or its contents, I started to get the heebie-jeebies as I flashed back to the embarrassing incident with the Pakistani phone books. The other Agents pitched in, removing the objects and piling them on the pavement, and throwing the broken wood from the crates against a fence that separated the parking lot from a car dealership next door. By the fifth crate, I was breathing hard, sweating like a pig, and starting to panic.

By the fifteenth crate with still no heroin, I was beside myself. Adding to my distress was the fact that for the first time in the case, we couldn't reach Rizvi. Both Malik and Brady had been calling all his numbers in Pakistan and leaving messages, and Rizvi wasn't returning their calls.

"What the fuck is going on?" I asked Brady.

"Don't know," he answered as calm as ever. "But it's strange."

By 7 PM we finished going through the last crate. *Nada.* Then we started the tedious process of rechecking every shoe and jacket—ripping out linings, heels, and pockets. No heroin. Not a trace.

Darkness had fallen, literally, and so had our mood. All of us who had searched the crates were bone-tired, and Brady and I sent the other Agents home.

Then I turned to him and asked, "What was the point of sending all this expensive shit and no heroin? And why send twenty-five fucking crates if it's just a dummy load?"

"Good question. Let's call it a day."

We were so exhausted that we didn't want to eat. Instead, Brady dropped me off at my hotel. I reached for the six-pack I had stashed in the fridge and started downing beers. I remember drinking one in the shower.

After the beer calmed me down enough to forget the fact that the day had ended in total failure, I stretched out on the bed and immediately fell into a deep sleep. An hour later, I bolted awake.

"It's in the wood!" my subconscious told me.

I called Brady and woke him.

"What the fuck, Mike? Can't we talk about this in the morning?" He sounded pissed.

"Chris, it's in the wood!"

"What's in the wood?"

"The fucking heroin!"

"What wood? The wood from the crates that we threw against the fence?"

"Exactly. We better go retrieve it before some garbage truck picks it up."

"Goddammit," said Chris. "I'll be there in twenty minutes."

On his way to pick me up, he called the Metro Dade County K-9 unit, which is something we should have done before. As we sped off, Brady and I worried that the wood had already been carted off. It was 4 AM by the time we reached the parking lot. As we burned rubber around the corner of the FBI building, I almost didn't want to look toward the fence. How was I going to explain to my new boss that a load of Pakistan heroin had been tossed into the sea or disappeared at a garbage dump?

I tensed up, and thank God, a hug pile of wood still rested against the fence. Two minutes later the K-9 unit arrived and we explained the situation.

"You mean you just threw the wood away?" the Dade County policeman asked, looking at us funny.

"Yup," I answered.

He let the German shepherd off its leash and the dog bolted straight to the pile of wood. The big dog was so excited it climbed on top of the wood and started jumping in circles.

I picked up one of the four-by-four posts and examined it closely. The center of the beam had been expertly doweled out and sausage-shaped bags of heroin had been stuffed inside. Brady and I started pulling out the bags and forming a pile.

We figured the wood from each crate contained about two kilos of heroin. Since each crate had been doweled out the same way that meant a total of about fifty kilograms of heroin.

"We've hit the motherlode!" Brady exclaimed.

"Why didn't Rizvi tell us?"

"Who gives a shit. Look at all this heroin!"

We were happier than pigs in shit. Days later, the DEA tested the heroin and found it totaled 50.01 kilograms (110 pounds) and averaged at more than 90 percent purity. They valued it at more than $200 million.

All the time I was in Miami, my supervisor Morse had been paging me constantly. The night before, he had even called my wife at home.

"Do you know where Mike is?" he asked her.

"Yeah," she answered.

"Where?"

"Working." Then she hung up. Her disdain of the FBI was even stronger than mine.

After we finished removing the heroin from the crates, an FBI Agent came up to me and said, "You'd better call your boss."

"Why?" I asked.

"I hear he's writing you up for insubordination."

"What are you talking about?" I asked.

"No, it's serious. He's writing you up now."

Knowing that a Special Agent could get fired for insubordination, I called Morse even though I had only slept an hour or two in the last three days.

He immediately started ripping into me. "Who the fuck do you think you are? You work for me! You'd better be here eight AM tomorrow. . . ."

If we hadn't just seized $200 million of heroin, I might have been in deep shit. Fortunately, the Rizvi/Khan and Malik seizures turned out to be two of the top heroin busts in U.S. history, totaling nearly $400 million in value. Both had been accomplished without fronting a dime of taxpayer money.

Not only wasn't I going to get fired, I was treated once again like an FBI Golden Boy.

But our work wasn't over. Malik and Brady finally made contact with Rizvi in Karachi and told him that they had received the heroin.

Brady said, "Give us a couple of weeks to sell it, and then we'll split the proceeds."

Mid-February 1996, Rizvi arrived in Philadelphia to receive his first cut of the cash. We booked him into a corner room at the Marriott Hotel in Center City, Philadelphia. The FBI gave us permission to use a suitcase filled with $500,000 in real cash to serve as a prop.

I'd been working dope cases for several years now, and planned to simply have Brady hand Rizvi the cash and arrest him on the spot.

Brady said, "No, Mike. We're going to bleed him dry, first."

"Sure, Chris. How?"

"Watch and learn."

I observed via video monitor from a nearby room as Brady entered Rizvi's hotel room with the suitcase, set it on the desk, and opened it in front of him. Brady positioned himself between the suitcase and Rizvi and asked him if he had spoken to the other members of the Pakistani drug-trafficking operation. As Rizvi answered, his eyes never left the cash.

Once Brady had gotten Rizvi to identify every defendant and link him to the criminal conspiracy as a form of irrefutable evidence, he shook hands with Rizvi and departed. By this point Rizvi appeared to be salivating.

On the video monitor I watched as a very happy-looking Rizvi walked over to the suitcase and fondled the money as though he was making love to it. A few minutes later, he locked the huge suitcase and carried it out of the room.

I stood waiting in the hallway dressed in jeans and a rugby shirt. Morse had wanted us to bring in SWAT to arrest him.

I argued, "We want this guy's cooperation. SWAT will stick a gun in his face and scare the shit out of him. Let me do it on my own."

Now Rivzi saw me standing ten feet away and froze in his tracks. He looked at me like he wanted me to move.

I stared back and said, "I'm not going anywhere." Then I walked up to him and declared, "FBI. You're under arrest."

He made a pained expression and groaned, "You're making a mistake," as I cuffed him.

I looked him in the eye and said calmly, "I don't think so, and Babu Khan isn't going to be happy with you."

Rizvi winced at the name of the Landi Kotal drug baron. With the half million in my hand, I escorted him down the hallway to our operational control room. Rizvi looked like a defeated dog in a business suit and smelled like he had shit his pants, which he actually had. Once we reached the hotel room, I told him to go into the bathroom and clean himself up.

When he emerged, I started to debrief him. The stench was so overwhelming that I told him to go back in the bathroom and take a shower.

I said, "When you're finished, wrap yourself in towels. I'll get you some clothes."

I was planning to take him back to the office and book him as I had with Nestor, Paz, Malik, and others.

Brady said, "What the fuck is wrong with you, Mike? Five minutes after you sit down with him, you want him to get someone else on the phone. That's when these guys are their most vulnerable. Lock in his cooperation before he changes his mind."

So when Rizvi emerged, I said, "Get me one of your guys on the phone."

Rizvi responded like a puppy dog, "I'm supposed to deliver this money to someone in New York."

"What's his name?" I asked.

"Tariq Jawed."

"Alright. Get him on the phone."

From that day forward, I always had a phone recording kit with me whenever I made an arrest. Later in my career, I became known around the office as "Telephone Mike."

A few days later, we arrested Tariq Jawed in New York, who turned out to be part of a Hawala money broker network employed by Afridi and Babu Khan. He told us that he had been instructed to forward the money to another member of the network in London. We arrested that gentleman, too, and a fourth member of the drug-trafficking ring during a trip to London with the help of Her Majesty's Revenue and Customs.

Ayub Afridi Khan remained out of reach in the tribal area of Pakistan, but based on information we got from Rizvi, we managed to seize another twenty-one kilogram heroin shipment of his, this time on a Pakistani ship named the *MV Craigmore* bound for England. Eleven members of the crew were arrested.

Rizvi, Babu Khan, Javed Ahmed, Tariq Jawed, and one other Pakistani defendant were indicted in U.S. federal court on conspiracy to import heroin, importation of heroin, and eight other counts. All faced mandatory minimum sentences of twenty years to life.

A $180 million heroin seizure in '92 had resulted in the FBI accusing me of being a despicable drug dealer in March '94. The anguish I had gone through before I was exculpated had motivated me to prove my detractors wrong. Two years and two heroin seizures later, I had won back my reputation.

I'd gone from FBI Golden Boy, to Public Enemy#1, back to Golden Boy. The amounts of heroin we'd taken off the streets were unprecedented—over $400 million worth—and probably would never be matched again!

To the FBI big shots and the others who accused me back then, I silently salute them with a big middle finger. You can't make this shit up.

10

THE RUSSIAN MOB

By mid-1996 it was time for a change. For the past ten years I'd been a successful FBI Case Agent in four major undercover drug cases. Yet, two years after being accused of stealing heroin, I was still getting funny looks from people in the Philadelphia office. Most of the managers who had accused me of making off with the drugs were still in place, and I couldn't stand being in the same room with them.

Additionally, I wanted to spend more time with my wife and three children, who were now ten, eight, and six. Running a UCO as a Case Agent involved working twelve hours a day, sometimes seven days a week. That didn't leave much time or energy for anything else. My wife wasn't complaining, but she made it clear I was missing the unique experience of seeing our kids grow up.

I'd been fascinated watching Chris Brady work as an undercover Agent in the Rizvi/Khan case, and wanted to try taking on a major undercover role myself.

I'd actually done some undercover work earlier in my career and I knew I liked it. A few years out of Quantico, I was assigned to go undercover and frequent clubs owned and operated by members of Italian Organized Crime (hereafter called the Mob or LCN—"La Cosa Nostra"—this Thing of Ours). The Case Agent, a former national championship football player from Notre Dame, gave me very specific instructions: Go "hang around these joints and find shit out."

Sure, Boss. I was clueless and unprepared. Today, an FBI UCA about to go on an undercover assignment would receive a five-page written Operations Order clearly defining the specific goals, objectives, and targets. But in the late '80s, there was no formalized FBI undercover training. I'm lucky I didn't get killed.

The Case Agent had two kinds of clubs in mind—illegal gambling joints and strip clubs. The first usually featured video poker machines, horse race simulcasts, card games, and sports betting. The people who frequented them were middle-aged or older, and all of their last names ended in a vowel. I was in my early thirties at the time and I immediately stood out. Problem #1.

Problem #2: Even though I had the street smarts to talk myself into the clubs, my lifelong aversion to gambling due to my father's problems in that area, meant that I had never wagered money or understood the games. Over the course of a couple of weeks, this caught the attention of other gamblers, who were watching me like a hawk and would stop speaking to each other whenever I approached. One night while guys were placing bets and throwing dice, a kind gentleman of around eighty came up to me, patted me gently on the back and asked the obvious question: "You're a nice kid, but what the fuck are you doing here, son?"

I got the hell out of there, fast.

In the second kind of establishment—strip clubs—I experienced a similar problem. These were Mob-owned dive bars stocked with naked dancers grinding to blaring music, and pop-ulated with long-haul truckers, dope dealers, manual laborers, and sketchy characters. Everyone from the bartenders, to the bouncers, to the dancers and customers were completely shit-faced most of the time, fights broke out frequently, and de-bauchery ran rampant in private booths, under tables, and in all corners of the parking lot.

Because I needed to keep a clear head to takes notes, I was the only one in the joint sipping a diet soda rather than banging back beers and shots. Other dead giveaways included the fact that I never indulged in any form of depravity and sat alone. You didn't have to be a genius to figure out that I was either some kind of weirdo serial killer, or undercover law enforcement.

One night, the Notre Dame alumnus Case Agent instructed me to go to a particular strip bar and look for a fugitive. He pro-vided me with a photo of the suspect, which I folded in half, and stashed in the inside pocket of my jacket. While a drugged-out bleached blonde gyrated to "Pour Some Sugar on Me" by Def Leppard, I left the jacket on the back of the chair and retreated to the men's room. When I returned the photo of the fugitive was missing.

Oops! I'd either dropped it on my way to the table, which I know I didn't do, or someone in the joint had taken it out of my jacket. Suddenly, I felt more naked than the dancers. I was lucky I didn't get the shit beaten out of me, or worse.

I'm not being overdramatic. Agents and cops have been killed working undercover. Less than three months earlier, on March 22, 1996, a colleague of mine, Philadelphia FBI Special Agent Chuck Reed—forty-five years old and married with three small sons, and a highly respected investigator—was shot and killed while negotiating a cocaine transaction during an undercover operation.

I distinctly remember the inconsolable grief of Chuck's family, and the pall his death cast over the Philadelphia office.

Chuck went down a hero. Although mortally wounded, he managed to shoot and kill the prick that blasted him. Two of Chuck's sons, Josh and Todd, went on to become FBI Agents. God bless 'em.

Knowing all this, and green and unskilled, I was still completely hooked on undercover work. Maybe I needed to have my head examined. Criminal psychology and the characters populating the underbelly of society have always fascinated me.

During my youth in Haverhill, I spent endless hours on street corners and dive bars listening to local hoods and observing criminal behavior. It was part of the environment. Guys I knew and played ball with were always getting into trouble. Once, in the middle of an eighth-grade baseball game, the police hauled away our first baseman for armed robbery. Another brain surgeon I knew who didn't like sitting in class had a habit of calling in bomb threats so we'd be dismissed. To this day he's known as "Boom-Boom."

I was also intrigued by the psychological challenge. Consider this for a moment. You're a guy who has spent his entire life on the straight and narrow to become an FBI Agent, and now, it's your job to convince real bad guys that you, a good guy, are a bad guy just like them. You're hanging with them for hours and they're watching your every move. Not easy to do, and unlike in the movies, there's no "take two."

Years later after I'd completed many UCOs, a federal prosecutor told me I was "one chromosome away from the other side." I'm not sure if he meant that as an insult or a compliment. For me, it's served as a reminder of how close to the line you get as an undercover—a line that has to be crystal clear in your mind and never crossed.

In 1996, I wanted to play in the major leagues of law enforcement and give undercover work another shot. Since my wife wanted to move back to Boston where we had friends and family, I started looking for an undercover assignment in the Boston area. A month later, I heard that the Boston office wanted someone to work undercover in a case targeting Russian Organized Crime.

The FBI, at the time, was focusing most of its attention on the far more established Italian LCN Mob, and were just beginning to investigate Russian OC, which was involved in various types of sophisticated financial fraud schemes, including money laundering and daisy-chain gasoline tax schemes. Our New York office had recently launched a case against the Russian Mob that some of my friends were involved in. So I checked in with them to get a sense of what I would be going up against, swallowed hard, and threw my hat in the ring.

In the fall of '96 I traveled up to Boston to be interviewed for Operation Full Service. The Case Agent, Shawn Bartlett—a quiet, scholarly type—hoped to develop a criminal case against a Kazakhstan-based businessman and former rocket scientist named Zhalgas Amanbayev, who now headed a sophisticated criminal gang mostly involved in financial crimes.

"Can you start now?" Bartlett asked.

"Yeah. But how long to you expect the case to last?"

"Six months," Bartlett answered.

"Where is Amanbayev now?" I asked.

"He's in Russia, but he'll be back in Boston in a couple of months."

After my disastrous early forays into undercover work, I

wanted ample time to prepare, but the Boston office told me to remain in Philadelphia until Amanbayev returned. New Year's Day 1997, I was in my living room watching football when the phone rang. It was Bartlett.

He said, "Amanbayev's here. Can you come up tomorrow and meet him?"

I sensed this was coming. I said, "Shawn, tell your bosses that I knew this was going to happen. You want me to meet this guy tomorrow and I'm not ready. This isn't the best way to start."

The managers sitting in the various FBI offices rarely understood the challenges of undercover work. If they did, they wouldn't have asked a UCA to prepare to go up against a major criminal on one day's notice.

The informant in this case was a Boston-area businessman named Matt Cowens, who did a lot work in Russia. He was one of what we called "the good Americans" who volunteer to help the FBI with no strings attached. Amanbayev had approached him recently about getting his hands on legitimate U.S. documents that would enable other Russian Mob associates to work in the United States.

When I spoke to him for the first time, Cowens said, "I'm afraid if I don't help him, something bad will happen."

The meeting with Amanbayev was scheduled to take place at a restaurant in a Marriott hotel in downtown Boston. Literally thirty minutes prior, Cowens and I worked out a plan where he would introduce me as a fellow businessman who was willing to operate outside the law and might be able to get his hands on the immigration documents Amanbayev wanted.

My first question to Cowens was, "How do I dress?"

"When you do business with these guys, you have to dress like them," he answered. "They all wear business suits."

Bartlett, the Case Agent, suggested that I complete the outfit with a black beret, which were fashionable at the time in Moscow. I nixed that right away. No way a fucking beret is going on my head.

Cowens and I entered the restaurant together. Waiting for us were Zhalgas Amanbayev and his brother Yuri, both dressed in expensive suits. Amanbayev, age forty-two had been born in Kazakhstan—part of the former Soviet Union—and currently maintained a residence in Fort Lee, New Jersey. He didn't speak English. Nor did Cowens speak Russian, so Amanbayev's brother served as the translator. It made for a very long conversation.

Right away the arrangement proved awkward. The guy I wanted to establish eye contact with and get a fix on was Zhalgas Amanbayev. Instead I was spending most of my time focused on his brother Yuri.

Zhalgas started by asking me a series of questions about U.S. immigration laws that I couldn't answer since I had no time to prepare. He would speak to Yuri for five minutes, then Yuri would turn to me and say, "He says, 'That sounds good.'"

Yeah, sure. I didn't have a clue what they were saying among themselves, nor could I feign to know things I didn't know. I said to myself: *Control what you can control.*

Alright. I couldn't pretend to speak Russian, but I could come across as a shady businessman. So when the waitress came over to our table, I grabbed her wrist and asked, "Hey, Sugar, what time do you get off?"

Tacky as hell, I know. And not something I would ever dream about doing in my normal life. But my behavior seemed to convince Amanbayev I was a low-life businessman who might be willing to break some laws.

The FBI had lots of knowledge about how Italian mobsters

conducted themselves, but knew very little about the Russians. I learned in that first meet that the Russians didn't like sitting around eating veal, drinking Chianti, and cracking jokes. Instead, they were as serious as a sore knee and got right down to business.

At the end of our meeting, Amanbayev told Cowens that he wanted to sit down with me again. Great. But where, how, and under what circumstances?

So when I saw Bartlett, I peppered him with a series of questions: Am I married, or divorced? Do I have kids? What kind of business am I involved in? Where do I live? Where do I work?

His answer was priceless: "I figured you would figure that out."

"Thanks a lot."

My prickly attitude still intact, I wanted to tell him to go fuck himself, but held back. I thought back to working with Brady, who did all his own backstopping well in advance of ever meeting a bad guy. I needed to do the same. I would never make that mistake again.

Now I had to figure things out on the fly. We quickly rented a beautiful house on the beach north of Boston. It was near where I grew up, so I knew my way around and could show the targets different points of interest. We rented an office in downtown Boston, wired it for audio and sound, and brought in a female FBI Agent to play the role of my secretary.

Amanbayev and his cohorts soon became regular visitors. Before I knew it, I was smack dab in the middle of my first full-time FBI UCA assignment, and learning something new each day.

Cowens told us that Amanbayev was involved in more serious criminal activities than procuring documents illegally. Our plan was for me to provide him with the immigration documents initially and then try to get him to segue into more serious crimes.

The case developed slowly because Amanbayev traveled to Russia often and was away for months at a time. That made it hard to establish rapport. He wasn't into small talk or sports, and we didn't seem to have common interests. An added impediment was the fact that the only way I had to communicate with Amanbayev was through his brother Yuri, who didn't seem to like me.

Also, I knew that members of Amanbayev's local gang were keeping an eye on me. So I had to remain in Boston and continue living in deep cover as the businessman I was pretending to be. Meanwhile, my family was a six-hour drive away in Philadelphia. During the first three months, I snuck home one weekend to find complete chaos. The house was a mess and my son had gotten school detention after reacting poorly to another student's barb about his parents being divorced and his father leaving home. I remember praying I hadn't made a monumental mistake.

It was a difficult adjustment for the entire family. My wife and I couldn't share a bed for months at a time, and because I couldn't reach out to friends and family in the Boston area, I was spending a lot of time alone. As a loner that was fine with me at first. But there were only so many hours I could spend at the gym, reading, or walking on the beach.

Nor was I permitted to enter the Boston FBI office, or associate with other Agents in public. The one thing I did do was ask Jarhead in Philadelphia to call the SWAT supervisor in Boston. Being an undercover, I couldn't go live on actual missions, but at least I could train with them. Soon, I had a new group of friends to shoot, train, hang, and bullshit with before heading back to the solitary beach house.

They were the only contact I had with the FBI except for Shawn

Bartlett, who met me once a week in local bars or at the gym to hand over my FD-302s and plot strategy.

Turned out the green cards Amanbayev wanted could only be secured through the Immigration and Naturalization Service (INS), which wasn't willing to cooperate at first. The FBI had its own concerns, because it knew that once the green cards were issued to criminal associates of Amanbayev, those individuals would be operating in the United States and would be hard to track. We could end up looking really bad if people found that we allowed individuals into our country who then went on a major crime spree.

I tap-danced with Amanbayev for almost a year, trying to learn everything he and his associates were up to, meeting other members of his gang, and convincing them that I wasn't lily-white.

During that same time, I got what's known in the FBI as a "Specialty Transfer" for my family to move with me to Boston, where my wife was near her sisters and my kids could spend time with their cousins for the first time in their lives. We bought a beautiful home we could barely afford, set the kids up in new schools, and I volunteered right away to coach whatever sport was in season.

After months of bureaucratic wrangling, we finally secured two green cards for Amanbayev's brother Yuri and another member of his organization, which proved to them that I knew the right kind of people. As a result, the case picked up steam. Over the next several months Zhalgas, Yuri, and I met in my office, parking lots, and suburban motels and he talked about his involvement in various complicated financial schemes, many of which I couldn't comprehend.

Fortunately, the one thing I did understand from my old Colombian drug cases was money laundering. Every criminal organization, regardless of their choice of crime, usually faces the problem of laundering funds. Legally, the FBI can function as a money-laundering "facilitator." In this case, we wanted Amanbayev to launder FBI funds—a practice known as "reverse money laundering."

Chris Brady had taught me that after a certain point in the tap dance, you had to make what he called the "awkward jab." In other words, the UCA needed to be direct and blunt. So one day, a year and a half into the case, I told Zhalgas Amanbayev through Yuri that I made most of my income as an international heroin trafficker and asked him if he could help me launder the proceeds of drugs sales through legitimate banks. It was a difficult conversation to have in a foreign language, but I managed.

I said, "I have tons of cash from dope deals that need to be cleaned."

Yuri asked, "What's a dope?"

This was going to take awhile.

Knowing what I know now about being undercover, I should have had a brick of heroin in my office to use as a prop. What I did understand was that legally I had to be cagey. A crucial element of making a money-laundering case is the need to establish something called SUA (Specific Unlawful Activity). With a tape recorder running either in my office or concealed on my body, I had to make sure that Amanbayev understood clearly that the dollars I was asking him to clean for me were profits from illegal drug sales.

I explained to him that I wanted to avoid DEA scrutiny and I didn't want to pay taxes to the IRS. Amanbayev bit, suggesting that we draw up a dummy contract between my fake company and another he would form in Kazakhstan. Then I would start wiring small amounts of money to him and he would reroute them through various accounts he maintained overseas, and then send the money to a second company I established in the United States. If investigators started asking questions, Amanbayev would say that he had been investing my money in foreign securities and forwarding me the profits. For this service, Amanbayev would receive an 8 percent commission—the average rate for international money launderers. Pretty clever.

He said he could launder as much as $10 million at a time. There was no way the FBI was going to allocate that amount of money. Instead, telling him it was a test run, I wire-transferred four separate payments totaling $500,000 to Amabayev between March and July of 1998, and he cleaned the money through foreign banks and financial institutions including the Royal Bank of Scotland in Nassau, the Capital Bank of Latvia, The Latvian Trade Bank 4, and the Kazakh Bank Credit Center in Almaty. Two weeks later, minus his commission of 8 percent, the money arrived in an account set up in the name of our fictitious company. The speed with which Amabayev completed the transaction proved that he had a sophisticated system in place and had laundered serious amounts of money in the past. Every part of the process was monitored and recorded by the FBI.

Legally, he and his associates were screwed. They knowingly took what they believed to be heroin trafficking profits and made them appear to be legitimate funds—a serious federal crime.

In December 1998, almost two years after our initial meeting, I called Amabayev and asked him to meet me at a restaurant in New York City. This time I didn't show. Arriving in my place were several burly FBI Agents who arrested him and charged him with immigration document fraud and money laundering. Facing a maximum sentence of twenty years in federal prison, Amabayev pled guilty. I never saw him again.

On the FBI scorecard, the UCO was a success, but I knew that we could have accomplished a whole lot more. We should have continued getting the names of Amabayev criminal associates for green cards, and we should have penetrated deeper into his criminal organization by tracking the foreign currency transfers and accounts.

But people high above my pay grade wanted to wrap up the case and tell the world that the FBI had infiltrated a Russian organized crime group and arrested the ringleader.

I chalked the case up as a valuable learning experience and was eager to take on another undercover assignment. The problem I faced was that according to FBI rules, once an Agent had completed a long-term undercover (of six months or more), he or she was required to return to regular office duty, working as a Case Agent on a traditional investigation. The Amabayev UCO, which was supposed to last six months, had stretched out for more than two years.

As of June '97, I had been officially assigned to the Boston office. Seeing that Boston had no Undercover Coordinator (UCC), I asked for and was assigned that job. So even though I wasn't allowed to go into the office while I was the UCA in the Amabayev case, I was officially coordinating the other UCAs working out of Boston. In my spare time, I read the FBI Undercover Operations Policy Guide manual inside and out, and memorized all the rules. After ten years in the FBI, I'd figured out that if you wanted to get ahead of management, you needed to use their ammunition against them.

So when a Quantico classmate called from the Philadelphia

office in late December '98 and told me that he needed me for a major LCN UCO between the Philadelphia and Boston offices, I had to say, "Thanks, John, but I just came off a gig and have to go back into the office."

He responded, "When the fuck do you ever do what you're told?"

Good point. Then he told me that the target was Robert "Boston Bobby" Luisi, who operated in the Boston area under Philadelphia Mob Boss Joseph "Skinny Joey" Merlino. It was a very odd arrangement in LCN circles in a couple of ways.

First, there was the unusual circumstance of why a Mob captain in Boston was reporting to an LCN Boss in Philadelphia. It had to do with the fact that the New England Mafia was in complete disarray after a series of successful federal prosecutions, and since Luisi's father, brother, cousin, and another man were shot to death in 1995 in the infamous 99 Restaurant massacre. Bobby Luisi Jr., who was in jail at the time and had been feuding with his father, did not seem upset that a number of his family rivals had been hastily removed from the Boston criminal scene.

Blocked from becoming a "made man" in Boston, Luisi had petitioned Philadelphia Mob Boss Joey Merlino for permission to join the Philadelphia family. Merlino agreed and made Luisi a Capo in Boston in 1998. Under their unusual arrangement, Merlino protected Luisi's criminal money-making activities in Boston in exchange for a piece of the action until Luisi could achieve his goal of creating his own crime family in Boston.

The case was also exceptional because the main target was Joey Merlino in Philadelphia, a Mob Boss and a real pain in the ass. Since the statute of limitation on other crimes Merlino had committed was running out, Philadelphia told Boston we only had six months to make our case against Bobby Luisi.

Fair enough.

The informant in both cases was a six-foot, 350-pound corrupt cop-turned-Mob-Captain named Ron "Big Ron" Previte (according to other published sources). Previte operated out of Philadelphia but was willing to travel to Boston and introduce me to Luisi, ASAP.

Like I said before, Italian Organized Crime was the FBI's number one criminal priority at the time. This unique opportunity to go after major Mob figures wasn't something I wanted to pass on. The big obstacle remained the FBI restriction on an Agent doing back-to-back UCOs. But I remembered from my study of the regulations that an undercover could meet with a potential target up to five times before notifying FBIHQ that it became an official undercover operation. Citing that provision of the rules, I prepared to meet with Previte and Luisi in mid-January '99.

I'd caught the undercover bug and was super excited. I also knew that this was deadly serious business. The undercover skills I'd learned so far were about to be tested in the lion's den of Italian Organized Crime. This time I would be going up against a Mob Boss and Capo. The slightest slipup could cost me my life.

11

**THE ITALIAN
MOB—CASE #1**

In early January 1999, two weeks after wrapping up the Russian case, I met with six-foot, 350-pound Mob informant Big Ron Previte. A self-proclaimed "general practitioner of crime," he was a character straight out of *The Sopranos* before there was *The Sopranos*—Big Pussy only tougher, funnier, and smarter.

A West Philadelphia native, Previte had a long and colorful criminal history. Among other things, he had admitted to selling government-issued gear out of a supply depot while serving in the Air Force, extorting bribe money from criminals as a Philadelphia police officer, stealing from the Tropicana Casino and Resort in Atlantic City as a security guard, and making money by swapping horse urine while working for the New Jersey Racing Commission. Since 1997 and while a "made man" in the Philadelphia LCN Mob, he'd worked as a paid informant for the FBI. His current Mob Boss was "Skinny Joey" Merlino—an ambitious young gangster who was trying to expand his crime empire into New England.

Funny thing happened. I liked Previte as soon as I met him.

He made no bones about his life of crime, and was fearless, despite the fact that he'd been wearing a wire for years. When asked if he worried about getting whacked by the Mob, he answered, "Why think about dying? You're alive. Enjoy the day. In fact, a bullet to the head is very quick."

Previte liked that I wasn't an Ivy League type, and had been a knock-around kid myself. In terms of working together, neither one of us had a problem with the other. He knew his role, and I understood mine.

The investigative plan was straightforward—the Boston office would focus on Luisi and his Boston crew, and the Philadelphia office would continue to investigate Merlino and his cronies in Philadelphia as they had for the past couple of years. If the Boston investigation provided more evidence for Philadelphia, so much the better.

Unlike in the Russian UCO, I spent hours and hours with Previte beforehand, working out our past history. We sat in hotel rooms, restaurants, and barrooms talking and prepping, with him tutoring me in all things LCN. Soon it was if we had known each other for years.

In a book written after the case by crime reporter George Anastasia entitled *The Last Gangster,* Previte said, referring to me: "This guy knew what he was doing . . . he and I worked perfect together . . . it was like we didn't have to talk about anything . . . we just played off one another . . . he was smooth . . . he understood. . . ."

I was going to be "Irish Mike," a guy in the Irish export-import business with an office near Logan Airport who "colored outside the lines." In other words, I had no qualms about selling things "that fell off a truck" (stolen property). To add a touch of authenticity to the offices of my company, Irish International, I purchased hundreds of leprechauns and other Irish-themed trinkets and scattered them everywhere. More importantly, the office was wired for audio and sound.

The plan was for me to start by offering Luisi and Merlino stolen property, and then move into dope deals, specifically cocaine, because the FBI knew Luisi had been a supplier in the past. We had learned from Previte that because of the unusual LCN alliance between Philadelphia and Boston, everything Luisi got his hands into had to be approved by Joey Merlino first. Again, here was a golden opportunity to gather critical evidence against top Mob players in both Philadelphia and Boston.

On January 11, 1999, less than a month after wrapping up the Russian case, I welcomed Previte, Bobby Luisi Jr., Robert "The Cook" Gentile, Tommy Caruso, and Paulie Pepicelli into my office. They all looked like Mafia extras from central casting. I saw the outline of an automatic pistol under Paulie's shiny wool jacket.

Previte made the introductions. He said, "This is Irish Mike. He and I go back forever. He knows my family. I've worked with this guy for years in Philadelphia. He's an earner. Now you can use him here. Here you go, Bobby." Not a bad start.

Luisi was stocky with a square face and thick dark hair brushed back. He didn't look like the sharpest pencil in the box, but struck me as dangerous and canny. According to Previte, he was a hustler and sometime drug dealer, who talked a better game than he played. He also had to pay Joey Merlino $10,000 a month in tribute, so he needed to make money. That's where I came in.

I sat behind a desk piled with papers and stuffed leprechauns facing Previte, Luisi, and the other mobsters, trying to keep my shit together. As Luisi started to talk, the phone rang and I picked it up. It was the Case Agent watching on video from a nearby office. He said, "I want you to start asking them—"

I cut him off. "No, thanks." And hung up. I had to stay focused. I'd learned that once a UCO went "live," you were on your own. You, and no one else, had to make split-second decisions to advance the case the best way possible. If you waited for help from the sidelines, the bad guy would grow suspicious and walk.

I described to Luisi how as part of my business I was sometimes presented with "opportunities" and I needed help in taking advantage of them.

Nodding to Luisi on his right, Previte said to me, "Bobby controls everything here in Boston. You can deal with him the same way you deal with me in Philadelphia."

Luisi said, "You're with us." Those are magic words to an FBI Agent.

In Mob-talk that meant he was offering me protection under his name. In other words, I didn't have to worry about any other Boston criminals bothering me or shaking me down, if I worked with him. It was a very big deal to have a Mob Captain offer something like that on the first meeting. But I had Previte vouching for me, and Previte was one of Merlino's main guys, and Luisi wanted to make Merlino happy.

I played dumb and said, "Yeah, Bobby, but I don't want to have any hassles with other guys who are doing the same thing."

"I just told you," Luisi responded. "You're with us. You're not gonna have any problems."

The meeting went so well that at the end Luisi said, "Come on down to the North End." The North End was the Italian section of Boston—a small neighborhood featuring narrow cobblestone streets and brick townhouses that dated back to the seventeenth century. Paul Revere's home stood there, as did other historical landmarks and many Italian restaurants and cafés.

We reconvened at the Caffé Vittoria on Hanover Street, which

I learned later was one of Luisi's favorite hangouts. Previte remained in Boston for a couple more days to make sure that the handoff went smoothly. Then I was on my own and officially assigned to Luisi's LCN Boston crew as an "earner," or someone who was expected to make money for the Mob.

Unlike the Russian UCO, where Amanbayev would return to Russia for weeks at a time to give us a break, this UCO required my daily attendance and focus. I was expected to make quick money for Luisi and had to be available at a moment's notice to meet with him or one of his associates. Luisi and his crew usually woke up at around noon and drifted into their social club at three or four in the afternoon. And they could go all night, drinking coffee and sambuca, playing cards, watching TV, busting balls, shooting the shit, and above all else, hatch schemes to make some money.

I had to develop a new routine. I started getting up early, having breakfast with my kids, and then taking them to school. They loved it, because they basically hadn't seen me for two and a half years. From school, I'd drive to the gym and work out for an hour or so to clear my head. I'd drift into my Irish International office at around 1 PM, read the paper, and wait for the phone to ring. Almost every day Luisi or one of his crew would page me, and I'd arrive at their favorite hangout Caffé Vittoria ten minutes later.

Even though we knew Mob guys were watching me, I had no backup team to swoop in and save me should I get in trouble. The North End was isolated and the type of place where everyone knew one another. The ever-vigilant Mob assumed any strange face was associated with law enforcement. That meant I had to "clean" myself before I returned home at night. I did this by taking different routes through downtown Boston. The narrow city streets made it impossible for anyone to follow me without being seen. Once I reached the Tobin Memorial Bridge, I transitioned from "Irish Mike" to husband/father/baseball coach.

I made a conscious effort to separate the two, though in many respects the difference between them was minimal. That's something I teach UCAs today: When creating your UCA profile, mimic your own personality and interests. My interests included dogs and sports, so Irish Mike's interests were dogs and sports. Irish Mike didn't pretend to be a car expert or a wine connoisseur because I wasn't one either.

The good part about the case was that I was sleeping in my own bed at night. I didn't get weekends off, but I hadn't as a Case Agent either. The disturbing part was that some of my FBI bosses were constantly on my ass about my work hours.

FBI office hours are 8:15 AM–5 PM and many Agents arrive and leave on the dot. My hours as Irish Mike were completely different and some bosses had a problem with that. Since they didn't see me in the office, they automatically assumed I was dicking off.

Early into the case one of them called me and said, "You're nothing fucking special."

"I know I'm not special," I retorted, "but this is what I've got to do to work the case."

I also had to learn another new language, because Italian mobsters don't talk like regular people. A typical conversation with them might go like this:

MOBSTER: "Hey, Mikey, what's new? How're they hangin . . . ? Listen, Mikey, I need to talk to you about those things, you know. Them things that I need."

IRISH MIKE: "What things you talking about?"

MOBSTER: "You know, those things. . . . Not the other things. Those things I told you about."

IRISH MIKE: "Those things, yeah. . . . What do you need? Because I got those things and not the other things. Those the ones?"

MOBSTER: "Yeah, perfect. That's exactly what I need. You're a good guy, Mikey. How's your dog doin'?"

IRISH MIKE: "The dog's good. Real good. You wanna get a sandwich?"

These guys might be cold-blooded killers, but they were also fun to be around. Both Merlino and Luisi had recently served stints in prison and both were petrified about going back. So I had to earn their trust. In addition, having been part of a Merlino arrest team when I served in Philadelphia, I couldn't meet with Merlino for fear of being recognized. So I was continually making excuses to Luisi why I couldn't go to Philadelphia. The truth is that I'd arrested a lot of bad guys in Philadelphia and couldn't risk a chance encounter with someone who might recognize me as an FBI Agent and compromise the case.

After my first couple of meetings with Luisi, the Case Agent said, "I want you to start buying dope from them." Like most Case Agents, he was laser-focused on making a case against Luisi as quickly as possible. And like I said before, we were under a six-month time restraint.

I answered practically: "I can't do that right away. It won't work. Find me some stolen property and I'll sell them that first."

In February 1999, the FBI supplied me with five furs that they had seized in another case. I told Luisi they had been stolen from a high-end store in Connecticut. They retailed for about $100,000 each. As stolen property, they were worth somewhere in the neighborhood of $20,000. I offered them to Luisi for $5,000 each. He gave one to his wife and another to a relative, but couldn't sell the other three.

So he didn't want to pay me. Knowing that I couldn't let myself be played for a mark if I wanted to appear real, I approached Luisi one day and said, "Hey, Bobby, what the fuck. I just gave you five fur coats worth twenty grand a pop. I gotta get something, too."

He replied, "Of course, Mikey. You're right. Here ya go."

Next, I sold Luisi and his crew cases of Kodak 110 and Polaroid 600 film that I told him had "fallen off a truck." I provided them with stolen cigarettes, showing them I would do anything to make a buck. Then I gifted him a $5,000 Rolex Oyster Perpetual Date Submariner watch that I said I'd gotten from a contact with more of them that he wanted to move. It was a token of my appreciation, I told him, for letting me "join his crew." He loved it, and showed it off everywhere we went.

The first week of March '99, three months into the case, while Luisi was in my office, I made what we call in undercover work "the awkward jab," as discussed earlier. In other words, I brought up the subject of dope, but went about it in a roundabout way.

I said, "Bobby, I got some diamonds."

"Great, Mikey," he responded. "I want to get them. I will bring them to a jeweler friend of mine, if he likes it . . . boom. We'll get the deal done."

"The problem is that the owner wants three bricks for them."

At the mention of the word "bricks," which we both understood to mean three kilograms of cocaine, Luisi stood up, pointed to the ceiling, and walked out. I sat behind my desk wondering if he would ever return, when I noticed him signaling me through a glass partition. I met him in the lobby of the remodeled factory building. Without saying a word, he indicated for me to follow him down a back stairway. Two floors down, he stopped, leaned into me, and whispered, "I want to, but I can't get caught."

I was wearing a body recorder, but Luisi uttered the words so softly that we couldn't hear him when we played back the tape.

The deal had to be approved by Merlino in Philadelphia. On April 28, 1999, while a secret recorder was running, I sat in my office with Luisi and Previte and the three of us called Merlino to get the green light for the cocaine deal. Here, word for word, is what Merlino said:

> MERLINO: "Bob . . . is that guy . . . ya know . . . do what he's got to do over there for him . . ."
> LUISI: "Oh, yeah . . ."
> MERLINO: "All right . . ."
> LUISI: "Yeah . . . that's . . . that's gonna be . . ."
> MERLINO: "All right . . ."
> LUISI: "Ya know . . ."
> MERLINO: "You got it . . ."

I know it sounds cryptic and ambiguous to the general public. But to LCN members and FBI Agents, Merlino's message was clear: Do the deal.

Less than forty-eight hours later, on April 30, four months into our six-month deadline, a young man carrying a briefcase knocked on my office door and said, "Hi, I'm Bobby Carrozza Jr. Bobby sent me."

I'd never met Robert "Bobby Russo" Carrozza Jr. before in my life, but knew the reputation of his father who had been indicted in 1990 for murdering an underboss of the Patriarca crime family. In fact, Carrozza Sr. had been Merlino's cellmate when they both were in a federal prison in Pennsylvania. Small world.

Minutes after Carrozza Jr. sat down, the phone rang. It was the Case Agent, who had been listening from another location.

He asked, "Do you know who you're dealing with?"

I started laughing. "Yeah, I know. Thanks." And hung up.

Bobby Carrozza Jr. had been sent by Luisi to do his dirty work. He spent the next couple hours talking about himself, and asking me questions about my background and my business. In his own way, Bobby was vetting me, because he knew that as far as Luisi was concerned, he was expendable. Among the things he said was that he was a stickler for punctuality, a trait he had learned from his imprisoned father.

"If you were late to a meeting," he said, "he'd either, number one, break your jaw, or number two, you were left out and he didn't care."

Carrozza Jr. liked to talk, which was fine with me. I would pump him for information on his coconspirators and use him to tie the cocaine conspiracy together:

ME: "The Philadelphia side talked to the Boston side . . . and everything was . . ."

CARROZZA JR.: "Copacetic."

ME: "If I can make everyone some money . . . and if I can make everybody happy . . . and no one's pissed off at one another . . . why not take a shot?"

CARROZZA JR.: "Right . . . as long as everything's all right. . . ."

ME: "I don't know if you realize . . . they talked to Joey that day. . . ."

CARROZZA JR.: "They did . . . I know that. . . ."

ME: "The guy . . . he had needed his okay on it . . ."

CARROZZA JR.: "Right . . . the thing . . . would be a very good grade. . . ."

ME: "If Joey Merlino and Bobby Luisi are talking on the phone . . . and say it's going to happen . . . I ain't about to fuck it up . . . you know what I mean?"

CARROZZA JR.: "Absolutely. . . ."

Finally, he popped open the briefcase he was carrying and handed me two bricks of cocaine wrapped in plastic. The plastic on most of the bricks of dope I'd seen were stamped with some kind of identifying marker. On one he handed me, I saw 215, which I recognized as the area code for Philadelphia. That indicated that the two bricks had come from mobsters in Philadelphia.

I said to Bobby, "Tell Joey, thank you," referring to Joey Merlino.

One thing I'd learned about doing dope deals was that you never keep the money and dope in the same place. Keeping them separate reduced the risk of being killed or ripped off.

So I locked the bricks in my desk, and then looked up at Bobby and said, "Okay, I owe you fifty grand. It's down at the hotel."

We walked together a few blocks to the Long Wharf Hotel. Waiting there was a huge Rhode Island cop and former Golden Gloves boxer who worked with the FBI. He had a face that looked like it had been pushed through a meat grinder.

I pointed at him and said, "That's my cousin. He's got your money."

"Hey, Irish Mike," Bobby Carrozza Jr. responded, "you know some serious people, too."

The entire transaction was recorded on videotape. The Massachusetts State Police lab consequently tested the bricks and found them to weigh 2,093.7 grams (a little more than 2 kilograms) and contain 42 percent cocaine. Like true mobsters, they'd tried to increase their profit margin by giving us mediocre cocaine that had been "stepped on," or diluted with a cutting agent. They thought they had gotten one over on us, but in reality, as long as we had at least 1 percent purity, they were all legally cooked. And the joke was on them, not us.

In my opinion, we had enough on Joey Merlino, Bobby Carrozza Jr., Bobby Luisi, and another Luisi associate named Shawn Vetere to indict them. But when we presented the case to the Assistant United States Attorney, he started poking holes and wanted more evidence.

In the world of federal law enforcement, FBI Agents investigate crimes on the street. Federal prosecutors review and prosecute cases from inside a safe office. The two worlds and viewpoints knock heads all the time.

"Luisi wasn't there," the Assistant U.S. Attorney complained.

"I know that. But we've got phone transcripts of him discussing the deal with Merlino. Besides, Carrozza acknowledged that he was sent by Luisi."

"Also, you never used the word cocaine."

"You people don't understand how real life works," I responded as I felt my head getting ready to explode. "You never use that word when discussing drug deals. It's always bricks or anything other than cocaine."

"We need more evidence against Luisi," the AUSA concluded.

"I already told you that he and I discussed the dope deal in the stairwell."

"Yeah, but we can't hear it on the tape," countered the AUSA.

"Are you calling me a liar?"

"No, I'm just saying that we need better evidence. We need to put the dope in Luisi's hand."

"Again, you don't understand how real life works," I said. "That's never going to happen. LCN guys like Merlino and Luisi never touch the dope."

The AUSA didn't know how the street worked.

"There's a way to do it," I added.

"How?"

"Luisi won't handle the dope, but he will touch the money."

"Okay. Let's get that on tape."

I contacted Carrozza and said, "Tell Bobby I need another present."

A week or so later, I was sitting at home on Memorial Day weekend when the phone rang. It was the Case Agent telling me that the SAC wanted to see us immediately. I knew this couldn't be good.

As I drove to the office, I asked myself, *What did I do wrong? Did someone see me using my FBI car to drive the kids to school?* It was like going to the principal's office when you were a kid.

Upon reaching the SAC's office, the Case Agent and I, asked as matter-of-factly as we could, "What's up, Boss?"

He answered, "You're done, Mike."

"What do you mean, I'm done?" I asked, thinking: Is this the fucking stolen heroin case all over again?

"You're done with the case. Pull your shit. It's over," the Boss said.

I asked for an explanation. The SAC, who was old-school and very well respected in the office, eventually offered one: "We have information that someone has tipped off the Mob that you're an FBI Agent."

"What information?" I asked. "What did you hear?"

"I can't tell you," he answered, "other than to say that we were told they know that you're an FBI Agent."

Quickly, I marshaled my arguments to be allowed to continue. After pointing out that we were close to wrapping up the case, I suggested, "How about I don't meet the wise guys in the North End anymore where I could get bundled (slang for kidnapped.) Instead I'll only meet them outside in public."

The Boss wasn't buying it, but gave us the long holiday weekend to come up with a plan. Meanwhile, Luisi paged me nonstop. In the past, if I didn't respond within ten minutes, he'd lose his shit. Now days went by as we tried to convince my FBI Big Boss to let me continue with the case.

Much later and after the UCO was over, I found out that two days before Previte had introduced me to Luisi in January 1999, a law enforcement officer from a different agency had knocked on Luisi's door, told him he knew Luisi was involved in drug trafficking, and asked him to become an informant for his organization. Luisi turned him down.

As the law enforcement officer left, he said, "Bobby, not for nothing, but be careful who your new friends are."

For whatever reason, this asshole had decided to burn the FBI, which was completely unprofessional and exceptionally dangerous. We knew that he knew about the FBI undercover operation, because he was present during a coordination meeting held in the USAO. Every local, state, and federal agency wanted a shot at Luisi, and he was pissed that he had been instructed to stand down while the FBI took a shot.

This disclosure came from another member of law enforcement who was so bothered by what had occurred that he eventually came forward and told the FBI. Had we known about the earlier statement to Luisi, I would have never been sent in under-cover. For four months, I'd been rubbing shoulders with Luisi and his wise guys without any hint of what had been said.

By Memorial Day 1999, I was determined to finish the case despite the possible danger and confident that there was a safe way to wrap it up. On Tuesday morning, the Case Agent and I convinced the SAC to let me arrange one more public meeting with Luisi. If I picked up on any suspicion from him, I promised to quit.

I approached a young man named Carl who had just joined the Organized Crime Squad, and said, "Carl, I want you to make a call to a mobster." Again, in the small world department, I had been trained in Philadelphia by Carl's uncle. If Carl turned out to be half the Agent his uncle was, he'd become a superstar.

His eyes bulging out of his head, Carl asked, "What did you just say?"

"Here's the story," I started. "You're my cousin. I want you to tell this guy that over Memorial Weekend I went to the Cape, got fucked up, and was arrested on a DWI. Tell him I've spent the last three days in the can."

While Carl made the call to Luisi, we contacted a local police department on Cape Cod, and told them what we wanted them to say about the arrest of "Irish Mike," and asked them to prepare a fictitious DWI report. They were great and helped immediately.

Then I made arrangements to meet Bobby Luisi on Hanover Street. I figured he couldn't kill me in that busy area in broad daylight, but he sure looked like he wanted to when he saw me. In the LCN world, an underling, especially an associate, never disrespects a Capo. Luisi immediately started cussing me out. When we stopped at a streetlight, he slapped me hard in the face.

I fought the impulse to punch him back by biting my lip until it bled, telling myself that if I did, the case was over. Five years earlier, I would have jumped his shit in the middle of the block.

Luisi said, "You dumb fuck. . . . When are you going to court on the DWI?"

"Next month," I answered. "Can you believe those mother-fucking cops? What's their fucking problem? A guy can't even have a couple drinks on the holiday?"

He snarled, "Let me see your papers."

Thank God for being prepared. I reached into my jacket pocket and handed him the fake DWI report. Turned out, Luisi wasn't upset that I'd been arrested. He was pissed that I had missed three days of making money for him.

"How are you going to make this up to me?" he asked.

I used this opening to mention the offer I had made to Carrozza to buy another kilogram of coke. A week later, on June 3, another Luisi associate named Tommy Wilson showed up at my office and handed me a third brick of cocaine on video.

The AUSA had told me that he wanted Luisi on tape handling either money or dope. So as Tommy sat waiting to be paid, I said, "Tommy, do me a favor. Go back and tell Bobby that I'm not paying anyone but him."

"No," Tommy pleaded. "Bobby told me to bring back the twenty-four grand."

"No disrespect, Tommy, but I've got my reasons. Tell Bobby what I said."

Twenty minutes later, Bobby Luisi called and sounded pissed. "You motherfucker. . . ." he started. "What the fuck is going on now?"

I said, "Bobby, I'll explain to you in person."

He agreed to meet me in front of the Custom's House on State

Street in an hour. With FBI video cameras rolling, I packed $24,000 cash in a FedEx box and set out for the financial district. I got there early and coordinated with the guys in the surveillance van so I knew exactly where they were going to be stationed across the street. Twenty minutes later, Luisi came bounding down the sidewalk looking annoyed.

As we stood talking, a teenage girl passed in front of us, and Luisi made a lewd comment about her behind.

I hated stuff like that. He was staring at the box under my arm, waiting for me to hand it over, and I was bleeding him dry just like Chris Brady had taught me.

Just as I was about to hand him the money, a delivery truck passed, blocking the line of sight from the surveillance van. Cognizant of the distraction in my peripheral vision, I pulled the box back and waited. Soon as the truck passed, I handed the cash to Luisi and he was cooked.

I was sick of dealing with Luisi and his crew, and mentally exhausted. When I met with the AUSA in mid-June, he said, "We have Luisi for dealing three kilos, but if you can get him to talk about more, it's a bigger charge." Federal drug charges and sentencing are dictated by the amount of weight of the drugs involved, and the AUSA wanted us with more than five kilograms, which mandated a minimum sentence of at least ten years. Fine.

A week later, I called Bobby Carrozza and Tommy Wilson to my office and discussed buying two or four more kilograms of cocaine at a cost of $48,000 to $96,000. The tape recorder that was running captured Carrozza implicating Luisi, Shawn Vetere, and Joey Merlino, his coconspirators, over and over again.

Carrozza said, "I can tell the other guy, Shawn. I'll see him after. He wants the results of this conversation. They like this thing here, and they want it to work. In conversations with the guys down south, everybody's happy with this . . . the guy Joey . . . everybody's real happy with this, and they're happy with you. Everybody. Bobby's happy. That's the way we want it to be . . . a system, a pattern. I'm good at that. Shawn put me in this position, because I'm a good talker. I know what I'm doing. Shawn says we're off to the races."

A couple days later, Luisi summoned me to the Caffé Vittoria to discuss the purchase of the four additional bricks of coke. As I entered a dark entryway, I heard someone bolt the door. The sound of a door locking behind you has got to be the worst thing an undercover can hear. It's almost always the prelude to a violent act, or the law enforcement equivalent of a shotgun being racked.

It had to have been done by either Paulie Pepicelli or Shawn Vetere who had entered behind me. I assumed one or both of them were armed. This was not the way I wanted the case to end.

Luisi stared at me with dead eyes from two feet away, his face unreadable. When he turned to scan the traffic outside on Hanover Street, I noticed a birthmark near his left eye for the first time. I heard an espresso machine hissing from an adjoining room and a chair scrape against the floor.

We were four big men squeezed in a dark hallway. Cold sweat started to form on my chest near where the microphone was taped. I had to fight back the urge to piss my pants. I knew that if they searched me, I was done. I had a feeling I was fucked anyway.

In milliseconds my mind raced through several escape options. I could try bull-rushing Luisi, but that would be like trying to knock over a small sequoia tree. I could go for Pepicelli behind me and try to grab his gun, but with Vetere standing next to him, I'd probably get pummeled to the ground first.

Luisi whispered in a gravelly voice, "Something ain't right, Mike. . . . I don't like what I'm seeing."

"What's up, Bobby?" I whispered back, trying to keep my knees from knocking together. "What's the matter? We good?"

"Come inside," he whispered, motioning me forward with his hand. "Get away from the door. Come in the backroom."

I didn't like the way this was going. I said, "Bobby, let's talk here. Let's figure out where this is going. Is there a problem?"

"Yeah, we got a problem," he responded in a flat tone of voice. "Come back inside. We need to go down to the basement."

The basement was one place I definitely didn't want to go. I scolded myself for not heeding the SAC's warning. I figured Luisi had discovered that I was really an FBI Agent, and once we reached the basement he was going to put a bullet in my head.

My legs shook as the four of us shuffled to the backroom and down a flight of steps to a dark room I'd never been in before. Luisi indicated a chair at a round table. I sat. Then he settled his big body in the wooden chair to my left. Vetere and Pepicelli sat across from us. Pepicelli sneered at me as if to say, "What the fuck you lookin' at?"

I turned away and heard music coming from a jukebox in the corner. It was playing "My Way" by Frank Sinatra.

I couldn't help myself. I started to chuckle.

Luisi leaned into me and asked, "What is it, Mike? What's so funny?"

"That was my father's favorite song. It's the only one I ever heard him sing."

Don't ask me why, but I took it as a sign from my father that everything was going to be okay, and I was going to walk out of there in one piece. It was as if my father was watching my back twenty-five years later.

I relaxed and Luisi started talking about the upcoming dope deal. I quickly realized that he hadn't summoned me to the basement to whack me, but to discuss terms and future business, and to avoid law enforcement scrutiny, as he believed we were all under surveillance from Hanover Street. We finalized another deal for four more kilograms of cocaine.

Now the AUSA had all the evidence he needed, and I was counting the hours until the case was over. My job now was to make sure Luisi, Carrozza, Vetere, Pepicelli, and Wilson stayed in town so they could be arrested at the same time. The arrest was set for Monday, June 27.

I called Luisi and said, "I got my hands on some more Rolexes. If you're around on Monday, I'll give them to you. If you're not in town, I'm going to have to sell them to someone else, because I need the money."

"I'll be here," Luisi said.

Six AM Monday, FBI Agents spread out into Philadelphia, Boston, and four other locations and arrested Merlino, Luisi, and nine other mobsters.

I was sitting in my Irish International office while the arrests took place. Shortly after six, my phone rang. Instinctively, I reached for my FBI phone. Then I realized it wasn't the one that was ringing. Instead it was the "bad guy" phone I had reserved for Mob business.

I picked it up and recognized one of the bad guy's voices. He said frantically, "Mike, get the fuck out of there. The FBI is coming!"

He was warning me, because he still thought I was with them.

The following day, the front pages of *The Philadelphia Inquirer, Philadelphia Daily News, Boston Globe,* and *Boston Herald* announced the spectacular arrests of eleven mobsters. News channels led with footage of the mobsters being taken into custody. A high-profile FBI press conference was held, but when I saw the photos of the speakers later I didn't remember any of them accompanying us on a 2 AM meeting with Luisi and his associates. They had their jobs and I had mine. While they were bragging about the arrests, I was at home sleeping.

I took the greatest amount of pride not in the media coverage or newspaper headlines, but in a simple paragraph in the sworn arrest warrant for LCN Boss Joey Merlino, filed with the District Court in Philadelphia on June 17, 1999, which stated:

> On June 10, 1999, the CW (Cooperating Witness, or Ron Previte) met Merlino in Philadelphia and paid him $1,000 for Merlino's role in authorizing the cocaine deal. The CW also told Merlino that he had a $25,000 to $50,000 deal set up in Boston. After being told about the deal, Merlino told the CW that he would tell Robert Luisi Jr. to take care of the UCA like "he was one of us."

A Mob Boss telling his crew to treat an FBI undercover Agent like one of them. Not bad.

A year later, I testified against Merlino, Luisi, and the other defendants in federal courts in both Boston and Philadelphia. Representing them were the best attorneys money could buy. Boston defendants Carozza, Vetere, and Wilson pled guilty and received double-digit sentences. Luisi elected to go to trial, and had to be convicted twice because of a court procedural error. He was later sentenced to sixteen years in federal prison. There he wrote a book entitled *From Capo to Christian*. After agreeing to testify against another mobster, he was released in 2012, changed his name to Alonso Esposito, and moved to Tennessee to become a Christian minister. Yes, you read that right. You can't make this shit up.

In the Philadelphia trial, Merlino was convicted of racketeering, illegal gambling, and extortion in the 2001 trial, but beat the drug charge. His defense attorney Edwin Jacobs argued that the evidence against Merlino in Philadelphia was not as clear as that collected during the Boston UCO, which he called a "textbook example of an undercover operation." Citing the Boston UCO where every conversation, negotiation, and transaction was recorded on video and/or audio, Jacobs argued that Merlino's Philadelphia conversations were open to interpretation or not recorded at all. In the end, Merlino was sentenced to twelve years in prison.

After his release in 2011, Joey Merlino relocated to Boca Raton, Florida. In 2015, he was accused of violating his parole and put back in prison. He was arrested again a year later for entering into an illegal business arrangement with New York–area organized crime figures. Apparently, he hadn't read Luisi's book, or if he did, chose not to follow his path to redemption.

Ron Previte retired from his dual occupations of mobster and FBI informant, and passed away in August 2017. To this day, I consider him a good friend, and one of the funniest guys to ever roam this earth.

12

THE ITALIAN MOB—CASE #2 (DOUBLE SESSIONS)

The summer of 1999, after completing two difficult UCOs back-to-back, I was mentally and physically wiped out. I needed time to recharge and my FBI bosses understood that. So I spent the rest of the year working out daily; going into the office to prepare evidence for the upcoming trials of Luisi, Merlino, and their associates; and then returning home to spend time with my kids.

By January 2000, I was eager and ready to jump into a new case. Opportunity came in the form of an experienced Organized Crime Agent who walked up to my desk one day and said, "Nice job on Luisi, Mike. Are you ready for something else?"

"Sure," I answered. "What have you got?"

"You know who Matty Guglielmetti is?" he asked.

"Who doesn't know who Matty Guglielmetti is?" I asked back.

"Well, we got a shot at him."

"Sign me up," I said without hesitation. I was totally hooked on undercover work at this point, and was being offered a chance to infiltrate the Mob a second time—something that almost never happens in the FBI.

Matty "Good-Looking" Guglielmetti was a very interesting character—a second-generation gangster who began his criminal career in 1984 when he and his father were arrested for hijacking a load of Canadian whiskey. On October 29, 1989, he crossed from Rhode Island to Massachusetts to attend a Mob induction ceremony in Medford, Massachusetts. It turned out to be the first time ever the FBI bugged an entire Mob initiation and listened as New England mobsters like Robert "Bobby" DeLuca and Vincent Federico had their fingers pricked and swore an oath of loyalty to La Cosa Nostra.

One of the mobsters at the ceremony was recorded as saying, "We get in alive in this organization, and the only way we're gonna get out is dead. No matter what. It's a hope. No Jesus. No Madonna. Nobody can help us if we ever give up this secret to anybody. This thing cannot be exposed."

In 1991, as a result of his attendance at the 1989 Medford induction ceremony and other crime activities in Connecticut, Guglielmetti pleaded guilty to federal racketeering and was sentenced to five years in a federal prison in Sandstone, Minnesota. We knew that following his release Guglielmetti, who was now a Capo in the Rhode Island faction of the Patriarca family, had resumed his criminal activities and was now positioning himself to become the new Boss.

The infamous Raymond Patriarca had reigned over all the family's various criminal activities from his base in Providence, Rhode Island, for three decades starting in the 1950s. Since his death in '84, the Mob in New England had been in serious disarray. Internal warfare had claimed many members, and others were serving time on extortion and racketeering charges. The current Boss, Luigi Giovanni "Baby Shacks" Manocchio, was in his seventies and under constant federal investigation. My job was to gather evidence on Guglielmetti and lock him up before he established himself as the new Boss.

In January 2000, when I joined the case, Guglielmetti was fifty-one and extremely paranoid about returning to prison. He'd worked with John Gotti in New York and was reputed to be a lot smarter and more cautious than Bobby Luisi. That meant I had to be at the top of my game. One of his closest associates—a thug named Bobby Nardolillo—had a blood relative named Vinnie Salvatore (not his real name) who was an FBI informant. He would be my way in.

One of the first things the Case Agent asked me was how long I thought it would take me to get close to Guglielmetti.

"Two years," I answered.

"Luisi took six months," he responded. "Why so long?"

"Because Ron Previte brought me in at the top level of the Philadelphia Mob and was trusted by the Boss. Your informant doesn't have that kind of access. It's going to take me a year to gain the trust of Bobby Nardolillo, and another year to get to Guglielmetti, maybe."

Unlike almost all other FBI Agents, I'd spent six months kibitzing with wise guys on a daily basis. I knew how they acted and thought, and understood that the biggest hurdle to doing business with them was gaining their trust.

"We want to do this in six months," the Case Agent concluded. "We'll find someone else."

"Okay, no problem."

A week later, the Case Agent came back to me and said, "Okay. We want you to meet the informant."

Vinnie Salvatore turned out to be a whack job—a wannabe

street hustler, who grew up stealing cars and breaking into houses and couldn't keep his mouth shut. He was cooperating with the FBI because he was jammed up on charges of selling stolen property.

I went back to the Case Agent and said, "I'm going to try to get Vinnie to bring me somewhere where I can meet Nardolillo and some of Guglielmetti's guys. I don't want him vouching for me for obvious reasons."

The Case Agent agreed.

Vinnie Salvatore told me about gambling games the Mob was running throughout New England, including the town of Rochester, New Hampshire—in the middle of nowhere. The people who attended them were hicks with nothing else to do. The Mob would basically set up gaming tables and steal their money. I considered it a perfect place to start.

First, I had to prepare and do the requisite backstopping. Who was I in my undercover role? What were the details of my background? And most importantly: What about me would attract Guglielmetti and the Mob?

Like I said before, I'd learned a massive amount about the LCN during the Merlino/Luisi case. The prime motivation for all mobsters was to make money. Easy money was their Achilles' heel—and the only way I knew for an outsider to gain access.

I also knew that Guglielmetti, like lots of other wise guys, was involved in the construction business. He actually came from a construction background and had served as a steward with the local Laborers' Union while an LCN member. He was very tight with both local and national officials of the Laborers' Union, and well as some Rhode Island politicians. At the time, Rhode Island was one of the most corrupt states in the country and the focus of many federal law enforcement investigations.

Armed with this knowledge, I chose to become Michael Jameson—a highly successful businessman from the Midwest, who had recently moved to the Northeast and was now looking to get into construction and possibly invest in strip clubs. He also loved to gamble. Since we wanted Jameson to be involved in an all-cash business, we decided that he had made his fortune in parking garages. Cash businesses were ideal for money laundering, which often led to drug trafficking—my favorite violation.

We spent about six months creating our undercover company, which included joining the Parking Garage Owners of America, preparing fake tax returns, renting office space, and printing business cards. I also bought a new expensive wardrobe to suit the role.

On a frigid night in March 2000, I launched what the FBI called Operation Double Sessions by walking into the Mob gambling den in Rochester, New Hampshire, dressed to the nines. The fifty or so patrons and a dozen or more mobsters stopped what they were doing for a second to check me out. I felt like I was in a Joe Pesci movie.

Poker machines lined three of the four walls of the smoke-filled room and lights blazed and bells rang. Games were underway at the four or five cards tables at the center of the room as a horserace simulcast played on a monitor overhead above. Rochester, New Hampshire, would never be confused with Las Vegas. The women present, to be kind, were not anyone you have ever seen in any fashion magazine, and the men tended more toward flannel than Hugo Boss. It didn't matter, the bad guys were in the room, and that's all I cared about.

With many eyes on me, I reached for my wallet and joined in. I'd come a long way from my days as a green Agent in the

Philadelphia social club. I knew the role I was there to play and I had a very defined target and purpose.

Minutes after entering, Vinnie Salvatore introduced me to Bobby Nardolillo—a huge biker type with a Fu Manchu mustache. I shook his hand and blew past him. Subconsciously, I was telling Nardolillo that he wasn't important to me. I had a successful life and money and he should be more interested in me, than me in him.

Nardolillo dressed all in black, smoked nonstop, and thought of himself as a tough guy. Eventually, we grabbed a table away from everyone else and started to bullshit for three hours about our backgrounds. We even discussed potential business deals. Bobby dropped Guglielmetti's name often, which led me to believe we were on the right track.

One of the deals we discussed was my potential investment in gentlemen's clubs. This had been strategically planned by the FBI after many hours of discussions. By way of preparation, I had already traveled to another city and trained to run a strip club by an FBI informant club owner. He taught me the nuts and bolts—how to order the booze, hire girls, schedule shifts, monitor the cash register, manage the floor, etc.

What I didn't know that first night was that it would take more than a year and half of gaining Bobby Nardolillo's trust before he introduced me to Guglielmetti. I was prepared to take as long it took and was backed this time by FBI management, which appreciated the importance of patience when it came to infiltrating the Mob.

Most of those days and nights I spent hanging with Nardolillo took place in a high-end strip club in Providence called Centerfolds, run by Guglielmetti's crew. They were trying to get me to invest.

Most red-blooded heterosexual males would probably consider getting paid to spend time in a club in the company of attractive naked women a dream job. It was for the first couple weeks, but after that it became a headache—a real headache, in fact, because I have a severe allergic reaction to cigarette smoke. Minutes after Nardolillo lit up, which he did every time we met, day or night, I'd develop a splitting headache. Sitting in a car with him was almost unbearable.

Another problem was that as an undercover trying to gain evidence about illegal Mob activity, I had to wear a recording device every time I went to work. But with the state-of-the-art music system in Centerfolds blaring rock music nonstop, it was hard for the device to pick up what Bobby and his associates were saying. Also, my relationship with the young, attractive dancers working in the club, many of whom saw me every night hanging with mobsters and throwing around money, had to be strictly above board, because everything I did in the club would later be scrutinized by defense attorneys, and a judge and jury.

Since I was trying to win the trust of a gallery of rough characters, I couldn't act like a prude either. I solved this problem by introducing Bobby and his associates to an attractive female FBI UCA, who played the role of my out-of-town girlfriend. She'd show up at Centerfolds every so often to let the dancers know I was off-limits. I made it clear that as a potential investor I wasn't interested in mixing business with pleasure.

Another problem was the booze. I'd learned during the Russian UCO that I couldn't slam back shots of vodka with my targets and still be effective. So I established with Nardolillo right away that I enjoyed an occasional beer, but wasn't a big drinker. I'd also learned mobsters, for the most part, were light drinkers, and many didn't touch the stuff at all.

Night after night, Bobby and I would meet at Centerfolds and talk. I was the savvy businessman who was willing to stretch the law to make a buck. He was the Mob insider who introduced me to a number of his associates and explained the workings and nuances of organized crime. His thorough course in Mob culture and practices was captured in more than three thousand body recordings, which were eagerly listened to and analyzed by the FBI.

In addition to my undercover role in the Guglielmetti case, I was still the Boston Undercover Coordinator, which meant that I had to report several times a week to the Boston office, usually in the dead of night sneaking into an underground basement to avoid being seen. There were plenty of other UCOs going on, so I was essentially basically working two jobs at once. On top of that I had responsibilities at home, which included coaching my kids' baseball games and getting the car fixed.

I wasn't getting a lot of rest, but I wasn't complaining. At least I got to go home every night and sleep in my own bed. I tried to keep Michael Jameson and my real life as a husband and father separate.

As in the Luisi case, information began to surface in early 2001 that my real identity might have been compromised. The fears this time were based on the release of certain court documents in Luisi's and Merlino's upcoming trials, and my required appearance in court to testify against the Boston and Philadelphia defendants. When our SAC heard about the problem, he summoned the Case Agent and me into his office to discuss. Obviously, if I testified in the Luisi trial and one of Guglielmetti's associates walked into the courtroom, I was done as an undercover and the Guglielmetti UCO was toast.

The SAC, who was a kind man, had a brilliant recommendation: Shave off the bushy walrus mustache I had worn for years. The Case Agent and I looked at one another in shock. Did the SAC really think mobsters I had been sitting in a club with for the past year wouldn't recognize me if I shaved off my mustache? Apparently so.

We told him we would consider his recommendation and left. The Case Agent, who was a complete wiseass, decided to make fun of the SAC's suggestion and drafted the following memo on official FBI letterhead:

3/14/2001—Request for approval for case expenditures in the amount of $11,820.63 for UCA identity concealment.

Referenced meeting discussing concealment of the identity of the UCA during his testimony during the XXXXX trial, and remains an outstanding issue. Numerous methods have been discussed to attempt to obfuscate the UCA's appearance to include: the use of multiple screens to block the gallery view, the use of blue dot technology during televised testimony, and the utilization of brown paper head apparatus during the actual testimony.

After a long and somewhat heated debate, in conjunction with SAC endorsement, it is recommended that the UCA change his physical appearance. Although the SAC has mandated that the UCA remove his facial hair, it is believed that stronger and more proactive measures should be taken.

Therefore, it is requested that the following procedures be approached at the estimated amounts that have been quoted by (local hospital). Assurances have been given that these are government rate figures and that the recuperation period should not exceed 2–3 weeks.

1. One year enrollment (HAIR CLUB FOR MEN) $426.50
2. Hair removal (Facial and Posterior) $142.67
3. Face-Lift $1,372.83
4. Tummy/Fanny Tuck $3,594.21

5. Selective Liposuction $6,239.42
6. Bikini Wax $45.00

FBIHQ has opined that it will reimburse the Field Office for 60% of the overall cost of $11,820.63 for the UCA's alterations due to the fact that he may be a more valuable asset in future UCOs once additional augmentations are performed. Therefore, it is requested that these funds be approved for the UCA's makeover.

When the official memo appeared on my desk, I laughed so hard that I almost pissed my pants. Continuing the sophomoric nonsense, the Criminal ASAC, who was a good guy and a practical joker himself, initialed the document and passed it on to the SAC for approval.

Days later, I opened my office mail and saw the memo with the SAC's signature on it. Was he fucking with us? Was he goofing back at us because we had goofed on him? I found that hard to believe, and think he simply signed it after seeing the ASAC's signature. But I never found out for sure. Bottom line, I had (and still have) official FBI approval for a physical makeover to include a bikini wax, a face-lift, and liposuction.

You can't make this shit up!

In late 2000, after spending nearly nine months with Nardolillo and his disgusting smokes, it was time to ramp up the game. Guglielmetti still remained in the background, despite the fact that Nardolillo floated his name all the time.

A couple of weeks later, I walked into Centerfolds with a six-foot-two, 350-pound Cuban friend and fellow FBI UCA who I introduced as a dope dealer named Manny. The purpose of this: I wanted Nardolillo to know, so that it would get back to Guglielmetti, that I occasionally dabbled in the dope game to make a buck, and usually with my friend Manny, who was a big-time supplier. I also made it clear that I routinely cleaned Manny's drug profits through my business.

It didn't take long for the LCN to respond. In April 2001, Nardolillo offered to provide an LCN security detail consisting of him and four of his associates to guard seventeen kilos of Manny's cocaine that was purportedly passing through Rhode Island. In legal terms, providing security to illegal narcotics was almost the same as possessing and distributing cocaine.

The dope dealers were really FBI UCAs and the cocaine had been seized by the FBI in other cases. The security detail lasted twelve hours and was carefully staged. After haggling with Nardolillo over money with audio and video equipment running, I paid him for his services. Our hope was that he would report the easy deal to Guglielmetti. If he did, Guglielmetti didn't bite.

After a year and a half of hanging with Bobby and paying for protection to operate under Guglielmetti's name, it was time to flush Guglielmetti out and push for a direct meeting. Again, all of this was carefully strategized and planned.

Shortly after the first cocaine protection detail, I told Bobby that I was interested in investing in a strip club in Tampa, Florida. The problem was that some Mob guy in Tampa was giving me a hard time and demanding a cut. I asked Bobby if Guglielmetti could help.

This time Guglielmetti bit, and agreed that for a piece of the action in my new club, he would represent me in Tampa. What he didn't know was that the Tampa mobster I had accused of threatening me was really another FBI undercover. We knew that if Guglielmetti checked with real mobsters in Tampa, we were screwed. But I'd learned that most mobsters were lazy. We chose Tampa specifically because the current Mob hierarchy was in tatters.

The Trafficante family, which included Santo Trafficante senior and junior, and Vincent LoScalzo, had controlled the Tampa Mafia since the 1940s. Now, after the deaths of both Trafficantes and the arrest of LoScalzo in 1997, some individual mobsters were involved in small-scale criminal activities, but most were either in prison or had moved into legitimate businesses.

Bobby arranged a meeting between him, Matty Guglielmetti, the Tampa "mobster," and me in early 2001. I arrived there two days early to meet with the undercover who was acting as the Tampa bad guy. One overcast very hot and humid day, the two of us, who were good friends, decided to sit by a lake and catch some sun.

As soon as I eased back in the lounge chair, I fell asleep. I was wearing sunglasses, but hadn't put on suntan lotion. When I awoke an hour later, I was as red as a lobster, except for a band of pale skin around my eyes. The burn was so bad I had trouble walking. A day later, the dead skin started to peel, and the Tampa undercover started referring to me as "Scales." He still does.

By the time the Providence mobsters arrived two days later, I looked ridiculous and felt like shit—not the way I wanted to present myself to Guglielmetti for the first time. If he bit on the gamble and liked me, I'd be well positioned to saddle up next to him and make the case. If I failed to convince him I was Mike Jameson, the operation was over and my life could be in danger.

The night before the meeting, Nardolillo took me up to his hotel room to coach me on Mob etiquette. The body recorder I wore captured our conversation.

NARDOLILLO: ". . . he [Guglielmetti] may say okay, and they
    may work out what they [Guglielmetti and the Tampa
    mobster] gotta work out. 'Cause he [Guglielmetti] will

know . . . and they will know how to talk to each other. Even I don't know all that."

ME: "My fucking head's spinning, Bobby."

NARDOLILLO: "Even I don't know all this."

ME: "That's between those two."

NARDOLILLO: "There's things that I don't even know. Because there's things I can't say to him. Do you understand? If he's real [a made man] . . . I can't. There's things I can't say to him."

ME: "No, he's real. He's real. I'm telling you. I think that's what you'll find out."

NARDOLILLO: "I've seen real cops that are real, too."

ME: "He's gotta be good then."

NARDOLILLO: "How about the ones right inside?"

ME: "Inside where?"

NARDOLILLO: "Your organization. Why? You don't think there's none in it? Sure there is."

ME: "There's cops inside your place?"

NARDOLILLO: "Not our place. We know there's none in ours, 'cause we know everybody in our circle. But there's other circles they get in. Look at fuckin' Joe Pistone . . . what he did."

ME: "Who's that?"

NARDOLILLO: "What he did to those guys in fuckin' New York. They got a million-dollar bounty on his head to kill him. He's a fuckin' federal agent. He went in."

ME: "Was that a movie?"

NARDOLILLO: "It's a true story."

ME: "I didn't know that."

NARDOLILLO: "That's a true story. They are real people. That's a true story."

ME: "I didn't know that. I thought that was Hollywood."

NARDOLILLO: "No, no, no. That's true."

ME: "He got in with those guys?"

NARDOLILLO: "Oh, yeah."

ME: "And they treated him like one of their own?"

NARDOLILLO: "Yeah."

ME: "And nothing happened to him?"

NARDOLILLO: "Well, they got him out, before something happened. He testified, and then they moved him. Changed his name, witness protection, the whole thing."

ME: "What would they have done if they found out?"

NARDOLILLO: "Killed him."

ME: "Who was he?"

NARDOLILLO: "He's fuckin' . . . I mean, there's a million-dollar bounty on his head."

ME: "I saw that on HBO one night. I didn't know it was a real story."

NARDOLILLO: "Oh, yeah. It's a true fuckin' story."

ME: "How could that happen?"

NARDOLILLO: "He portrayed himself on the street . . . just like a guy. All you need is one guy."

Nardolillo was a mobster, but he wasn't a made man. He was explaining to me that made men speak and act differently.

I obviously knew Joe Pistone, but played dumb. Ten years earlier had I been with a Mob associate who brought up the subject of an FBI Agent working undercover, I probably would have panicked. Nardolillo's admission that the Mob would kill the real-life Donnie Brasco if they ever got their hands on him, was later played in court to juries numerous times to demonstrate the violent mind-set of the LCN and their fear of infiltration.

The meeting between Guglielmetti, the FBI mobster who called himself John, and me was held at Castaways Restaurant inches from the Tampa Bay, the next afternoon. John played his role brilliantly. Not only did he manage to convince Guglielmetti he was a real mobster, but he did this in part by challenging Guglielmetti as only a real Mob guy would do.

Guglielmetti responded strongly. He told John, "I'm not gonna just lay down, because you showed up and said this is your area. . . . We have an interest in this club. . . ."

At the end of the meeting Guglielmetti was recorded describing his impression of John to Bobby and me this way: "He seems to be okay. . . . He seems to be around (organized crime) people. . . . He apologized if he stepped into anything. . . . He's a kid who's on the street. Goes in and grabs it; it's a feather in his cap."

Turning to me, Guglielmetti said: "I like you, you're all right. You handled yourself well considering that you were put in a fuckin' situation you knew nothing about. . . ." He also said to me, "You're with us. . . . No question."

That was music to my ears, and meant our gamble had paid off. Now eighteen months into the case, I had direct access to Guglielmetti and could start to nurture a relationship. Back in Rhode Island, I made sure I saw him on a daily basis.

Matty Guglielmetti, I learned, wasn't into drinking or chasing women. We'd often meet for dinner, where I'd play the part of a savvy businessman, who knew how to make money and could keep his mouth shut. Matty was cautious at first, but after months of conversations started to take me into his confidence and explain how the Mob did business through legitimate and quasi-legitimate businesses aided by a complex and nefarious web of relationships between mobsters, union officials, and politicians. One of Guglielmetti's sources of income was from his position as a shop steward for Laborers' International Union of North America (LIUNA) Local 271, which we knew was controlled by the Mob.

Since I was Mike Jameson, a shrewd businessman always looking for financial opportunity, Matty Guglielmetti and his associates pitched me business prospects all the time. At one point, Guglielmetti suggested that I invest in an adult entertainment club run by one of his associates. He arranged a personal tour. Ten AM on a Tuesday morning, I entered the establishment assuming that that there would be little sex activity taking place at that early hour.

The proud owner met me outside, buzzed me through two security doors, and started to escort me through rows of porno movies, dildos, and other sex devices, speaking the whole time about the financial benefits of operating an adult sex shop. While my body recording was running, I passed a private room and made eye contact with the customer inside.

"Hey. How's it going?" I asked.

What my body recorder didn't capture, but has been seared into my brain since was the sight of the man inside. He was a good-looking gentleman of around forty, average build with a full head of hair, completely naked except for the pair of leather chaps and a ball gag in his mouth. Was he a sex worker getting ready for his shift, or a customer waiting to be abused? I didn't ask.

All I know is that as I exited the shop, I muttered one word, which was captured by the body recorder—"Wow."

Mike Jameson took a pass on that investment opportunity.

A month later in August 2001, I met with Nardolillo to propose a second cocaine protection detail, in the hope that Guglielmetti would take the lead. My dope dealer friend Manny returned to Rhode Island with eleven kilos of coke to guard, and the second staged scenario worked as perfectly as the first one— all captured on tape. We now had enough evidence to file serious criminal charges against six of Matty's associates, but not the ringleader and prize catch himself. But we were getting close.

13

September 11, 2001, I was sitting in the back of a classroom at the FBI Academy in Quantico, Virginia, waiting my turn to teach an undercover class to new FBI UCAs when a friend entered and said a plane had crashed into the World Trade Center in New York City. I remember feeling bad for the pilots and wondering how they could have made such a horrible mistake on such a clear, beautiful day.

When the same friend returned a short time later to tell me that a second plane had hit the Trade Center, I realized immediately that our country was under attack, and we were headed for war. I rushed back to Boston, where two of the suicide planes had left from on that fateful day.

Like most Americans, I was shocked and horrified by the terrorist attacks on the World Trade Center and Pentagon. As an FBI Agent responsible for protecting our country, I immediately shifted my focus from hanging out with mobsters to chasing down leads and hunting for other possible terrorists. Frightened citizens were calling our FBI office day and night with tips, and we investigated all of them—three suspicious Middle Eastern men living in an apartment outside of Boston, who turned out to be students, a relative of Osama Bin Laden who resided in an exclusive apartment tower and might have information, a strange van parked near a federal building.

Like all other Agents, I was working sixteen-hour shifts investigating the terrorists and trying to prevent future attacks. As a result, all my other responsibilities fell by the wayside. They included coaching football, family time, and hanging with Guglielmetti. I had to be smart. I couldn't just go radio silent on him without raising suspicion. So I made sure to call him and leave messages when I knew he would not be there to pick up, explaining that I was away from Rhode Island on a business trip.

But I couldn't keep that up forever. So after six weeks of nonstop 9/11 duty, I convinced my superiors to let me cover the midnight antiterrorism shift, grab a few hours of sleep, and spend some time in my undercover role with Guglielmetti. If that meant working eighteen hours a day, so be it.

They agreed, and I picked up with Guglielmetti where we left off. Within weeks, he agreed to become a silent partner in my company Hemphill Construction and I gave him a set of keys to our Rhode Island office. In order to keep up the impression to Guglielmetti and others that we were legitimate, Hemphill Construction started bidding on contracts. Using FBI approved and vetted subcontractors, we actually won an asbestos abatement removal project. It marked the first time in history that the FBI actually completed a legitimate construction project, and went a long way in establishing the company's presence in Rhode Island.

Guglielmetti, who seemed to be on friendly terms with every state official in Rhode Island, introduced me to numerous union and public officials, including Arthur Coia Jr.—the former general national president of LIUNA—who later became a subject of our UCO. At first, Guglielmetti had me grease the palms of a couple union guys, either by slipping them some cash or paying for a vacation or rental car.

It gave us a firsthand look into how the Mob maintained control over the Laborers' Union. We learned that if you were a laborer who wanted employment on a construction site, you didn't go to an employer. Instead you went to the union hiring hall. There, local officers decided who worked and who didn't. Those laborers who got employment never saw the complicated kickback schemes, real estate frauds, and other misuse of their dues. Those "investments" were made by union leaders, beholden not to the rank and file, but to bosses who reported to the general president's office and, from there, to the Mob.

Two years in, Operation Double Sessions was pulling me in multiple directions. To further establish the legitimacy of Hemphill Construction and lend me needed help, I brought in more FBI UCAs.

My first "employee" and right-hand man was brand new to the undercover game and came highly recommended by my old friend Jarhead. Assuming the undercover name Mike Sullivan, this recent graduate from the FBI's Undercover School had previously served in the military and still maintained a stiff manner and bearing. He transferred from Philadelphia to Boston, bought a house near mine, and the two of us carpooled three hours every day back and forth to the Hemphill Construction offices in Providence.

I doubt Sullivan remembers those drives as heart-warming and fun, because I spent many of them critiquing his performance bluntly as I tried to quickly school him in the nuances of undercover work. For example, the first time he met Guglielmetti as the mobster passed through our office, Sullivan addressed him as "sir." Guglielmetti reacted with a strange expression. The only people who had previously called him "sir" were federal judges— or in this case a new FBI UCA from a military background.

I took Sullivan to the woodshed, told him this was not "fuck-around time," and explained that even the slightest mistake could cost us our lives, or at least, compromise the case.

Like the good soldier he was, Mike took my corrections, learned, and eventually proved himself invaluable. We added two more FBI UCAs from outside the Boston area—Ken Jones and Doug George—one was a financial wizard and could cook the books for us, and the other had pre-FBI experience in construction management. They were both quiet professionals who supported me when I was overmatched with business, financial, or union details. They could talk the talk and walk the walk when I had trouble banging a nail in straight, let alone posing as a construction magnate.

At times during the Guglielmetti UCO, I needed a quick break from the LCN and used that time to lend a hand in other cases. One such opportunity came in early February 2002, when one of the Agents in the Boston office approached me about acting as an undercover in a murder-for-hire case.

Trying to avoid being pigeonholed as an Organized Crime undercover, I welcomed the opportunity to branch out into other areas. Apparently, the Case Agent thought I looked like someone who would commit a murder for pay, so I gave it a shot.

An informant had approached our office with information about a man who wanted to hire someone to rob and possibly murder an elderly man who ran gambling games in Hudson, New Hampshire.

Taking a day off from Mike Jameson, I left my suits in the closet, dressed in jeans and a sweatshirt and drove out to Methuen, Massachusetts, where I met a small-time New Hampshire crook named Donald Blake.

The informant introduced me as—what else?—a mobster from Rhode Island willing to whack someone for pay. I basically impersonated Matty Guglielmetti, adopting the same swagger, language, and attitude I'd been observing daily. Blake bought my ruse hook, line, and sinker, especially after I braced him against my truck and searched him for a wire before introducing myself. Then, I pulled my shirt up to show him I wasn't wearing a wire, being careful not to reveal the recording device concealed elsewhere on my body.

Blake wanted to hire someone to rob and possibly kill a seventy-one-year-old man named Michael Gosselin, who lived with his seventy-year-old wife in the town of Hudson, New Hampshire. According to Blake, Gosselin had been skimming money from the gambling games he ran every Thursday and Saturday for twenty-five years. The two-to-three thousand he ripped off each week was kept in a safe in his house.

On Thursday nights, a local police officer would escort Gosselin directly to the bank where he would deposit the proceeds that averaged between $20,000 and $25,000 cash. On Sunday evenings, however, the banks were closed, so the police would follow Gosselin home. It was Gosselin's practice to deposit the money from the Sunday night game on Monday morning.

Blake wanted me to jump the old man early Monday morning before he had a chance to go to the bank. That way I could grab the previous night's take as well as the money he had skimmed over the years, which he stored in his safe. He instructed me to carry a gun and warned me that Gosselin kept a small pistol in his house and owned a small dog. He suggested that I might have to pistol whip Gosselin before he relinquished the combination to the safe. And he warned that the stress of the robbery might cause Gosselin to have a heart attack.

Should that "worst-case scenario" occur, Blake said he could "live with it." This admission was important from a legal standpoint.

We agreed that if I recovered less than $100,000 from Gosselin, my share would be 70 percent. If the amount was more than $100,000, I would be paid an entry fee and we would split the remainder of the stolen money fifty-fifty. I needed to haggle, negotiate, and establish that a violent crime was about to occur at Blake's direction for legal reasons.

Naturally, our conversation was recorded. A day later, Blake was arrested. The whole case took less than twenty-hour hours and thwarted a potentially violent crime—a slam dunk for the FBI.

Most of the time, I had no problem wearing a wire. I took exception when Matty Guglielmetti's father passed away in late 2003, and, as his business partner, I was expected to attend the wake and funeral service. Since this was a highly personal event that had nothing to do with the case, I asked my FBI bosses if I was still required to wear a wire. They answered with an emphatic "yes." The rule was that once you wore a recording device in a case you had to continue wearing it unless you could justify taking it off for security reasons.

Matty Guglielmetti had been extremely close to his father, and the wake was extremely emotional. FBI Agents and police officers waited outside the funeral home photographing everyone who entered—many of whom were members of the Mob. My photo was snapped, too, by State Police officers who had no clue about my real identify.

Then, with my body recorder running, I approached Gugliel-metti and his family and expressed my condolences. With tears in their eyes, they thanked me for coming. I couldn't help it, I felt like a heel.

The following day, I attended the church service, and then drove in the funeral procession to the cemetery. It was a very cold winter day, and the burial took place in a family crypt where standing room was very limited. I was about to turn and leave, when Bobby Nardolillo escorted me inside. I stood shoulder to shoulder with Guglielmetti's family and his close associates as they struggled to contain their grief.

Since it was impossible to turn off the body recorder without attracting attention, I moved away as far as possible to allow the family some privacy. I felt like a complete shit bag. Yeah, Guglielmetti was a bad guy, but on this day, he was simply a grieving son.

By the fall of 2004, as Double Sessions approached the five-year mark, it was time to make the awkward jab. The Christmas holidays were approaching—a time when Mob guys liked to entertain and throw around money. I explained to Matty that our construction business wasn't doing so well, and we had to consider other ways to make money. As my silent partner, I told him I wouldn't do anything without getting his approval first.

Matty stood looking at me from a few feet away. I could tell from his face that he knew where this was going. I half-expected him to turn and walk out, but he didn't. So I told him about my relationship with Manny—the Cuban drug dealer who was really a UCA. Guglielmetti indicated that he'd heard Manny's name before, and even mentioned the past protection details Bobby Nardolillo had provided.

I said, "Matty, the quickest way I know to make a buck is to clean some of Manny's money. I've done it many times in the past."

What I was doing was tying money laundering to an SUA (Specific Unlawful Activity)—in this case drug trafficking—so the charge would hold up in court.

Guglielmetti nodded and said, "I know but I don't want to know." He later added, "Mike . . . you've been more than direct with me . . . you've told me more than I want to know. . . ."

His dilemma was simple: He wanted to do things, he just didn't want to get caught. It was Bobby Luisi five years earlier whispering in the stairwell.

I left the dilemma squarely in Guglielmetti's lap by telling him I wouldn't do anything with Manny without his approval. Legally, I was whacking an entrapment defense by giving him the opportunity to say no and walk away.

But Mob guys can't help themselves—they only see the green. And Matty gave me the green light to clean up Manny's money. Less than two weeks later he happily accepted $18,000 in cash, which he believed were laundered funds from Manny's drug-trafficking business. He was now legally cooked.

We pushed a little harder. On December 6, 2004, I told Guglielmetti that Manny had a huge load of cocaine that would soon be transiting through Rhode Island on its way from New York City to Canada. While it stayed overnight in Rhode Island, Manny needed someone to protect it. Guglielmetti wanted to know how much he would get for babysitting the drugs and how many people were required. I told him that Manny was sending

sixty-seven kilos of coke and was offering $1,000 a kilo for pro-
tection—a $67,000 payday for a night's work!

I could see Guglielmetti doing the math in his head. Contrary
to my regular undercover practice, I used the specific words
"coke" and "kilos" so a jury wouldn't be confused.

Matty didn't flinch. During a conversation a week later, he gave
me instructions on how he wanted the drug protection detail to
work: "I don't want people in and out of there . . . I don't want a
guy taking three . . . running out . . . coming back . . . taking
four. . . . You might as well just hang a sign out and say we're
doing drugs." A jury wouldn't need help interpreting that either.

On December 22, 2004, I informed Guglielmetti that the shipment would arrive in Rhode Island the week of January 17 and
would be kept under guard in a hotel room. Then I gave him
another chance to walk away. He looked at me like I was crazy
and said, "I trust you, Mike . . . who would walk away from
$67,000?"

January 18, 2005, I handed Guglielmetti the key to a hotel
room in Cranston, Rhode Island, and told him to make sure his
boys were there at 6 PM. When his associates Alan Blamires and
Anthony Moscarelli entered the hotel room, they were met by
four undercover FBI Agents who opened up one of the suitcases
to show them the cocaine.

A couple of miles away, Matty and I sat in another hotel room,
coordinating our teams from afar while we watched TV, ate a
leisurely dinner, and talked about future plans. At one point,
Guglielmetti said, "Relax, Mike, everything will work out fine."
He was right.

Two days later, he settled into a chair in my private office looking pleased with himself and expected me to hand $67,000 in

cash for babysitting the shipment of coke. I actually had about ten bucks in my pocket.

As he sat facing me, I saw two FBI Agents arriving to arrest him. Hearing them approach, Guglielmetti turned and recognized one of the Agents as someone who had interviewed him before. A look of sheer panic came over his face.

I stood and said, "Matty, do the right thing."

He looked back at me in complete shock. We had worked together for more than three years and he had no clue that I was an FBI Agent.

Guglielmetti's arrest and the arrests of a number of his associates including Bobby Nardolillo, and other subordinates and union officials made national news, and destroyed a dangerous faction of the Patriarca crime family. Later that same day, January 20, 2005, I took a deep breath as I exited the office of Hemphill Construction for the last time.

After almost five years, I no longer had to pretend I was someone I wasn't, or carefully monitor every word I said for fear of being discovered and shot. Double Sessions was over. I went home to my family, played basketball with my sons, then put my feet up and sipped a gin and tonic with my wife.

Guglielmetti was so embarrassed by being duped by the FBI that he pled guilty within days of his arrest. He was sentenced to twelve years in federal prison.

The next time I saw Bobby Nardolillo was a year later when I testified against him in court. As I sat in the witness box reciting the facts of the case, he glared at me like he wanted to choke me to death. He later pled guilty and was sentenced to fifteen years in federal prison, three more than Guglielmetti because he had instructed the protection detail to carry guns.

Their half-dozen or so LCN underlings all received double-digit sentences ranging from ten to thirteen years. One of them told us Nardolillo considered shooting the undercovers and stealing the cocaine during the second protection detail. Thank God they didn't.

Three local Laborers' Union officials, including Nicholas Manocchio, nephew of LCN boss Luigi Giovanni "Baby Shacks" Manocchio, pled guilty to labor law violations and accepting cash bribe payments from me. In a separate civil action LIUNA's General President Emeritus Arthur Coia Jr., who I had hired as a consultant at the direction of Guglielmetti, was charged and found guilty of allowing LCN Capo Matthew Guglielmetti to exercise control or influence over the Union and other charges.

As a result, Coia's membership in the national union and status as General President Emeritus were both revoked. A 2004 news article by a nationally syndicated columnist written at the exact same time the FBI was investigating the relationship between the LCN and Laborers' Union described Coia Jr. as a close associate of former President Bill Clinton. I wonder if they're still friends.

14

THE ITALIAN
MOB—CASE #3

As the primary undercover in Double Sessions, I had just completed one of the longest undercover assignments in FBI history. Five years is a long time to pretend you're someone else and parry with wise guys on a daily basis without committing a potentially deadly slipup. It was also my second infiltration of a Mafia family, and although the FBI didn't keep a scorecard, I knew I was one of a very few, if not the only FBI Agent, to infiltrate the Mob twice.

The FBI didn't hand me a trophy—nor was I expecting one. My reward, starting in January 2005, were the free nights and weekends I got to spend with my family.

That didn't mean I didn't have work to do. With more than three thousand recordings of Guglielmetti, Nardolillo, and their associates to transcribe and analyze, and other evidence to categorize, I spent the rest of 2005 and most of 2006 either prepping for their various trials or testifying in court.

Additionally, I was still the Boston Undercover Coordinator—a full-time job in itself—responsible for assigning, training, and

mentoring UCAs and developing credible scenarios in various
UCOs. And I squeezed in time to bust balls around the office,
and go out after work with other Agents for beverages, compan-
ionship, and laughs. I was back to being a normal FBI Agent, and
it felt good.

Sometime in the fall 2006, Mike Sullivan, my right-hand man
in Double Sessions, approached my desk with a gleam in his eye.
He'd pretty much avoided me since the end of the case, which
didn't come as a shock since I'd browbeaten the poor bastard
day and night for several years.

"What's up, Mike?" I asked.

"I need a little help in another case."

"What case is that?" I knew that Sullivan was now the Case
Agent of an operation targeting Boston's current Mob Underboss.

"We have a case against The Cheese Man," Sullivan answered.
"You in?"

I didn't hesitate. "Of course I'm in. What have you got?"

Carmen DiNunzio—aka The Cheese Man or Big Cheese—was
notorious in Boston for taking over the local Mob after a series of
recent successors had bit the dust and Bobby Luisi and his
crew had been locked up. He tipped the scales at four hundred
pounds and owned and operated the Fresh Cheese Store on En-
dicott Street in the North End of Boston. The cheese store had
allegedly been given to him by organized crime associate Steven
(Stevie Junk) Giorgio to repay a gambling and loansharking debt.

Fifty-year-old Carmen and his younger brother, Anthony, were
straight out of Mob central casting. Born and raised in East
Boston, they were schooled in criminal activity at an early age.
After a falling out with famed Boston Mob Underboss Gennaro
"Jerry" Angiulo in 1983 and having a murder contract on his

head, Carmen DiNunzio fled to the West Coast. There he and his brother worked as bookies and collectors for the Chicago Mob's California and Nevada crews.

In 1992, both brothers were indicted and charged with racketeering and the attempted takeover of a casino on a Native American reservation in San Diego. They pled guilty to extortion and were sentenced to four years in federal jail. During their stint in prison, the DiNunzios befriended some influence-heavy New York wise guys, who helped them regain their standing in the Massachusetts underworld, which they returned to in '97.

By 2006, when Sullivan approached me, The Cheese Man was big, made, and in charge of the decimated Boston Mob. And like most Organized Crime bosses, he was willing to do practically anything to make a buck. Recently, he'd gotten involved in a scheme with a local dirt farmer named Andrew Marino and Mob associate Anthony D'Amore to sell 300,000 cubic yards of toxic loam (soil composed of sand, silt, manure, and clay) to the State of Massachusetts to be used in the Big Dig project—a massive multibillion construction project that involved rerouting Interstate 93 through the heart of Boston and connecting it with the Thomas P. O'Neill Jr. Tunnel. The problem was that the soil was highly contaminated.

DiNunzio spoke to an associate named Dominic about the dirt scam and the challenges they faced because it was toxic. What The Cheese Man didn't know was that Dominic was an FBI informant (another guy jammed on other charges who offered to cooperate with the FBI).

Like I said before: You can't make this shit up.

All of this had been set up before Sullivan approached me. He and I came up with the idea of me playing a state official willing to take money under the table in exchange for fudging the paperwork and approving the soil.

Sullivan liked the plan, but expressed a concern: "You sure you aren't too exposed to the Mob already?"

He had a point. In the roles of Irish Mike O'Sullivan and Mike Jameson, I was well known to the New England Mob. No doubt, associates of Luisi, Merlino, Nardolillo, and Guglielmetti would like nothing more than to get their hands on the FBI Agent who had fucked their bosses. And since I had never taken up on the offer of the physical makeover approved by the FBI, I was still easily identified by my bushy walrus mustache.

On the other hand, I'd never played a state official before and my exposure this time would be minimal—less than a dozen meetings at most.

Whether it was out of foolish pride, or because of something in my blood since my days of playing baseball in Haverhill, Massachusetts, or the adrenaline rush I got from working undercover, I've always found it hard to turn down a professional challenge.

But something unexpected and somewhat less challenging came up first. In January 2006, just before I started preparing to take on The Cheese Man, I was asked to take on a "quick hitter" type case. This was a situation like the Blake murder for hire where the FBI needed a UCA to intervene quickly to prevent a violent act that could endanger the public.

Since this one involved a planned bank robbery, and my FBI superiors apparently thought I looked like a bank robber (Thanks, guys!), I was asked to pitch in. The subject this time was a suspected bank robber named Joel Adam Drown, who had approached an FBI informant for help in robbing a bank in New Hampshire.

The informant had convinced Drown that the two men needed a third accomplice to procure weapons and drive the getaway car, while they went inside to steal the cash. I was to play the role of the third accomplice.

Why not? I always keep a suit and tie in my car, as well as an all-black "wise guy" outfit, in case I was needed for a quick UCO. On this occasion, I again chose to model myself on some real wise guys I'd been associating with recently and had studied carefully. Dressed in black, I assumed a tough guy, asshole attitude. Basically: Don't fuck with me, I'm a professional criminal, and do this bank robbery shit all the time.

I had two days to secure the getaway and switch cars, prepare the informant, coordinate with FBI SWAT and the local PD to make the arrest. I also had to procure the guns, which included a .45 caliber Smith & Wesson for Drown that had to be mechanically disabled without being visible to the naked eye. We wanted to make sure no one was shot.

On a bitter cold day in January 2006, the informant drove me to Drown's house—a ramshackle doublewide trailer perched above a frozen lake. Joel Drown turned out to be a pale, fidgety man in his midtwenties. According to the informant, he was also a drug user.

Drown bought my wise guy act hook, line, and sinker, donned his "work" outfit—Jesse James reversible hat, black bandanna, red stocking cap, black leather gloves, jeans, a blue sweatshirt, and sunglasses—and we took off to rob a bank. Not your usual nine-to-five job.

I showed him where I had parked the "switch" car, then the three of us spent the next three hours driving around, shooting the shit, and casing banks on Route One in Seabrook, New Hampshire. The recording device I wore ran the entire time.

I knew where we wanted the arrest to take place, and which bank would work best from the FBI SWAT point of view. But I had to be careful not to appear to be directing Drown to that particular bank, since his lawyer could potentially use that in court as part of an entrapment defense. So my brain had to be working on several levels at once—hard-ass criminal, FBI Agent, prosecutor. It was a form of multitasking that came natural to me now—talking with bad guys about committing serious felonies with one part of my brain, while going through a checklist of FBI evidence needs with another.

As we were casing the bank we wanted—TD Banknorth on Route One—an armored car pulled into the parking lot and started unloading bags of currency. Totally unplanned. Imagining he was about to make a big score, Drown decided to hit the bank immediately.

My adrenaline soared. Realizing that I needed to control the subject instead of letting the subject control me, I calmly informed Drown that before rushing the bank we had to change into our disguises and get our weapons ready.

"Yeah, right."

I drove to the SWAT arrest position I had selected the previous day, then handed Drown the inert .45 Smith & Wesson, all the time talking to him calmly about what was going to happen next.

Turning to him, I said, "Joel, you wait here while I make sure the license plate is covered up."

I stepped out of the car taking the keys with me so Drown had no means of escape. As I walked to the rear of the car, I signaled to the SWAT team to move in and make the arrest.

Drown initially pleaded not guilty, but changed his plea to

guilty when he was told that the guy he tried to rob the bank with was an FBI Agent. I never saw him again.

After Drown's arrest, I changed out of my black wise guy clothes and went back to preparing to go up against The Cheese Man. In my third Mob case, I was going to be a state official assigned to inspecting loam, so I had to bone up on soil science and learn the terminology—PH, anion and cation exchange capacity, clay mineralogy, etc. Real Massachusetts state officials were cooperative, providing me with a huge lime green state transportation truck. For my wardrobe, I selected a yellow hard hat plastered with union stickers, a lime-green vest, and shit-kicker boots.

I knew by this time that the Mob was tough to penetrate, and DiNunzio was going to try to remain in the background. It was my job to lure the big man out of his cheese store and get him to incriminate himself on tape.

The first meeting between me—calling myself Michael Moretti—and one of the DiNunzio's Mob associates named Anthony D'Amore was set to take place at the dirt farm called Acton Sand & Gravel in September 2006. Knowing the first impression I made would be important, I drove the huge green state transportation truck into the farm like a bat out of hell and tore right past D'Amore and farm owner Andrew Marino, who were standing with our informant waiting to meet me. I spent ten minutes circling the mounds of dirt, then stopped and took a long piss against the wheel of the truck.

Then without bothering to wash my hands, I walked over to D'Amore and Marino and greeted them with handshakes. On purpose, I addressed D'Amore, a Mob tough guy, by the wrong name.

"Hey, Lenny, how's it going?"

He looked fit to be tied. Then I walked away and pretended to make a ten-minute phone call, while the two of them simmered.

There was no scientific term for what I was doing. I borrowed some of my techniques from previous UCOs and others from my favorite TV show at the time, *Dog Whisperer with Cesar Millan*. In the show, dog trainer extraordinaire Millan gave endless examples of how to tame the meanest, nastiest dogs by simply establishing that you (not them) were in control.

I used a different term when applying the technique to bad guys. I called it *mind-fucking*. In this instance, I wanted these knuckleheads to think I was an asshole state official who didn't give a shit about them. I was strictly in it for the money, and wanted to be the last person on earth they'd suspect of being some tight-assed FBI Agent.

It's amazing how well dog control techniques work on human beings. Fifteen minutes into our conversation, D'Amore and Marino offered me a $15,000 bribe for approving the 300,000 cubic yards of contaminated loam and fudging the state paperwork. Now we had to tie the bribe back to The Cheese Man.

Mike Sullivan and the other FBI Agents working the case didn't think there was a chance in hell that DiNunzio would agree to meet me. I disagreed.

Knowing that Mob guys were always hot to make a buck, and there were as many as six million to be made in the sale of the tainted loam, I told D'Amore and Marino that I didn't trust them and wouldn't agree to any deal unless I got a direct guarantee from DiNunzio himself.

Everyone in the office except me was shocked when The Cheese Man agreed to meet me in the parking lot of the Hilltop Restaurant in Saugus, Massachusetts, a week later. I chose this location in the burbs because I wanted to avoid the North End or Providence, where I might run into one of the Mob guys I had met during previous UCOs.

While I was preparing for the initial encounter, Mike Sullivan said, "I really want you to push DiNunzio's buttons. Fuck with him big-time and get him upset. Maybe he will threaten you, too."

"My specialty," I replied. "As you know, I'm really good at pissing people off."

I call it "poking the beast." Knowing how much stock Mob guys put into punctuality, I deliberately showed up to our first meeting fifteen minutes late. The Cheese Man looked like he wanted to wring my throat. Weighing four hundred pounds and standing in the hot early October sun, he was already sweating through his shirt.

The atmosphere was tense, and Dominic (our informant), also in attendance, looked like he wanted to disappear into the parking lot asphalt. I remained relaxed and ornery—my default mode.

I started egging the big mobster on, and questioning whether Marino could deliver on the promise of the 300,000 cubic yards of loam.

DiNunzio was captured on tape assuring me that Marino would come through. At one point, he said, "You need to understand. I'm not even supposed to step out like this, my friend. I was going to throw this fucking kid off the roof for fucking up something like this. I never met him, but he's going to go along on a number of things. If you know anything about me, we're taking a beating so you can get your end."

Was The Cheese Man actually trying to convince me that he had come out of the shadows to deal with me like this out of a sense of altruism? Yes, he was.

I pushed him further by bringing up the subject of the $15,000 bribe money. I said to him: "I had a number. . . . My end is now the same as the first time, and that's all I give a fuck about. We haven't started out on a good note here. What about my 5 percent?"

"Yeah, 5 percent," The Cheese Man responded. "You're getting 20, 20, and 20. He gave you 15 already. And then 5 percent. If you want to take 4 percent and leave us something, that's fine."

Already, in a first meeting with a complete stranger, we had DiNunzio on tape verifying all of the criminal elements of a serious federal criminal violation.

He was asking me to take less of a percentage on the entire deal to "leave us with something," as though he and his associates wouldn't be making a substantial profit on a $6 million contract. Unbelievable. In my role of corrupt state official and asshole, I turned him down.

His head had turned beet red, and his eyes narrowed as though he was imagining plunging a hatchet into my head. I'd never seen a Mob guy so pissed off.

DiNunzio pleaded, "We're taking a beating here. That's why we went and grabbed this other kid (Marino) earlier. We're talking to him, and we're not talking normal, like we're talking here. You know what I mean?"

I did. The Cheese Man was saying that if the dirt farmer Marino didn't do what he wanted and consent to being extorted, he was going to hurt him.

Poking the beast a little more I said, "What I need on my end. . . . I need a guarantee."

DiNunzio looked like he was a second away from exploding all over the parking lot. He took a deep breath and responded, "I don't ever come out. . . . I'm The Cheese Man. You ask anybody about me. We straighten out a lot of beefs, a lot of things, and Marino's gonna do what he's gotta do."

The conversation lasted approximately twenty minutes. When Mike Sullivan listened to the tape, he not only laughed his ass off, he also acknowledged that in those twenty minutes we accomplished more in terms of making a case against The Cheese Man than the traditional investigation had in the past two years.

At a follow-up meeting with DiNunzio held three days later at the Green Tea Restaurant in Newton, Massachusetts, I tied up a couple of legal loose ends. This time I told him how I had switched samples gathered from Acton Sand & Gravel with uncontaminated ones in order to get the contract approved. But since D'Amore and Marino hadn't submitted the necessary paperwork in time to meet the state's fall 2006 deadline, we would have to wait until spring 2007 to sell the loam.

The Cheese Man's face turned beet red again.

"You know how much money, at a minimum, walked out of your pocket?" I asked him, continuing to embarrass him and piss him off. "Three hundred thousand, minimum. You guys fucked it all up . . . blew a simple straight deal."

I got up and threw a twenty on the table. The Boston Underboss sat stunned in his chair as a $6 million deal was about to walk out of the restaurant.

Not only was I killing the loam deal on the spot, which the FBI obviously never had any intention of completing, I was also keeping the bribe money for my time and troubles.

"This is a shame," The Cheese Man groaned, dumbfounded. "You're not going to find a bag of money tomorrow. You know what I mean? He (Marino) just fucked everything up. What a shame."

Pretending that I felt bad for him, I returned to my seat and discussed other possible illegal schemes we could run in the future. At the end, I reminded him: "Carmen, in the inspection business, the man who holds the pencil wins. Just remember that, please. I'll be happy to help you, or anyone you refer."

"One good thing came out of it," DiNunzio responded, "I got to meet you, Mike. It's not dead yet."

I said, "I consider I got a friend in the North End now."

"And a good friend, too."

Having completed my undercover role, I went back to my Undercover Coordinator work. Meanwhile, Sullivan and other Agents continued collecting the last bits of evidence needed to prosecute a major LCN prosecution. The Cheese Man, D'Amore, and Marino were arrested early the morning of May 2, 2008.

Unaware of the timing of their arrests, I was in the office early for my customary 5 AM workout. When I exited the gym an hour later, I walked past the elevator just as it pinged opened. I turned and saw two of my fellow Agent friends with their arms around Carmen DiNunzio.

He looked at me standing in workout gear and I looked back at him.

Using the morning salutation I give to most acquaintances, I said, "Hi, Carmen. How's it going?"

At that point, The Cheese Man hadn't been to court yet and didn't know why he'd been arrested. It took a split second for the implications of what he saw to sink in.

Then The Cheese Man turned to one of the Agents and said, and I quote: "I'm so fucked."

All of us, including DiNunzio, had a good laugh.

He was right. We had him firmly by the legal short hairs, which is why despite the fact that he hired the best defense attorneys money could buy, he pleaded guilty to conspiracy to commit bribery concerning programs receiving federal funds. The Cheese Man was sentenced to six years in federal prison. D'Amore and Marino followed his example and pled guilty, too.

I'd had quite a run. Over the course of nearly ten years, as the primary UCA in three major Mob cases, I'd helped deliver a series of debilitating body blows to Organized Crime in New England. Nobody was keeping score, but the Case Agents, other UCAs, and I were directly responsible for putting a Mob Boss, an Underboss, two Capos, corrupt local and national Union Officials, and dozens of Mob associates behind bars for a cumulative total of well over a hundred years. Some of them never returned to a life of crime.

The Case Agents, my UCA colleagues, and I were just doing our jobs—jobs we loved doing. We didn't get parades or trips to Disneyland when we successfully concluded a case, we simply rolled up our sleeves, rubbed some dirt on it, drank some beers, and went to work on new ones.

15

THE OUTLAWS

By 2007, I was at the top of my UCA game. The skills I'd acquired going up against a series of heavyweights in the Italian and Russian Mobs gave me a new level of professional confidence. I loved the psychological gamesmanship of undercover work, and the thrill of the hunt.

Physically, I wasn't the same. Twenty years of chasing bad guys, combined with a serious leg injury suffered while on SWAT had left me with a permanent limp, and taken a toll on other parts of my body. My colleagues marked this new stage in my career by giving me another nickname—"The Old Man," or *El Viejo* in Spanish.

Mentally, I was as eager and ready as I'd ever been. After concluding my UC role with The Cheese Man, I jumped into two very different investigations—one involving Public Corruption subjects in Florida, and another against the notorious Outlaws Motorcycle Club.

The first one, known as "Flat Screen" had been underway for some time when I got involved. It started back in October 2003, with a tip from a Blood gang member informing the Miami FBI that Miramar, Florida, City Commissioner Fitzroy Salesman (Yes, that's his real name) had been buying drugs, stolen property, and soliciting prostitutes—sometimes in the city hall parking lot. You can't make this shit up.

The tip precipitated a meeting between Salesman and a respected FBI UCA I'll call Victor in a Miami strip club. Over the next several months, Victor and other Florida UCAs discussed possible money laundering and real estate deals with Salesman, who bragged that he was someone who "could get things done in Miramar"—meaning that he was open to do business at a price. I was brought in as the veteran UCA to make the Public Corruption aspect of the overall case.

August 2005, I traveled to South Florida, where Victor introduced me to Salesman at a barbeque joint in the Seminole Hard Rock Hotel & Casino near Hollywood. I was Michael Moretti again, but instead of a Massachusetts state soil inspector, this Michael Moretti was a wealthy construction contractor from the Northeast who was looking to retire in South Florida and didn't care whose palm he had to grease in order to secure lucrative Broward County government contracts.

I dressed in a $1,500 Armani suit, exuding money and confidence, while everyone else plopped around in flip-flops and Tommy Bahama flowered shirts.

Fitzroy Salesman struck me as a typical criminal, despite the fact that he was wearing a well-tailored business suit and had an impressive public official title. His favorite subject—like that of so many criminals—was himself. He regaled me with story after story about how important and impressive he was, and like all good UCAs, I keep the tape recording running and my mouth shut.

Over the next several months, Salesman introduced other

UCAs, who played the role of local lobbyists and financial managers who reported to me, to school board members, Broward county commissioners, and other politicians who might be willing to grant State government contracts for money under the table. One of them, County Commissioner Josephus Eggelletion of Lauderhill, offered to secure a contract to build city sidewalks for our FBI-created company, but ultimately never delivered. He later bit on a parallel $900,000 FBI-created money-laundering scheme we developed in the Bahamas, and ended up pleading guilty to state corruption charges. School Board member Beverly Gallagher was also convicted of accepting bribes.

Fitzroy Salesman took a little longer to snag.

The Miramar City Commissioner chose to remain in the background until April 2006, when he came up with a plan to start our company off with smaller jobs, and then move us up into the higher million-dollar range contracts.

"You take the shit nobody else wants," he explained to me during one of my visits. "When the big shit arrives, I say: 'They earned their turn.'"

First, Salesman convinced Miramar City Manager Robert Payton to hire our backstopped firm to build a city gazebo for $34,000. Then, we were given a contract to install a gym floor at the city recreation center. For his services, Salesman took a 1 percent bribe of the total projects costs. It didn't amount to much in the beginning, but would become extremely profitable for him when the big jobs came, or so he told us—on tape.

Needing a legitimate contractor to do the work and keep his mouth shut, we turned to the family friend of one of the other UCAs, who ran a licensed construction firm in Fort Lauderdale. All the contracting work was completed to specifications and done above board.

By the summer of 2007 it was time for us to take on the "big shit" in Salesman's terminology. On July 28, he and I met in my oceanfront room at the Westin Diplomat Hotel. With audio- and videotape recording equipment running, Salesman told me about an upcoming county building renovation project that could be worth as much as $500,000 he wanted to push our way.

"Can we get our hands on that?" I asked.

"That is what I'm working on," answered Salesman. "There is growth," he added. "As a matter of fact, we're building a $22 million state-of-the-art cultural center right now." He then went on to boast about how he could help our company secure part of $80 million in capital improvement projects earmarked for Broward County in the upcoming year, including a new police department building and a command center for fire rescue.

He said, "I'm in there, and that is what I do. I have a good relationship with the rest of the commission and the city managers."

"You're my special friend in Miramar," I offered.

"You give as much as you get," Salesman responded, leaning back in his chair as relaxed as a snake sunning itself in the warm Florida sun.

Before I got up to pay Salesman the bribe money he'd earned so far, I offered him a chance to back out. In order to avoid a later entrapment defense, I literally pointed to the door and told him to leave if he was uncomfortable with accepting a bribe.

Salesman responded with his peculiar philosophy of right and wrong. "I'm not interested in right or wrong in the world," he explained, "because right or wrong can be perceived, depending on who you ask. It's a perception. My greatest concern is what works. There's no right or wrong in the world. We're not talking about going out and murdering a child."

No, we weren't. But we *were* talking about Public Corruption.

Following his little speech, I stood up, and slowly counted out three stacks of hundred-dollar bills, amounting to $1,000 each, and set them on a table next to him. I intentionally didn't hand him the money. Salesman picked up the stacks one by one without hesitation, and slipped them in his pocket. All of this was captured on videotape.

Five minutes later, Salesman left my room $3,000 richer. At the same time FBI paperwork was being drafted for his federal indictment. After an eight-day trial in which I testified for two days, a jury found him guilty of two counts each of bribery and extortion.

At his sentencing, Salesman made a teary appeal to the judge. "I will never, ever be the same. It doesn't matter what I do. If I could give my life to reverse it, I would."

He was sentenced to three years and four months in federal prison, a major hit for a Public Corruption conviction, which usually involved a slap-on-the-wrist and little, if any, prison time.

Concurrent with impersonating different versions of Michael Moretti with Salesman and The Cheese Man during 2006 and 2007, I was also playing the role of a long-distance trucker in a Boston UCO called "Road Kill."

The FBI investigation into the notorious Outlaws Motorcycle Club began in November 2005, when an FBI UCA (who I'll call Pete Smith) infiltrated the Taunton, Massachusetts, chapter of the gang posing as the owner of a trucking company in Texas who visited Massachusetts on a monthly basis, and was willing to bend the law to make a buck.

The Outlaws were a rough bunch. According to a Department of Justice report, the most violent motorcycle gang in the country with more than ninety chapters worldwide, and three

Massachusetts chapters headquartered in Brockton, Taunton, and East Boston. Their logo, which they referred to as Charlie, featured a skull and crossed pistons. The FBI and local law enforcement were targeting them because of their known involvement in drug trafficking, firearms violations, and other criminal activity in the Boston area.

Starting in 2006, Smith began purchasing cars, trucks, and motorcycles from members of the Taunton chapter of the Outlaws as part of an insurance fraud scheme. The Outlaws or their associates would either steal the vehicles outright, or report the vehicles stolen, collect the insurance settlement, and pocket a portion of the money when Smith purportedly resold the vehicles in Mexico.

In support of Smith, a longtime UCA buddy named Gonzo and I played the role of long-distance truckers, who worked for Smith, and used an FBI big rig to transport the vehicles to Mexico. Gonzo, a licensed CDL (Commercial Driver's License) operator, drove a monstrous eighteen-wheel tractor-trailer, and I was his trusted passenger sidekick "Pancho," pretending to speak Spanish, handing out sandwiches and drinks, and working the radio. We both wore baggy canvas shorts and wife-beater T-shirts topped off with huge floppy Panamanian straw hats. Geriatric versions of Cheech & Chong complete with huge handlebar mustaches and tanned skin.

One Agent drily commented that when together we looked like "walking probable cause"—meaning we appeared to be up to no good. Gonzo and I took that as a compliment.

We were working an undercover biker gang case, and I could barely ride a bicycle, let alone a motorcycle. I figured as long as we gave the bad guys what they wanted, we'd be fine.

Gonzo hailed from Puerto Rico, had served honorably as a U.S.

Army Captain, and was the second funniest guy I knew in the FBI after Jarhead, which is saying a lot given the cast of FBI misfits I tended to associate with. He had the ability to make the most hardened criminals laugh their ass off within minutes of meeting him. He was also a merciless mimic of FBI management officials. We'd met in Miami twenty years earlier and had both cut our undercover teeth under Chris Brady's astute tutelage.

With Gonzo as my partner, I knew this was going to be a blast, we'd have to stay in Hampton Inn hotels (don't ask), and the bad guys would get caught.

About a year and a half into the UCO and after many successful meetings, Smith was dragged into a basement by the Outlaws one night and strip-searched. They were looking for a wire that he was in fact wearing and that, incredibly, they didn't find. Smith walked out of the basement, quit the next day, and never returned to Massachusetts. I couldn't blame him.

But he did agree to telephone the Outlaws and tell them his truckers (Gonzo and Pancho) would be back in the area if the Outlaws wanted to continue to do business. Gonzo replaced Smith as the lead UCA, and I played second fiddle. It was up to us to push this difficult and violent case across the finish line.

The next time Gonzo and I met the Outlaws in Taunton, Massachusetts, we let them know that we also used our semi to transport large shipments of cocaine from Mexico into the United States and Canada. That got their attention. On November 30, 2006, in a variation of the FBI drug sting we had run on Matty Guglielmetti in Rhode Island almost two years earlier, we got six Outlaw members, including the current president, to serve as a protection detail for forty kilograms of cocaine and a thousand pounds of marijuana that Gonzo and I had supposedly driven up from Mexico.

They were hired to guard it while the drugs were transferred to other trucks for transport to Canada. The cocaine and marijuana were real and provided by the FBI from other criminal cases.

As Gonzo and I drove away after delivering the drugs, a State Police cruiser pulled behind us and flashed their lights. My partner and I looked at one another and laughed. Gonzo summed up the situation with a shit-eating grin and a two-word expletive, "We're fucked."

Not only did our truck have Florida plates, but the trailer reeked of weed. On top of that Gonzo and I were wearing the ridiculous Panama straw hats and, not having shaved in several days, looked like a couple of burned-out hippies on a dope run. Since we were working undercover, we weren't carrying badges or anything that identified us as FBI Agents. And, we also both had loaded guns under our seats.

Gonzo pulled to the side of the highway loudly ranting about racial profiling. In the rearview mirror, I saw the State Troopers eyes light up at the first whiff of ganja. I also noticed that the younger of the two troopers had his gun out and concealed behind his leg. He seemed very, very nervous. Not a good sign.

The senior trooper approached Gonzo's window.

"Hi, officer, what's the problem?" Gonzo asked in broken English, acting like a wiseass and impersonating a stereotypical Mexican.

"Your rear license plate appears to be blocked. We couldn't read it," the trooper responded

"Really? Don't think so." Gonzo was positive our license plate was highly visible and properly affixed.

The officers ordered us out of the truck and handcuffed us each, for "our own safety."

I knew what they were doing. They were looking for an excuse to search the trailer. As a law enforcement officer myself, I understood that they couldn't do that without producing a search warrant or getting our consent.

The younger trooper and I kept feeling each other out, and the more I chatted with him, the more fidgety he got, sometimes carelessly pointing his pistol in my direction. Meanwhile, Gonzo complained to the senior trooper about how often he was pulled over because of his Hispanic background.

All of this was taking place on the side of the highway. The traffic behind us had now slowed to a crawl and rubberneckers paused to see what was going on. I couldn't help laughing when a yellow school bus passed with schoolkids' faces pressed against the window looking at us like animals in the zoo, not knowing we were actually on Team America.

"What's so funny?" the junior trooper asked.

"Inside joke."

Bad things can happen when law enforcement gets nervous. So I made a battlefield decision, got the attention of the senior trooper, and told him Gonzo and I were FBI Agents and that our guns were loaded and concealed under the front seat.

He didn't buy the FBI part, and I couldn't blame him. They grabbed our guns immediately. The younger trooper was now visibly shaking. I asked the senior one to call our FBI office so that someone there could identify us.

He refused.

I mentioned the name of a Massachusetts State Trooper who had assisted us earlier in the day. The senior trooper recognized the name, but when he called him, the trooper who had assisted us didn't answer his phone.

Still highly suspicious of who we really were and what we were up to, the nervous troopers instructed us to proceed slowly to the next exit and pull over.

We did as instructed. Over Gonzo's continuing complaints about being a victim of ethnic profiling, I heard sirens approaching. Three marked units and an unmarked cruiser surrounded our truck when we stopped. Passersby continued to gawk.

"Hey, Gonzo," I remarked. "Look on the bright side. We must be real convincing as drug dealers."

He didn't find that funny, which made me laugh harder.

Several cops were now conferring in front of our cab. Some had their guns drawn. An aggressive plainclothes detective walked to the driver's side window and started throwing FBI and State Police names at us.

"You know Sergeant McCloskey?" the detective asked.

"Yeah."

"What's his first name?"

"Bob."

"What department does Doug Kinzer work for?"

"FBI—Squad C-3."

I answered all his questions correctly. Finally, he mentioned the name of a good friend of mine, a State Police undercover named Pete Davidson.

"Sure, I know Davidson. He thinks he's a comedian. He tries his lousy jokes out on me every time I see him."

The detective smiled. Turned out Davidson and he had been roommates at the police academy. The detective got Davidson on the phone, and after Davidson identified me by my signature bushy walrus mustache, the detective and I took turns busting his balls.

After an hour standoff, Gonzo and I were free to go. From the expression on the face of the senior trooper, I could tell that he was still having trouble believing that we two extremely shady-looking characters were actually FBI Agents.

To fuck with the trooper's head a little more, Gonzo led him back to the back of the trailer to show him what he had wanted to get a look at for more than an hour. The trailer, reeking of ganja, was empty.

"Tough shit," said Gonzo, still fuming. "Go catch a real dope dealer." Then he fired up the diesel engine, blasted the air horn, and drove off with me beside him bouncing up and down on the seat with laughter.

Another time in a different UCO in Providence, Rhode Island, Gonzo and I were negotiating a drug deal with a Latin Kings gang member who went by the name Lucky, and had it tattooed across his neck.

I'd never seen a neck tattoo at that point, and stared at it fascinated by the intricate ink artwork.

Gonzo was trying to negotiate the particulars of the drug deal we were trying to make, but I kept interrupting him, pointing to Lucky's tattoo and asking questions. "You get that around here?"

"Yeah, Central Falls. Why?"

"It hurt?"

"Hell, yeah."

"Think I should get one?"

Lucky took one look at my white Irish skin and said, "Nah . . . I don't think so . . . ," while Gonzo just shook his head at my lack of focus.

It turned out that Lucky didn't live up to his name. He was shot and killed the night before we were scheduled to conclude the drug deal.

In May 2007, Gonzo and I were getting ready to drive a second haul of stolen Outlaw vehicles to Mexico, when Outlaws former president Timothy Silvia, fresh out of prison, asked whether we could provide him with marijuana or cocaine. It was an unusually brazen move in the drug world, but Gonzo had been so convincing, and charming, that the Outlaws were completely comfortable talking flat dirty to him.

"Sure," I said. "How much?"

"At least ten kilograms."

"That's all?" I complained, trying to make Silvia feel like a small fry. "We usually only do fifty or a hundred at a time."

His eyes widened. Then he said, "I'm just getting back on my feet," trying to save face.

I paused as if I was trying to decide, made eye contact with Gonzo who shot me a silent signal, and finally said, "Fuck it . . . why not? It's a quick score. We'll take care of you."

Silvia breathed a sigh of relief, and Gonzo and I slapped on our Panama hats and told him we'd be in touch.

On June 15, 2007, I met with Silvia in the parking lot of the Holiday Inn in Westgate Mall in Brockton to discuss the specifics of the drug deal. Silvia showed up driving a brand-new gray Hummer with Massachusetts plates and fit the profile of your typical biker—shaved head, all tatted up, and stocky, more fat than muscle.

He immediately got in my face and challenged me about being a cop. I countered by asking him, "How do I know that you're not a cop?"

He backed off and we started talking. During our forty-five-minute conversation captured by the body recorder I was wearing, we negotiated a price of $180,000 cash on delivery for ten kilograms of cocaine. Silvia told me that he had served twenty years in prison and had recently been released.

"I'm done with that for the rest of my life," he explained at one point. Next time he was arrested he said, "I'm shooting it out with them. I'm going out in a blaze of glory. I can't do twenty more."

I made sure to mention that to the SWAT team that was going to make the arrest.

During our confab in the parking lot, Silvia also claimed to have killed someone in a bar fight, beat two witnesses with baseballs bats, shot another individual, and conducted home invasions of area drug dealers. I assumed some of it was true, since his rap sheet consisted of 106 pages with 220 entries.

Silvia also discussed his involvement in stealing vehicles and his profiting financially from fraudulent insurance claims filed for other cars. He boasted that he had paid $100,000 for the Hummer he'd arrived in, and owned two additional Hummers, which he said he was willing to report stolen for resale in Mexico.

Timothy Silvia wasn't lucky, either. On July 30, 2007, six weeks after I recorded our conversation in the Holiday Inn parking lot, Silvia and his partner Todd Donofrio returned to the same parking lot to meet Gonzo and me and collect their ten kilograms of cocaine. After giving us $55,000 in cash as an initial payment, Gonzo lured Silvia into the back of the truck to show him the cocaine, while I lowered the electric door gate to prevent Silvia from escaping. Seeing my visual signal, the SWAT team did their thing.

Silvia never saw it coming and never had a chance to reach for the gun he had hidden in Donofrio's car. Instead, he was indicted for federal drug trafficking, possession of illegal firearms, armed carjacking, insurance fraud, and other charges. Nearly two hundred law enforcement officers from the FBI, State Police, Plymouth County Sheriff's Department, and the Taunton and Brockton police departments participated in the arrests. A raid of the Outlaws' Taunton headquarters resulted in the seizure of more drugs, $100,000 in cash, and more than a dozen firearms, including an AR-15 automatic assault rifle.

They went off to jail, while Gonzo and I hung up our Panama hats at his favorite restaurant, The 99, and dined on steak tips and drank beers.

Silvia, instead of going down in a blaze of gunfire as he had promised, instead ended up pleading guilty and was sentenced to twenty-one-and-a-half years in prison. Fourteen other Outlaws were convicted by trial or guilty pleas, and all received double-digit prison sentences, effectively obliterating the Taunton Chapter of the Outlaws Motorcycle Club.

The year 2007 turned out to be very busy for me. I traveled to Florida to make the $3,000 bribe payment to Salesman on July 28, and quickly returned to Boston, put on my shorts and hat, and teamed with Gonzo to snatch Silvia and Donofrio two days later.

My seventeen-year-old daughter had accompanied me to Florida to visit colleges. While I was paying off Salesman in an upstairs room at the Westin Diplomat, she was sunning herself downstairs beside the majestic pool. An hour after paying a cash bribe to a public official on videotape, my daughter and I went to tour a nearby college like normal families did, except I had a .40 caliber Baby Glock stuffed into the rear waistband of my pants.

Back in 2007, the United States was the only civilized nation in the world that didn't have a national law enforcement undercover team. All the countries in Europe, Canada, and most of South America deployed national teams with specific expertise in organizing, planning, and executing undercover operations to fight their most dangerous criminals and criminal organizations.

Instead, in the United States, the FBI had fifty-six field offices running their own undercover operations.

Change was past due and finally came in June 2007 when the FBI formed its first national undercover team known as NDURE (National Dedicated Undercover Response Element). Don't ask me where they came up with that name.

Experienced UCAs like Brady, Gonzo, me, and others had been lobbying for a national team for more than twenty years. To our minds it made absolute sense to find a way to match our best UCAs and other assets against our nation's most complex, dangerous, and challenging criminal targets.

In 2005, FBIHQ's Undercover Unit Chief had summoned me to Washington to brief me on his plan for a national undercover team. I agreed with everything he had to say, even when he asked me to run it. When he told me I had to transfer to Washington and work out of FBIHQ, I passed.

Two years later, in 2007, shortly before NDURE was officially approved, I got a call from the Criminal Investigative Division Assistant Director (CID AD) who was essentially the number-three official in the FBI and my former SAC in Boston. Again, he asked me to lead NDURE.

I told him I would accept under three conditions: One, I remain assigned to Boston. Two, I got to handpick members of the undercover team with no interference from FBIHQ. And, three, they would leave us alone.

He immediately agreed to the first two, and promised that as long as he remained the CID AD, he would adhere to my third condition as well.

I was honored to be named NDURE's first member, and accepted the position of Operational Senior Team Leader (STL). A good friend of mine and supervisor in the Undercover Unit, originally from the Atlanta Division, was appointed to handle the FBIHQ administrative side of NDURE, while I ran the operational end.

My obvious first UCA pick to join the national team was none other than Gonzo. After him I selected the cream of the crop of UCAs from the Atlanta, Minneapolis, San Francisco, Richmond, Seattle, San Diego, and Charlotte Divisions. It was a team of all-stars and our future seemed bright.

Within the first two years, we did UCOs in conjunction with twenty-three different FBI field offices, and made many difficult cases, especially in the area of Public Corruption. Soon we were getting more UCO requests than we could handle, and rave reviews from SACs all over the country.

Then we took on one of the most powerful men and criminal organizations in the world, and everything changed.

16

THE SINALOA CARTEL—PART ONE

Early 2009, I was sitting in my Boston office, when I saw a young Case Agent named Hank Tanner, who I knew to be a bright, eager kid by reputation and looked like a lumberjack, peek in. The straight-arrow Mormon kid from Utah had a frightened look in his eyes. For some reason, new Agents, even those like Tanner who towered over me, regarded me as an intimidating guy. Maybe it's because I was exacting of myself and others, or that I didn't smile a lot, or I had no patience with bureaucratic BS.

For whatever reason, Tanner appeared hesitant about entering my office. When he finally got up the nerve to do so, I greeted him with a simple, "What's up, Grizzly?" Tanner wore a beard, but the reference to the dated 1970s TV character Grizzly Adams went completely over his head.

He said, "I'm working a case with an informant."

"And?"

"I think I might have something important," Tanner said, "but

I'm not sure what it is, or how to develop it. I was told you could come up with something devious."

"Tell me about your informant."

"He's a two-time convicted federal drug dealer with ties to the Sinaloa drug cartel."

I'd been half-listening while leafing through some NDURE paperwork, but upon hearing the words "Sinaloa drug cartel" the hairs on the back of my neck stood up. Twenty-two years on the job, I knew a good case when I heard one. He had my full attention.

In 2009, the Mexican Sinaloa drug cartel was the most powerful criminal drug organization in the world. It had been founded in the late '60s in the Mexican state of Sinaloa, and according to the U.S. Justice Department had been responsible for importing more the two hundred tons of cocaine and heroin into the United States. It also supplied the United States and other markets with massive amounts of methamphetamine, marijuana, and MDMA.

Since the mid-'90s, the cartel had been run by pint-sized drug lord Joaquín Achivaldo Guzmán Loera, commonly known as El Chapo, or Shorty. Born the son of a poor cattle rancher, he was now worth billions and ranked by *Forbes* magazine as the forty-first most powerful person in the world—ahead of Steve Jobs and Israeli Prime Minister Benjamin Netanyahu. He was also the world's most wanted fugitive after escaping from a Mexican prison in 2001.

Tanner explained that his hard-to-handle informant, Gustavo (Gus) Vargas, who I later dubbed "the General," had been a very successful Miami drug trafficker and worked with Pablo Escobar's Medellín Cartel in the 1980s. Since then he had served two terms in federal prison on drug charges, and still maintained relationships in the world of drug trafficking, including contacts high up in the Sinaloa Cartel.

Vargas was willing to cooperate with us, Tanner said, because the U.S. government had seized some personal property that he wanted returned for sentimental reasons. I couldn't care less about the seized property. I just wanted this guy to work with us.

"Sounds like you might have a tiger by the tail," I offered as I felt adrenaline pump into my system.

I didn't have the heart to tell Tanner that the odds of us making a case against the Sinaloa Cartel and Chapo Guzmán from our Boston office were astronomically low. Since Boston wasn't a major drug supply or distribution city, we were going to have to come up with a scenario to convince the cartel that we were operating somewhere else. And since the FBI was prohibited from operating in Mexico, and Mexican government officials couldn't be trusted, we would have to rely on his informant, Vargas, in a big way.

Before I even considered those issues, there was another bureaucratic one I had to address. As NDURE's Operational STL, I knew every UCO we had underway. The truth was that we usually didn't take on drug cases, because they weren't considered the highest priorities. This would be the exception. If we were going up against Chapo and his cartel, we needed our absolute best UCAs.

So, begrudgingly, I traveled to FBIHQ to make a formal request to take on this unique drug case, which was going to require a good deal of time and money. Before the critical meeting, I made it a point to "accidently" bump into the CID AD and let him know the purpose of my visit to headquarters. It proved fortuitous, and to my great satisfaction and amazement, my request to pit NDURE against the Sinaloa Cartel was approved and Operation Dark Water was underway!

I had no doubt that we were embarking on a high-stakes gamble, and any chance we had to succeed in indicting El Chapo and his associates depended on meticulous planning, impeccable execution, and good luck.

Since Mexico was outside of the FBI jurisdiction and we couldn't even enter Mexico, we were going to have to depend on the Cuban-born drug trafficker informant to travel to Sinaloa, Mexico, and initiate discussions with leaders of the cartel. The first thing I did was to check him out myself.

Tanner—the young Mormon serving as the Case Agent—set up a meeting between Gus Vargas, other Agents, and me. My fellow Agents dressed casually in jeans and T-shirts. I deliberately wore a suit, sat to the side of the room and watched, and never said a word. My behavior clearly unnerved Vargas—which is exactly what I set out to accomplish.

As soon as the meeting was over and I left without speaking, Vargas turned to Tanner and asked, "Who was that asshole in the suit?" Perfect.

I wanted to see what kind of person we would be depending on. Gus Vargas fit the profile of most of the better informants I had met in the past—he was in possession of a massive ego. Despite the fact that he had been arrested twice and had served a total of seventeen years in federal prison, he considered himself the smartest guy in the room, and a major player in the drug world.

Given Vargas's criminal resume, which included working with Pablo Escobar's Medellín Cartel in the '80s, I didn't doubt that he knew his way around. At the same time, I understood that we were going to have to watch this guy like a hawk for any sign of betrayal. If at any point during the case he thought he could make a better deal for himself on the other side of the fence, he wouldn't hesitate to jump.

Not only did we need to be brutally realistic in terms of who we were working with, we also had to come up with a reasonable plan. The United States provided an enormous market for the cartel's product. Also, our law enforcement agencies (including the DEA and FBI) vigorously pursued drug traffickers, and the traffickers were aware of that. So we couldn't expect the leaders of the Sinaloa Cartel to do business directly with a U.S. criminal organization because of their fear of being arrested.

So how were we going to lure them into doing business with us? After weeks of brainstorming we came up with a plan to impersonate an Italian organized crime group headquartered in Sicily interested in opening a pipeline for illegal drugs into Europe. We were going to need a team of our best UCAs to pull this off.

I immediately recruited Gonzo and another Italian-looking, Spanish-speaking member of NDURE named Patricio. From the Boston office, I selected a third Hispanic Agent, Antonio, who had worked international undercover cases. To portray the head of the fictitious Italian crime organization, I tapped a good friend of mine from the Newark office who had done organized crime UCs in the past, spoke fluent Sicilian, and looked as intimidating as Marlon Brando in *The Godfather*.

It was a strong and very capable team. I would remain in the background, setting the stage with elaborate scenarios, defining and redefining the UCA's roles and responsibilities, pulling the undercover strings as the puppet master who remained out of sight.

But just as we were getting started, Murphy's law kicked in, and my friend from Newark was offered a lucrative private sector job, which he felt he couldn't turn down. I accepted his profuse apologies, wished him well, and started to look around for someone else to play the role of the leader of the ersatz international criminal organization. I racked my brain for candidates, interviewed several, and in the end, chose . . . myself.

I know, I don't speak Sicilian, Italian, or Spanish, and sometimes have trouble communicating in English. But the honest truth was, I was itching to get back into the action of another UCA assignment and knew I could pull it off.

Going forward and for the remainder of Dark Water, I would be known as El Viejo—The Old Man—a mature, successful, and sometimes irascible Italian crime boss, who wanted to make international dope deals and money and didn't give a shit about who he might offend in the process.

With our all-star UCA team in place, we spent the next six months doing the requisite tedious but essential backstopping. In this case, the UCAs were supported by other Agents like Mike Sullivan from Double Sessions; an anal-retentive but highly respected Agent we called the Stork; and a Boston PD detective we dubbed Tattoo because of his close resemblance to the diminutive greeter on the '70s and '80s TV hit *Fantasy Island*.

Those three, working with us UCAs, Case Agent Tanner, our supervisor Harry Wilson, and our ASAC Frank Johnson, set out to create the profile of a highly successful and sophisticated international criminal organization headquartered in Sicily. With help from international law enforcement friends from around the world, and some domestic FBI private sector friends, we developed international shipping companies and business entities to give the outward appearance of a legitimate international business, with absolutely no nexus in any way to the United States.

We deliberately erased any connection between us and the United States so as not to scare the cartel away.

In July 2009, Gus Vargas traveled to the Mexican city of Agua Prieta on the U.S.–State of Sonora border and adjacent to the town of Douglas, Arizona. What he saw around him was a dusty town of roughly eighty thousand and home to several *maquiladoras,* including Velcro, Levolor, and the Commercial Vehicle Group, which built cab systems for heavy-duty trucks and was headquartered in New Albany, Ohio.

In the lobby of one of the town's upscale hotels, he met with a former Mexican minor league baseball player with short dark hair named Alvaro Rivera-Pedrego—a representative of the Sinaloa Cartel. The two men discussed drug trafficking. When Vargas mentioned that he was working with an Italian crime family that was interested in importing cocaine and other drugs into Europe, Rivera-Pedrego's attention perked up. He said his boss, El Chapo, was interested in expanding into new markets in Europe and he thought he could arrange a meeting with Vargas and the drug kingpin himself.

This was music to our ears in Boston. Three months later, in late October, Vargas returned to Mexico and traveled farther south to the capital city of Sonora, Hermosillo. In this desert city of 800,000, Vargas met again with Alvaro Rivera-Pedrego, who introduced him to El Chapo's first cousin and business representative Jesus Manuel Gutierrez-Guzman—a good-looking man in his early fifties with bushy eyebrows and a perpetual scowl.

Again, Vargas talked about his connections to our fictitious Italian crime organization and his interest in brokering a deal between it and a major drug supplier like the Sinaloa Cartel. The United States was never mentioned. Gutierrez-Guzman asked him how much cocaine the Italians were interested in purchasing.

This was the opening we were looking for. Vargas answered that the cartel would have to negotiate the amount directly with the Italians and suggested that the Sinaloans send someone who could make decisions on behalf of El Chapo. As a blood relative of El Chapo's, Gutierrez-Guzman represented that he had that authority.

That's when the real work started on our end. We knew there was virtually no chance El Chapo would leave his safe haven in Mexico, where many U.S. officials believed he was quietly protected and supported by the government of Mexico. The FBI, and especially us in Boston, had fought vigorously against any notification to the Mexican government of our UCO, and we ultimately prevailed.

Under the best of circumstances, we were walking a daily tight rope, where one mistake could have fatal results. We didn't need some official in Mexico spilling the beans about our UCO to Chapo.

Communicating with the cartel through Vargas, we told them we didn't want to meet in Europe because there were too many law enforcement eyes on us there and we didn't want to expose the cartel to any new cop eyes. They appreciated our concern. We subtly suggested a location in Miami instead, where we weren't widely known, and where El Viejo could bring some of his Italian associates for some relaxation and fun in the sun.

Our plan from Day One was to mimic El Chapo's and his gang's practices. Since we knew Chapo Guzmán treated his employees well, El Viejo did, too. We also wanted to send him the subtle message that while he was stuck in Mexico with an international warrant over his head, El Viejo was free to travel anywhere he wanted.

The cartel agreed to meet us in Miami for two reasons: One,

it was close to Mexico. And, two, we weren't going to discuss importing drugs into the United States, so they felt safe.

With the upcoming 2009 holiday season, we pushed the date back to early 2010, to give us more time to prepare for this critical first meeting. In addition to the other three UCAs, I recruited a very attractive female UCA I had worked with before to play my glamorous girlfriend, Liquita. The Agent who played her was not only very pleasing to look at, she was also brilliant and in possession of a Ph.D.

Figuring that the cartel would be interested in our ethnic backgrounds and roles, we cast Gonzo as my Spanish-English translator and main Hispanic drug associate, responsible for our transportation needs. Antonio would act as our international business advisor and expert in port facilities in Spain. Patricio, who looked Italian but spoke fluent Spanish, would be my most trusted Italian advisor who was being groomed to take over my position.

The meeting of February 24, 2010, was set to take place in a luxury thirty-story oceanfront Florida condo rented by the FBI. Naturally we had it wired for video and sound. The bar was stocked and ready. The joint was staged with fresh flowers, photos, and clothes in the closet. Liquita sashayed around in a bikini, covered by one of El Viejo's opened white dress shirts, with a diet soda in hand. Our informant Gus Vargas stood ready to make the introductions. It was game time.

As we did a last-minute check of everything, I noticed that the other UCAs appeared nervous. This was natural going into a first undercover meeting. I had butterflies in my stomach, too. I always did, but I had never seen my friends this uptight.

Hoping to lighten the mood, I went to the bathroom, removed my clothes and replaced them with a loud purple velour bathrobe that I found hanging there. It barely tied around my ample waist. Then I slicked my hair back with water, checked my reflection in the mirror—I looked like a complete jackass, in my opinion, a smart-ass Marlon Brando godfather type, but perfect for the role.

I waddled into the living room where Vargas and the UCAs were nervously waiting with my hairy chest exposed and strutted around like a peacock. With the audio and video running, they all burst into raucous laughter.

"What's so funny? What's so fucking funny? You want a piece of this? You know who I am? I'm fucking El Viejo!"

The tension lightened considerably and for years later, prosecutors referred to this simply as "The Bathrobe Meeting."

El Chapo's first cousin Jesus Manuel Gutierrez-Guzman arrived minutes later, appearing scared to death. What we didn't know and quickly found out was that he was petrified of high places. After making a big show of how we had swept the apartment for listening devices, we tried to escort him out onto the balcony to show him the panoramic view. Even with the beautiful Liquita sprawled out on a chaise lounge, Gutierrez-Guzman looked like a man who was imagining what it would feel like to fall thirty stories and hit the ground.

He huddled in a corner as far away from the ledge as possible. We calmed him down by bringing him inside and sitting him on one of the sofas facing the FBI cameras.

We spent the next three hours discussing the possibility of transporting cocaine from Mexico to Europe like we were talking about importing potato chips. Gutierrez-Guzman maintained that the Sinaloa Cartel had the capacity of transporting up to twenty tons via cargo containers. Twenty tons! I sat trying to imagine the damage that could do to people's lives. The amount was absolutely stunning, but completely realistic in terms of the intelligence we had on the cartel's capacity to produce cocaine.

We told Gutierrez-Guzman we would be more comfortable starting with 1,000 to 1,500 kilograms—the exact opposite of what most cops would do. We knew that real dope dealers never complete a multi-ton deal the first time. If we had even entertained a multi-ton deal, we probably would have never seen the cartel again.

For the next several hours we discussed price structures, quality of product, and international distribution routes while the Atlantic Ocean sparkled in the distance. I chose to remain in the background, listening but not saying a word, motioning to Patricio when I needed him to clarify a point. It was my way of mind-fucking Gutierrez by letting him know that I was too important to crawl into the weeds with him on a first meet. El Viejo has *cojones*. Tell that to fucking Chapo. He didn't even bother to get dressed.

Almost four hours later, we had worked out the basic framework for a Mexican-European drug deal. As I usually did after an intense undercover meeting where every gesture, word, and facial expression was being noticed and measured by the bad guys, I stretched out on the floor and immediately fell into a deep sleep.

The chess match had begun in earnest. In reality, the rhythm of the case was more like a roller coaster with dramatic ups and downs. Now we waited weeks while Gutierrez-Guzman returned to the mountains of Sinaloa and reported to his leader. That report appeared to have been received favorably, because Gus Vargas received word in April that El Chapo wanted to meet him in person. We in Boston and DC breathed a collective sigh of relief.

On April 20, 2010, Gus Vargas flew with Rivera-Pedrego and Gutierrez-Guzman to a private airstrip in the mountains near Culiacán, Mexico. Tucked between the Pacific Ocean and the Sierra Madre mountains, Mexico's tomato-growing capital was also home to its most infamous narcotrafficker. The drug business was so ingrained in the soul of the region that local souvenir shops sold marijuana leaf belts, and machine gun buckles. Local musicians sang tributes to drug dealers known as *narcocorridos.*

One of the most popular ones, penned by Los Reyes de Sinaloa after Chapo's escape from prison went:

He's already gone to the sierra
He's going to visit his people to tie one on.
He got tired of being locked up
And so he went back to his homeland.
In the prison of Altiplano there is mourning
In Culiacán, it's a fiesta!

The patron saint of the area, worshipped by many drug traffickers, was known as Jesús Malverde—a local man who lived from 1870 to 1909 and was known as a bandit who stole from the rich and gave to the poor. Similarly, El Chapo won the loyalty of many poor people and farmers in the region by employing them, buying their products, and building schools and hospitals.

Vargas had some *cojones,* too. And, after the plane landed in Culiacán, Rivera-Pedrego, Guiterrez-Guzman, and Vargas were escorted by armed guards through military checkpoints to a heavily guarded compound high up in the mountains. El

Chapo welcomed them in something Vargas described as a hut. No, he wasn't wearing a purple bathrobe, but was casually dressed.

Vargas reported that the drug kingpin took an active role in the discussions that followed and expressed a keen interest in working with the Italians. Despite his reputation for flooding the world with illegal drugs and ordering hundreds of murders, part of him remained a humble, rural farm boy. But he wasn't shy about bragging to Vargas at one point: *I supply more heroin, methamphetamine, cocaine, and marijuana than anyone in the world. I have a fleet of submarines, airplanes, trucks, and boats.*

El Chapo proposed that his cartel ship an initial load of a thousand kilograms of cocaine to Europe. His group and ours would participate as fifty-fifty partners splitting all profits and expenses. The cartel would be responsible for expenses and security prior to the shipment arriving in Europe, and we would handle all costs and security once it landed. Should this initial exchange work out, he expressed interest in flying twenty tons of coke from Bolivia to Europe. Incredibly, the world's biggest dope dealer was negotiating directly with the FBI.

On June 10, 2010, Gutierrez-Guzman called Vargas in Boston to arrange another meeting between the cartel and Italians in the Virgin Islands. At one point during the phone conversation Gutierrez-Guzman said, "I'm going to give you to my cousin."

Vargas recognized El Chapo's voice on the other end of the line. Chapo said, "Say hello to your boss over there. Say hello to El Viejo."

A frantic week of preparation later, ten of us on the UC team traveled to the U.S. Virgin Islands. Since we had to look the part of a successful Italian crime syndicate, we rented a multimillion-dollar mansion on a cliff overlooking the ocean. It felt like we were preparing for our equivalent of the Super Bowl and World Series wrapped into one.

Manuel Gutierrez-Guzman arrived accompanied by a younger man named Rodolfo Alarcon Mendoza, who claimed to be El Chapo's personal representative—which we interpreted as another positive sign.

Over the next two days, June 18 and 19, we discussed amounts of cocaine to be exported, the intricacies of international transportation routes and methods, port locations, and emergency contingencies. As members of the Italian organization we agreed to a price of $2,800 per kilogram of cocaine—unheard of in the United States, where prices ranged from $20,000 to $25,000 a kilogram, but not unusual when buying in bulk from a Mexican cartel.

During the meetings, Mendoza was constantly on his Black-Berry, texting back to Mexico. At one point, his phone rang, and El Chapo was on the other end asking to speak with someone from our organization.

Both Antonio and Patricio took turns speaking to him. El Chapo assured them that the relationship between his organization and ours would be long and productive. He also said, "Make sure El Viejo is satisfied with our arrangement." He didn't need to worry.

Toward the close of the second day of meetings, I stood drinking from a bottle of water as I conversed with Gutierrez-Guzman and Mendoza, my old friend Mike Sullivan stood silently as one of my bodyguards. When I finished the bottle, I tossed it on the floor near Sullivan's feet. He stiffened for a microsecond. Had I dropped the bottle at his feet in our real-life roles back at the office, he would have thrown it back at my face. As El Viejo's bodyguard, he stooped to retrieve it.

This was Mendoza's first meeting with us, and he appeared extremely nervous, especially in my presence. Sitting in a warm room with members of what he thought was a major European crime syndicate, he started sweating through his shirt. Whenever I made eye contact with him, the young man would immediately look down at his smartphone and pretend to be tapping out a message, while beads of sweat flew off him and splattered onto the floor and table.

Gonzo glanced at me looking at Mendoza at one point and began mimicking his frantic finger tapping his phone. Seeing the grin on Gonzo's face, I almost burst out laughing.

A little humor always helped us relax. It also could cause us to lose focus. This was a complex international case with lots of moving parts. One minor slipup and we could all end up with bullets in our heads.

Two months later, in August 2010, we were introduced to two more members of the Sinaloa Cartel, Rafael Celaya Valenzuela and Sergio Lopez Alarcon, when we met them at the oceanfront Florida condo. Good, we thought, the more top cartel guys we smoke out the better.

Celaya represented himself as an attorney and financial planner, and Alarcon as an accountant. They arrived with Manuel Gutierrez-Guzman and Rodolfo Alarcon Mendoza to discuss the financial details of the drug deal. All of them were bright, educated, polite, and well dressed. It was like dealing with the executive board of a major corporation.

On our side, we brought in several more UCAs who were expert in the fiscal aspects of drug trafficking and money laundering. The Mexicans were so impressed with our financial expertise and internal discipline that at one point Celaya pulled Patricio and me aside and asked if we would consider laundering some of the cartel's money.

"How much are you thinking about?" Patricio asked, with the video and audio recorders running.

"A little bit to start," he answered.

"How much is a little?" I asked.

"Five hundred million dollars."

Seriously? The amount was staggering and underlined the difficulty the cartel had in transforming their enormous drug profits into legitimate assets. After careful consideration, the FBI decided not to pursue the money-laundering opportunities for a number of reasons, including the legal and logistical difficulties we would run into.

I told the cartel's lawyer we would consider helping them clean their money later, but our first priority was establishing the Mexican-European cocaine link.

Celaya was correct about one thing—our discipline. Every member of the team had been coached to keep up their specific cover and assignment and "stay in their lane." We structured meetings in a way that the cartel could clearly see the chain of command of our fictitious organization. At one point, Gutierrez-Guzman admitted that our organization was even more disciplined than Chapo's. Quite a compliment, coming from El Chapo's cousin and right-hand man.

As El Viejo, my job was to project power, so I left the day-to-day negotiating to the other three UCAs, who with their exceptional undercover skills set the table for El Viejo's carefully timed meetings with cartel representatives at key times.

Aside from the arduous preparation and staging we had to complete for the various meetings, and the stress of the meetings themselves, there was also a ton of FBI reports and paperwork that had to be filed. By the end of 2010 all the hard work everyone on the excellent Dark Waters team put in seemed to be paying off. We were in the process of setting up a major international drug deal with the leaders of the Sinaloa Cartel. All we needed now were patience and good luck.

17

THE SINALOA
CARTEL—PART TWO

In early 2011, two years into Operation Dark Water, we started to work with the Spanish National Police (SNP) to set up the European side of deal. The SNP controlled an airstrip outside of Madrid. In March, our team traveled to Madrid and I took Manuel Gutierrez-Guzman out to inspect the strip. On a cold, gusty morning, the two of us were greeted by SNP officials in dress uniforms standing at attention. I'd never seen so many shiny brass buttons and fancy police hats in my life. The scene created the impression that the SNP was in El Viejo's pocket.

I, as El Viejo, told Gutierrez-Guzman that if El Chapo ever got to a point where he had to flee Mexico, he could land at the private airstrip in Spain and my Sicilian organization would protect him. We called this "the Escape Hatch plan," and later learned that it was something El Chapo seriously considered.

The visit to the airport with Gutierrez-Guzman was a perfect prelude to subsequent meetings in Spain with more representatives from the Sinaloa Cartel. The previous five cartel associates were now joined by Jose Benjamin Locheo del Rio and Samuel Zazueta Valenzuela. Locheo del Rio identified himself as the cartel official responsible for daily operational decisions and the initial shipment of a thousand kilograms of cocaine from South America to Europe. Zazueta Valenzuela was in Spain to set up a front company for the cartel.

Like in almost all previous drug cases I had worked, we weren't going to be provided with millions of U.S. tax-payer dollars to buy drugs. So we got the Sinaloa Cartel to agree that we would handle the sale and distribution of the drugs once it arrived in Europe. In return, we would receive 20 percent of the load. Negotiations dragged on longer than usual because Gutierrez-Guzman was having trouble making telephone contact with El Chapo in Mexico.

As the meetings wrapped up a week later, I handed Gutierrez-Guzman a 100-euro bill with a personal greeting on it from me to Chapo. I explained that this was part of an old Italian crime tradition. Upon receiving it, El Chapo was supposed to tear the bill in half, retain the half with my note and send back the other half with a personal message from him to me. My message said:

> Señor, we finally meet this way. Sorry the call did not happen . . .
> no problem . . . Manuel will serve as the telephone between us. I
> look forward to a long and prosperous business relationship. You
> are welcome to be my guest in Europe if ever needed.

A month later, April 21, 2011, during a follow-up session in New Hampshire, Gutierrez-Guzman returned half of the 100-euro note with Chapo's handwritten message on it. It read:

> My friend, thank you for the support you are offering me, to
> receive me, and I am not discounting the invitation. Through my

cousin I send you a message. So when he makes a decision, he
will go with you. My friend, a big embrace.

As I read it, Gutierrez-Guzman stood and wrapped me in a bear
hug. The gesture was captured on videotape and confirmed the
partnership between us two heavyweight drug honchos.

Gutierrez-Guzman then informed us that the cartel intended
to ship a thousand kilograms of coke in a container from Ecuador to Spain as an initial load. After that, we would start receiving
a thousand kilograms of dope a month. As members of the FBI,
we only needed one major drug seizure to complete our large-
scale UCO.

We patiently waited throughout the summer of 2011 for the
first shipment to arrive. The unexpected delay had to do with
large seizures of Chapo's drugs that took place in South America. Although the cartel never suspected that we were involved,
they went dark.

Finally, in early August 2011, Gutierrez-Guzman and Celaya
Valenzuela arrived in Boston to tell us that a ship with a container holding a thousand kilograms of cocaine had departed
from Ecuador on August 1 and was scheduled to arrive in Spain
on or around August 19. Our collective mood went from bummed
to ecstatic. A day later, after a flurry of phone calls back and forth
to Mexico, the two cartel members said the container didn't
contain cocaine, but was designed as a test load to determine if
it would arrive safely through Spanish Customs without being
interdicted. Though disappointed, I recognized that they were
being cautious, professional drug traffickers, and we needed to
be patient so as not to tip our hand.

Two more test loads followed. One contained plantains and
another held pineapples. The logistics involved in having our

Agents track them from South America to Spain was a nightmare. All of us were frustrated. We had collected enough evidence to charge five cartel members (including Chapo) with conspiracy, but without having seized actual illegal drugs it would be known in legal terms as a *dry conspiracy*. And we didn't want to go up in court against an organization as powerful as the Sinaloa Cartel without real drugs.

At the close of 2011, the FBI had invested an enormous amount of time and money in Dark Water, and FBIHQ was growing increasingly impatient. While our ASAC Frank Johnson in Boston remained confident we would succeed and continued running interference with the pencil pushers in DC, I knew the clock was ticking not only in DC, but with our cartel partners in Mexico.

So in the early days 2012, after long and careful consideration, I called Case Agent Tanner into my office and told him gently that we had to inform Chapo's people that the Italians were walking away.

"What?" he asked in shock.

"El Viejo and his boys are moving off in another direction due to the delays and test loads," I said.

He looked so upset, I thought he was about to pass out. "Why?" he asked.

"I've been doing UCOs my whole career," I explained. "After awhile you start to think like the bad guys. I can tell you bad guys like the Italians would never tolerate delays and false promises like this. The only people who would hang around waiting for something to happen are cops."

Tanner was devastated. He'd worked his butt off for three years, and now I was telling him we had to walk away without ever getting any dope. I explained to him that this was a move we had to make, and to my mind, a calculated gamble that had an 80 percent chance of succeeding.

"That high?" he asked.

"I think so. We have to let 'em know that we're not screwing around."

Sometime in late April 2012, our informant Gus Vargas conveyed the message to Gutierrez-Guzman: The Italians are looking for other sources of supply, and they're pissed off that they've expended more than $70,000 paying off corrupt Customs officials and law enforcement personnel in Spain for letting the test loads in, and never receiving dope or any kind of compensation from the cartel.

After that we (the Italians) cut off communications. Vargas remained the only bridge between the two sides. Some members of our team feared we'd never hear from Sinaloa again. I disagreed, and hoped to hell I was right.

A long month later, Gutierrez-Guzman called Vargas to request a meeting with us in Phoenix, Arizona. Gus Vargas and another UCA went, but we decided that El Viejo and the other Italians should decline the offer. Vargas extended my (El Viejo's) good wishes to the Mexicans in their future endeavors, and told Gutierrez-Guzman that I had moved on.

Tanner remained upset. I told him to sit back and wait like a good fisherman to see if the bait worked. He looked at me like I had lost my mind.

Less than a month later, Gutierrez-Guzman informed us that if we could travel to Detroit in twenty-four hours, a cartel associate would front us some heroin and methamphetamine to cover some of the expenses we had incurred in Spain. It appeared as though our gamble had worked. No one was more relieved than me.

As El Viejo was believed to be in Europe, two new UCAs from

New York answered the call. At my request, they dropped what they were doing and grabbed flights to Detroit. Boston team members Mike Sullivan, Stork, Tanner, and I joined them in Detroit after taking an overnight flight.

On June 7, sleep deprived but charged with adrenaline, the two NY UCAs drove to a ramshackle restaurant in southwest Detroit that looked like it had been plucked out of the dusty Mexican countryside. As they entered, all eyes in the joint shifted to them. They were both big, heavily muscled, and had "don't fuck with me" written all over them. A short Hispanic man, half their size, bounded out of the kitchen, walked up to within inches of them, and snapped their picture with his cell phone.

Then without saying a word he motioned them to the rear of the restaurant. The two burly New York UCAs followed the little man through the kitchen and out the back. Parked in an alley behind the restaurant was an old red Honda. The Mexican simply pointed through the open passenger window to something on the floorboard.

One of the UCAs reached in and retrieved a white plastic bag that looked like a take-out order, while the other UCA stood guard. The exchange had taken no more than sixty seconds and not one single word had been exchanged.

The two UCAs then drove five minutes to a nearby hotel where Tanner, the other guys from the Boston office, and I were waiting. We gave Tanner the honor of opening the bag. Hands trembling with excitement, he carefully pulled apart the plastic opening and removed nine individually wrapped packages of crystal meth (1.76 kilograms) and heroin (3.56 kilograms). All of us collectively sighed with relief.

We'd done it! We no longer had a dry conspiracy. The expression of joy on Tanner's face was priceless.

The strange exchange outside the Mexican restaurant remains the largest seizure of methamphetamine and one of the largest seizures of heroin in Detroit law enforcement history. More importantly, we now had illegal drugs in our possession supplied by the Sinaloa Cartel, which strengthened our legal case by leaps and bounds.

The dramatic shift in momentum buoyed the spirits of everyone on our team. With the Italian criminal organization back on board, we pressed the cartel hard to finally deliver on their promise of cocaine. On July 2 they informed us that a shipment of cocaine sent through a Brazilian front company named Cristerlia Celta would be arriving at the port of Algeciras, Spain, on the 27.

On the night of July 27, FBI and SNP officials carefully opened the container from Cristerlia Celta in a police compound in Algerciras, Spain. Inside we found 346 kilograms (762 pounds) of cocaine in the form of bricks wrapped in bright blue, yellow, and pink plastic. It was the big score all of us had been waiting for more than three years.

In a little more than a month, we had seized $15 million worth of drugs from the Sinaloa Cartel without fronting a penny. Now, with the evidence we needed, we decided to summon the Mexicans to Spain and arrest them there. We did this for two reasons: One, if any of them ended up cooperating with the FBI, we wanted them in Europe so we could use them to go further up the chain of command, and, two, we wanted them as far away from Mexico and any other UC activity we might launch in the future.

In early August, Gonzo, Vargas, the other UCAs, case personnel on the Boston team, and I traveled to Madrid, Spain, and arrived before the Mexicans to coordinate with the SNP. The Sinaloans thought they were there to meet El Viejo and discuss a South American–European cocaine pipeline we were going to run for many years into the future.

We had other plans. First thing we did was to rent a massive eight-room suite in one of the city's finest luxury hotels. I took photos of myself standing in the elegant marble bathroom with gold fixtures to show my kids how far I'd traveled from the boy who grew up with one pair of dungarees and two T-shirts.

I had developed superstitions that went all the back to my days of playing high school baseball, including secretly wearing a St. Michael's medal—representing the patron saint of policemen—around my neck. Throughout my FBI career, I made it a habit to wear some subtle piece of law enforcement paraphernalia on my body the day of an arrest. The morning of August 7, 2012, I dressed in my best suit and tie, a crisp white shirt, and a pair of FBI cufflinks.

When Jesus Manuel Gutierrez-Guzman entered the hotel suite, I rose and embraced him. Reviewing the videotape later, the FBI cufflinks were clearly visible. I directed Gutierrez-Guzman to the suite's luxurious library, and with Gonzo at my side translating, we began what would be our last meeting.

With the video and audiotape running, I carefully reviewed every aspect of the case step-by-step. And I made sure that Gutierrez-Guzman confirmed that El Chapo had been the final decision maker in every overt act, including the planning and the shipping of the cocaine. After three hours of getting Gutierrez-Guzman to recount every act in the criminal conspiracy, I received a text message from members of the Boston team monitoring the meeting from another area of the hotel that read: "*No mas*" (No more.)

Next, I beckoned Zazueta Valenzuela, Celaya Valenzuela, and Jesus Gonzalo Palazuelas Soto—who had been sent by the cartel to Brazil to supervise the initial shipment of cocaine—up to my suite and went through their individual roles and responsibilities in the drug-trafficking conspiracy.

More than four hours after the FBI recorders had been activated, I thanked all the cartel members individually and asked them to wait for me in the lobby before I took them out to celebrate. Instead, when the four men reached the lobby they were discreetly arrested by members of the SNP and taken off in handcuffs.

Three years after the start of the case nobody thought we could make, we had four high-level Sinaloa Cartel members in custody, and enough evidence to arrest other members of the cartel, including Chapo Guzmán himself.

We were well aware that the cartel had a system in place whereby if one of their officials didn't report back in thirty-six hours, a red flag would go up. So we knew we had to work fast. One of the cartel members we had arrested agreed to cooperate and immediately started feeding us information. Some of what he told us pointed to corruption at the very highest levels of the Mexican government. He not only provided evidence that top Mexican government officials were in the pocket of the cartel, he claimed that some of those officials and potential coconspirators had played a role in the shipment of our cocaine to Spain.

When we quickly relayed this very important news to FBIHQ in Washington, we were told to "stand down" because what we were pursuing—namely the links between the Sinaloa Cartel and the Mexican government—were in HQ's words "outside the scope of your original objective." All of us were incredulous. What the hell did that mean? Additionally, we were ordered to conclude the UC portion of the case and return to the States immediately.

The whole thing stunk to high heaven. For one thing, the FBIHQ supervisor who ordered us to "stand down" was not the NDURE supervisor, and had never played any role in the case.

I argued strenuously with FBIHQ that we had a golden opportunity to identify and collect timely evidence against other coconspirators in this massive and now airtight drug conspiracy. If they happened to be powerful Mexican government officials, so be it. We'd simply done what we were trained by the FBI to do—follow the trail of evidence. Where it led had never been a problem in the past.

FBIHQ argued back that we had inadvertently stepped into another evidentiary realm—namely, international Public Corruption. They were out-of-their-minds wrong. We hadn't stepped into anything new. The case was what it had been all along, an international drug-trafficking conspiracy.

Those of us who had spent the last three years working on Dark Water were shocked and pissed off. Did the FBI not want to know about the collusion between high Mexican government officials and the Sinaloa Cartel? Had someone higher up in our government told the FBI to suspend that part of the investigation?

We never found out. What we did learn is that soon after we were told to conclude our investigation, the Justice Department announced that it had issued criminal indictments against Chapo Guzmán and eight other members of his organization. The story appeared on the front page of *The New York Times* and was the lead story on *NBC Nightly News*.

Meanwhile, Gonzo, other UCAs, case personnel, and I returned to Boston fuming that we hadn't been allowed to pursue the new leads we'd developed. We now began the very onerous extradition process with Spain. After that it took us two years to prepare evidence against all four defendants.

Three of them, including Gutierrez-Guzman, pled guilty and received sentences from ten to more than twenty years in federal prison.

The lawyer, Rafael Humberto Celaya Valenzuela, who had always thought of himself as the smartest in the group, was the only one who decided to go to trial despite the fact that the evidence against him was overwhelming. My cross-examination lasted a mere fifteen minutes. After a five-day trial, the jury deliberated only five hours before finding him guilty on all counts. On October 14, 2014, more than five years after Tanner first poked his head in my office Celaya was convicted and later sentenced to seventeen years in the can.

All of the Dark Water defendants had been arrested and convicted except one. January 7, 2016, I was roused from my sleep one morning by the sound of my pinging phone. I leaned out of bed and read the text message: "We got him!" I knew immediately who the message was referring to: El Chapo. He'd been arrested in Mexico. A year later he was extradited to the United States, and is now in U.S. custody awaiting trial in a U.S. federal court. I stand ready to do my part.

Shortly after Celaya Valenzuela's trial ended in October 2014, FBI Director James Comey traveled up to Boston to present awards to the team that had worked on Dark Water. At first, I didn't want to attend, because I'm not a fan of awards or ceremonies. But when I thought about how proud I was of Tanner, the other UCAs, and the rest of the team, and how hard they had worked, I changed my mind.

In front of five hundred FBI Agents and employees, Director

Comey spoke about the case and our remarkable accomplishment. When it was my turn to go up to the podium, I remember looking at the Director and thinking, *What the fuck does "outside the scope of your original objective" mean?*

That's how my demented mind works. On that occasion, I rubbed some dirt on it, kept my mouth shut, and shook his hand.

18

MURDER FOR HIRE

One unexpected result of Operation Dark Water was the death of NDURE. Yes, you read that right. On the heels of one of the most spectacular undercover operations in FBI history, FBIHQ disbanded the unit that was largely responsible for its success.

I got my first hint that trouble was brewing shortly after me and other members of our Dark Water UCO team were ordered home from Spain in mid-August 2012 and told not to pursue time-sensitive leads into drug trafficking at the highest levels of the Mexican government because they were "outside the scope of your original objective"—which was complete bullshit.

As we boarded the train to take us to the Madrid airport, all NDURE members received emails from the new regime in the Undercover Unit at FBIHQ telling us that changes were coming and that "we needed to remember what it is like to be a regular UCA."

What the hell does that mean? I remember thinking.

There was no question in any of our minds that the new system of managing and executing UCOs introduced under NDURE had been hugely successful. From 2007, when the system was first introduced, to 2012, we had made a series of very tough cases, especially in the areas of Public Corruption and Violent Crime, topped off with Dark Water and the indictment of El Chapo and top members of the Sinaloa Cartel. For the last five years we had been treated as FBI undercover rock stars, who could do no wrong and were loved in the field by hardworking street Agents who needed undercover help.

The dramatic swing in the perception of NDURE coincided directly with a change in Undercover Unit leadership at FBIHQ. Gone were the experienced and successful supervisors, Unit Chiefs, Section Chiefs, and my old Criminal Investigative Division Assistant Director who supported us. Replacing them were a group of supervisors who had been disasters in their prior Field Divisions and were clearly jealous of NDURE's success and popularity.

According to FBI policy, you now don't have to have UCA experience to become a supervisor in the FBIHQ Undercover Unit—which is ridiculous. And that's exactly what we got in 2012. NDURE was now being supervised by Agents who had never worked undercover and had no clue what it was like to be in the same room with a bad guy where one mistake could result in a bullet in your head.

George Bernard Shaw once wrote: "Those that can do; those that can't teach."

The FBI Undercover Unit version of that was: "Those that can make cases. Those that can't go to FBIHQ and obstruct Agents in the field."

By 2012, the new Undercover Unit at FBIHQ consisted of the

following management personnel with decision-making authority over NDURE:

1. A high-ranking senior official who was so inept that he/she was assigned to "Special Projects" only—a euphemism for sitting in an empty room all day and doing no harm.
2. A senior official who was so intimidated by the experience level of NDURE personnel that he/she was afraid to talk to them directly and would only communicate through a secretary.
3. An official who was later forced to retire from the FBI for failing multiple FBI security polygraphs.
4. An official who had been the subject of multiple OPR (Internal Affairs) investigations, and once quit an FBI UCO after being threatened—by voicemail.
5. An official who had the reputation for being one of the most incompetent UCAs to ever serve in the FBI and was loathed by the entire FBI undercover community. This doofus once ordered an $800 bottle of wine for subjects who did not drink alcohol, and a seafood buffet for other subjects who were allergic to seafood.

From the perspective of this new FBIHQ Undercover Unit, NDURE had become too successful and had to be destroyed. Since they didn't have the balls to tell us that to our faces, they did what many weak managers at FBIHQ do: They started a smear campaign. For more than five years NDURE Agents had been the pride of the FBI undercover world. Suddenly, we became the most reckless, out-of-control, and dishonest UCAs in FBI history. It would have been laughable if it weren't so sad.

Shortly after we received the email in Spain telling us "to re-member what it is like to be a regular UCA," the new members of the FBIHQ Undercover Unit fired their first shot, accusing an NDURE member of financial impropriety. His egregious crime in their opinion: the purchase of a $39.00 umbrella. He did so when it started to rain while he was playing golf with a target in a Public Corruption UCO. Despite the fact that it was per-fectly normal and appropriate to buy an umbrella in those cir-cumstances, he was accused of using government funds "for personal gain."

Only weeks earlier, this same NDURE Agent had been sum-moned to FBIHQ to act as a subject matter expert in a very sensitive Public Corruption investigative matter that was being briefed at the top levels of the FBI, DOJ, and the White House.

Days later, another member of NDURE was told by someone at FBIHQ that we "had become too big for our britches," and needed to be brought under control. The last time I'd heard that expression was forty years earlier on a grade-school playground.

They knew they had to be careful with me because I still had friends in high places, including a former Director. So they de-livered their message to me indirectly—denying a request I made for $149.50 to travel to another city where we were investigat-ing a suspected serial killer. Don't worry, I found another way to secure the funds.

Weeks later, when I returned a five-year-old laptop and the re-turn receipt was one serial number off in a seventeen-digit se-quence, they alleged I had stolen government property and referred the matter to OPR (Internal Affairs) for investigation. One digit off! OPR laughed in their faces, refused to accept the complaint, and told them not to waste their time over what was obviously a typographical mistake.

Every day brought another allegation, each one more ridiculous and petty than the one before. Meanwhile, NDURE members in the field were being pulled from important cases and summoned back to FBIHQ to conduct inventory assignments—like counting gadgets. I kid you not!

The sole purpose of these bureaucratic maneuvers was to humiliate some of the best and most successful UCAs in the FBI. Why? The monster was determined to eat its own, not in the interest of protecting the public or making the Undercover Unit better, but solely out of jealousy and spite.

Disgusted by what FBIHQ Undercover Unit leadership was doing and hoping to draw attention to the situation, I submitted my resignation from NDURE on November 13, 2012. My letter stated that I was leaving "due to the overall lack of support . . . lack of professionalism . . . and lack of respect . . . the recent FBIHQ treatment and character assassination of Agents XXX and XXX is deplorable . . . our experience and success level apparently frustrates certain personnel at FBIHQ . . . and recent edicts have been caustic in tone . . . bordering on adversarial in nature . . . and not productive . . . we have been regularly undermined by USOU personnel offering baseless allegations and inflammatory remarks . . . with no repercussions. . . ."

I ended by saying: "The current system is seriously flawed, if not broken, and needs serious repair." Then sent it off to the new Criminal Investigative Division Assistant Director.

The Criminal Investigation Division Assistant Director rejected my resignation letter and told my SAC that he wanted me to remain in NDURE to help fix the problems. What he didn't understand, or didn't want to admit, was that the problems weren't fixable as long as the current Unit "managers" remained in place.

A few weeks later all NDURE members were summoned via

email to a meeting at FBIHQ for "training involving a new financial accounting system." Having spent a lot of time rubbing shoulders with members of Italian Organized Crime, the meeting in my mind had all the hallmarks of a "two in the hat"— aka, a Mob hit. My SAC, a good guy who was petrified of FBIHQ, asked me to attend to see if things could be smoothed out. I went in deference to him.

The destruction of NDURE on December 12, 2012, took less than five minutes. Undercover Unit leadership sat on one side of the room, and all us members of NDURE sat silently on the other. Leadership delivered the coup de grace without once looking anyone of us in the eye.

As we got up to leave, Gonzo sarcastically asked, "What about the new financial accounting training?"

Leadership didn't react. Those goofs didn't even get a joke.

As we left, the most inept of the leadership officials actually invited us to the Undercover Unit's Christmas Party scheduled for later that day. I kid you not! We laughed in his face and repaired to a nearby joint for lunch.

We drank beer and reminisced about UCOs, great cases, and great friends, and how we'd kicked ass as an undercover group across FBI field offices all over the country, only to be administratively castrated by a bunch of inept fools. And I laughed harder than I had in years.

To Darryl, Anibal, Mike, Mark, Pat, John, Ron, Mark, and Mark, and our great RCMP friends, Steph and Eddie—thanks for the ride of a lifetime—we done good.

I resigned from NDURE for the second time the next day. Not one Undercover Unit leadership member had the balls to respond. Let the record show that after every possible allegation was thrown our way, not one NDURE member was ever found to have engaged in any improper or inappropriate FBI conduct, and no disciplinary action was ever taken.

Three months later, on March 25, 2013, the Undercover Unit's NDURE Supervisory Special Agent, and the only one who supported us until the bitter end, and the sole member of the Unit who had operational success as a UCA, sent out the following memo:

OBITUARY: National Dedicated Undercover Response Element: (fondly known to those that knew it as NDURE)

Born: June 2007

Murdered: March 25, 2013 (after months of torture)

On March 25, 2013, NDURE was finally killed with one final stake driven through the heart of its illustrious and storied existence. The new regime, ever so risk-adverse, could not tolerate this new concept and success in UCOs, so they set out one by one to destroy the individuals and finally, the institution. The men who started this worthy endeavor will go down in the annals of FBI undercover history as pioneers of a new and very successful technique, which was long overdue in the history of this storied program. They put in many hours on great cases. They started a new wave of interest in being better at this thing we do, even for those who never had the privilege of being associated with this great program. They were the light to the modern UCO and technique utilizing multiple UCAs to get the job done by saving numerous man-hours and thousands of dollars. But alas . . .

. . . Then came the final blow, with the wisp of a risk-adverse, frightened decision, the once most prolific and successful group of UCAs in the history of the FBI were thrown out with no respect, no accolades for a job well done, no thank you. Just one more cold-hearted and cowardly executive decision that is today's FBI.

This is to all the great warriors who fought the good fight and went down with the ship. Just know my friends, and never forget, you are all true heroes and we who know the truth will never let any of this history be forgotten. Sail on. . . .

For speaking the truth, this SSA was removed and transferred from the Criminal Investigative Division the very next day.

Thanks, Don. Back at you.

FBI bureaucratic politics remained as odious to me as ever. I spent the majority of 2013 on other cases, including the Boston Marathon bombings. On August 8, 2014, I would be celebrating my fifty-seventh birthday and also be reaching mandatory FBI retirement age.

After what I considered a great career and a long list of accomplishments, I started to prepare myself psychologically for retirement. In the past, when I ended one UCO, I started searching for the next one. Now, I began packing boxes in my office, and going through paperwork and names from cases I'd worked twenty-five years ago in Philadelphia that I couldn't remember.

I still had duties to fulfill as Boston's UC Coordinator, but besides that all that was on my plate were the Sinaloa Cartel trials in October. It was common practice for Agents to be called back to testify in court after they retired. Weeks before my retirement date in August, the FBI pushed my retirement back one year so I could help prepare exhibits and testimony for the upcoming trials.

Then a month before going to court, three of the defendants in the Sinaloa case pled guilty. Not wanting to hang around with little to do, I drafted my retirement papers, and started planning for the future.

In September 2014, I was sitting in my office counting down my last days when several members of one of the Boston Counter-Terrorism Squads asked for my advice about a potential undercover operation. They were concerned about a longtime criminal named Joseph Burke, who the Bureau of Prisons had designated as an international terrorist.

I knew Burke's reputation and the fact that he had been raised in the notoriously tough Charlestown section of Boston—a breeding ground for violent offenders depicted in the Ben Affleck movie *The Town*.

A week later, the Organized Crime Squad unit came to me with a different UC proposal targeting the same individual—Joe Burke. My job was to analyze both proposals and make recommendations to Executive Management.

Burke, I learned, had spent the last seventeen years in prison for a series of armed robberies and other violent crimes. He had also been convicted of drug trafficking in prison. He was scheduled to be released at the end of December 2014, and we knew from informants that he was plotting more violent crimes once he got out.

I ran my recommendations by the Criminal ASAC. They basically went: Proceed with caution. This guy reeks of violence and has to be watched carefully once he's back on the streets. If you decide to run a UC operation, you're going to need a very experienced UCA to go against him.

My undercover strength was in Organized Crime and Drugs, not Violent Crime, so I never really thought of myself as a candidate. But two days later the ASAC called me while my wife and I were walking our dog and asked, "Mike, how do you feel about climbing into the ring one more time?"

"Really?" I asked back. "You sure you want me to go after Burke?"

"You're the only one I trust given his background and the kind of guy he is."

I took that as a tremendous compliment, but for the first time in my career didn't immediately accept the challenge.

"I need to think about this," I said. "I need to talk to my wife."

Naturally, my wife didn't want me to do it. Her response, bless her heart, was: "You've given them everything. You're going out on a high note after El Chapo. Why would you want to go after some psychotic nut?"

The answer was simple: the thrill of the hunt. Additionally, I was honored to have been asked, and wanted this dangerous guy off the streets. Lastly, I started thinking of me against Burke, who was in his early fifties, as a battle of experienced heavyweights going to war for the last time.

When I told my wife I was going to accept the assignment, she wasn't happy, but gave me her support.

My boss, the ASAC, was surprised when I informed him of my decision. He said, "We want you to do this, Mike, but you sure you got one last fight in you?"

Joining me on this assignment would be Tanner—the Case Agent on Dark Water. Intrigued by what he had learned during that case, he attended FBI Undercover School, passed with flying colors, and was now a certified UCA looking for his first big undercover assignment. We were excited to work together as an experienced older UCA and protégé.

One of the things that convinced me we could make a viable case was the access we had to one of Joe Burke's associates who we had nicknamed Penis Head because of the funky-looking beanie he always wore on his head. He was a tough guy wannabe and a trust fund baby, who both Joey Merlino and Joe Burke had used previously as a human ATM. I planned to match Tanner against him.

Again, we were working with an informant, who knew both targets, and whose identify I can't reveal. He was able to arrange a meeting between Burke, Penis Head, Tanner, and me less than a month after Burke's release from prison on December 31, 2014.

This time I was Mike Cassidy, an L.A.-based financial investor offering an entertainment industry business proposition that Burke and Penis Head could profit from both financially and in terms of publicity.

The first meeting took place in an FBI-controlled location in the Northeast valued at around $15 million and steps from the Atlantic Ocean. The place screamed money.

As soon as Burke entered, the hairs on the back of my neck stood up. Not only was he imposing physically—at six feet two inches, covered with tats and thickly muscled from almost two decades of weightlifting in prison—he also reeked of violence. Square-jawed and good-looking, it was his eyes that gave me the heebie-jeebies. They were the eyes of a complete sociopath.

From that moment forward, I was careful never to get within arm's length of him. I'd almost never carried any kind of weapon on a UCO before, but this time knowing Burke's reputation for violence, I concealed a military self-defense knife in my pocket, provided by my eldest son who was now a fourth-generation cop and former member of the U.S. Marines.

At fifty-eight, I wasn't as agile and fit as I'd once been. Should Burke ever approach me in a threatening way, I planned to slit his throat before he got his hands on me. He was that intimidating.

Like I said before, we knew from the informant that Burke was planning new acts of violence. It was Tanner's and my job as members of the FBI to try to dissuade him from doing so. I told him the business proposition we were offering would be a way for him to make money and keep his nose clean at the same time.

Burke seemed to agree and the initial meeting went well. We exchanged phone numbers and promised to keep in touch.

During a follow-up meeting at the same location in mid-February 2015, I offered Joe some start-up money to get him back on his feet. Burke said he didn't need it, reached into his pocket, and pulled out $50,000 in cash. Tanner and I were both aghast.

Here was a guy only two and a half months out of prison and on parole, and he was already flashing $50,000 in cash. He didn't tell us where it had come from, but we suspected he had made it from some form of drug trafficking. Our FBI antenna immediately went up.

During this second meeting, Joe informed me that he was traveling to California in March to meet with Aryan Brotherhood and Mexican Mafia friends he had made in prison. Wanting to keep track of his activities, I told Burke that Tanner and I would also be in Los Angeles at that time to work out some of the details of our business proposition. I offered to introduce him to some of my business associates while we were all in L.A.

On March 7, Joe and I met in another swanky FBI location smack in the middle of the entertainment industry. As a sign of his growing trust, he told me about his relationship with the Boston mobster Whitey Bulger and other details of his criminal past. He also informed me that he was in California setting up a marijuana deal.

When the meeting ended, he walked with me outside into the Southern California sunshine and asked if he could join my fictitious company. It was another sign of our developing relationship and an indication that he had blown through the $50,000 he had shown Tanner and me three weeks earlier.

I answered, "We'll see what we can do."

Two weeks later on St. Patrick's Day, I met Joe Burke again in New England. This time I scolded him because we'd heard that Penis Head had expressed suspicions that my company was really an FBI sting. I'd learned from experience that whenever a target raised any doubts about your authenticity, you had to jump down their throats immediately. That's what I did with Joe.

He reiterated that he trusted me and wanted to work together. Then out of the blue, he told me he desperately needed money and was thinking of robbing an armored car.

I said, "Joe, that's a dumb thing to do. You'll end up back in jail."

Then he asked me for $500,000 to invest in a scheme to buy marijuana grow plants. I turned him down.

Next he said, "You might know some rich people who want to get out of a marriage. . . . This . . ." He made a hand gesture indicating firing a handgun. "I'll do this all day long."

"Joe," I warned, "you need to be concerned about going back to jail."

"How they gonna know, if I'm dumping some body in L.A. or Miami? You think I'm gonna leave fingerprints?"

"Are you talking about hurting somebody or just taking their shit?" I asked.

"No, just killing them," he answered. "You might know somebody who wants to get rid of a husband. I'll do that all day long. For a price, all day long. Not a problem."

Once again the hairs on the back of my neck stood up. It was clear that we had a ticking bomb on our hands and we couldn't wait to develop an international terrorism or drug case against him. We had to move quickly to get him off the streets.

That's when we caught a break. Burke's parole officer found out he had traveled to California in violation of the rules of his probation. So for the next several months he was confined to a halfway house in the Cape Cod area.

This gave us time to plan an endgame. I suggested that since

Burke had proposed doing a contract killing, we use that as a way to send him back to prison.

During the month of April, while Burke was at the halfway house, I met several times with Penis Head in New York City and got into some discussions with him about trafficking Oxycontin—a powerful synthetic opiate that had become the scourge of the Northeast. He even provided me with some sample pills for me to sell. So right away we had Penis Head's leverage over Burke should we need it.

My next meeting with Joe Burke was on May 16 on Cape Cod. He picked up where we had left off, bringing up the home invasion and murder-for-hire propositions again.

I said, "I might be interested in pursuing that if you can guarantee that no one will be killed."

"I can't guarantee that," Joe answered. "If there's a problem, someone will have to die."

He was hell-bent on using violence to make money, so we ramped up the investigation. A month later, on June 27, I invited Joe Burke to a fancy social event in the greater Boston area. It was actually completely staged and filled with UCAs. I selected one, who was a good friend I'll call Vincent, to serve as the target. His sole purpose was to piss Joe off.

My UCA buddy played his role perfectly. Within five minutes of meeting Burke, Vincent had insulted two female UCAs in front of him, and soon the two men were on the verge of exchanging blows.

Burke pulled me aside and said, "I'm gonna smash his fucking head in . . . and slap the piss out of him."

That night after I calmed Burke down, he returned to the halfway house. Four days after he was released on July 14, Joe brought up the murder for hire again. He whispered to me at one point, "I'll make it so he's never found."

On September 9, I met with Burke in Boston and told him about problems Vincent was causing me with the Internal Revenue Service, including freezing my business assets. I needed him off of my back and offered to show Burke Vincent's office in New York City. "You do whatever you gotta do," I suggested.

"Yeah," Burke responded.

"Are you going to do this by yourself?" I asked. "Are you going to do it with somebody?"

"Myself."

Burke said he had no qualms about killing him. "I'm gonna shoot him in the head. Fucking gonna shoot him in the fucking derby," he said. "Three in the derby and three in his chest. Don't worry, he ain't getting up."

I said, "Joe, I can't give you a lot up front. I'll scrape something together."

"Yeah."

"I'll pay you and I'll tell you anything you find in his office is yours."

Burke suggested another way to make extra cash. "You just borrow money from him. And then once you get the money from him, we got that, then we got the stickup and he's gone. That's how the wise guys do it. When the guy gets clipped, you ain't gotta pay it back. He's gone."

Ten days later we met in Manhattan so I could show him the location of Vincent's office. Burke brought a girlfriend with him who he said would obtain the murder weapons—a Glock .40 caliber handgun with a silencer and a Škorpion submachine gun Joe said, "The Glock, I'm using on him. All you hear is the hammer being pulled back . . . click, click."

That night Burke met me at my hotel room to discuss money. I told Joe that Vincent typically carried a bag with $100,000 in cash to his office every Friday night. I said, "If he doesn't have the hundred, I'll make up the difference because it's gonna be close." Then I added, "Tell me I'm not gonna go to jail."

"You're never gonna go to jail," Joe assured me. "As long as you don't tell nobody nothing you ain't got nothing to worry about. Never."

I handed him $2,000 as a down payment. Then the two of us went to a nearby theater to catch a midnight showing of the movie *Black Mass* with Johnny Depp playing Whitey Bulger. As the two of us sat side by side munching on popcorn, Joe occasionally leaned into me to tell which parts of the movie were inaccurate based on his association with the Bulger gang.

After the movie and before I took him to Vincent's office, Burke pulled me aside and asked me to procure two African American male masks that were manufactured in Hollywood. As an experienced bank robber, he even knew the store in L.A. where they were sold.

I delivered the masks to him during our last meeting on October 6. "Perfect," he said, after he tried one on with a concealed video camera recording everything.

"You need anything else from me?" I asked at that point.

"Nothing. I already got the piece; I got everything."

As I did before the arrests of the Sinaloa big shots, I reviewed with Burke all the aspects of the crime he was about to commit—time, place, weapons, etc.

He was explicit. "The first shot, I'm gonna hit him here." He pointed to his chest. "When he goes down, he's gonna grab his chest. And I'm gonna walk up to him. I'm gonna stick it in his mouth. I'm gonna say, 'Listen, this is for Mike.' Pop! And the back of his head will be all over the fucking place."

Before he left, I gave him a chance to back out. "A couple of things . . . ," I said. "One, is that I'm not having any second thoughts. And maybe I should."

"Why?" Burke asked. "He's a piece of shit."

"But I'm not. . . . So if you want to walk away, you wanna tell me to walk away, today is the day, because I'm ready."

"Full speed ahead, my man," Burke said.

His goose was cooked. Two days later, I called Burke to book a meeting with him for the following day, Friday, October 9, in Boston—a week before the hit was scheduled to take place. On Friday, I sat in a nearby hotel on standby, while other FBI Agents arrested Burke without incident.

He was charged with using facilities of interstate commerce in the commission of a murder-for-hire plot. Joe Burke offered to cooperate and, believing I was a bad guy, started to tell the FBI about me and my crooked business activities. In August 2016, he pled guilty and was sentenced to ten years in prison and three years of supervised release.

Joe Burke's arrest was headline news in the Boston area. From my perspective, it was just another undercover job done and another dangerous criminal off the streets.

BON VOYAGE

As I write this in July 2017, I'm still a member of the FBI after three one-year extensions beyond the FBI mandatory retirement age of fifty-seven. They must like me, or have just grown used to having me around, or think I have compromising photos of someone, because three one-year extensions are extremely rare. A month from now, I'm finally going to retire, turn in the badge and gun, and move on to the next chapter in my life.

I'll be going kicking and screaming. The truth is, I've loved being an FBI Agent, and especially a UCA. To my mind it's the best, most exciting, and challenging job in the world. I'd continue doing it into my nineties, if I could.

Not long ago, I got a call for a Violent Crimes supervisor asking for a female UCA to pose as an employee of a bank that was being targeted for a takeover. Bank takeovers are one of the most violent crimes we deal with. Heavily armed criminals force their way into a bank and take it over, disarming guards, threatening employees, and sometimes taking customers hostage.

None of the female UCAs available had much violent crime

experience. So as the UC Coordinator, I suggested maybe an older, less nimble male UCA instead.

The supervisor, who knows me well, burst out laughing and said, "I know where you're going with this."

You might think that nearing the age of sixty with a bum knee and other aches and pains, I might want to kick back and recommend someone else. Nope. I was excited to get back into the ring one more time and experience the adrenaline rush I get from going against dangerous criminals, the coordination and camaraderie with SWAT and the guys on the Violent Crimes Squad, and the "go-live" moment when anything can happen.

We had information that two experienced bank robbers were planning to bum-rush a bank employee as he or she arrived at work prior to the opening of the bank. After putting a gun to the employee's head, they planned to force the bank employee to let them in the bank, and then open the vault and safe-deposit boxes.

When I say these guys were experienced, one of the criminals had served twenty-three years in federal prison for *sixteen* bank robberies. These guys knew what they were doing.

We met with the managers of one of the target banks, explained the situation, and they gave us their permission to swap their workers with two FBI UCAs to protect the public. I would play the role of the manager/victim who would be bum-rushed and possibly held hostage. Fun job, right?

We knew that the robbers would be conducting surveillance on the target banks, so we spent days working with the real bank employees, learning codes and procedures and mimicking their behaviors. As the fake manager/target, I had to appear soft. In other words, an older man who wasn't going to put up much resistance.

My age and baldness worked in my favor. And to sell my weakness further, I borrowed a walking cane from the prop department of our local high school theater. It was a crooked masterpiece that looked like it once belonged to Ebenezer Scrooge.

When we moved into position the first day, we knew we were being watched. Like us, the criminals had employed disguises and props, and were pretending to be construction workers complete with a van, hard hats, and reflective vests. They'd set up twenty yards from my designated parking spot on the side of the bank.

The second UCA, a woman I'll call Natasha, entered the lot ahead of me. I drove in five minutes later, butterflies fluttering in my stomach. It was a feeling I was familiar with from twenty-five years of UCOs. It meant: I'm on full alert and ready for anything.

First thing I noticed as I parked was that the two bank robbers were sitting in their van exactly where we had expected them to be. But there was a third guy standing behind a dumpster, wearing a red baseball cap and white latex gloves.

WTF?

Who wears a pair of latex gloves in a bank parking lot before the bank is open? What the hell is this guy up to? Is he with the robbers or operating on his own, and maybe planning to rob the bank before they do?

All these thoughts rushed through my head as I used the Ebenezer Scrooge cane to slowly get out of the car. FBI SWAT wasn't on the scene. Since this was supposed to be a surveillance run, I was more or less on my own. The pistol hidden in the small of my back offered some protection, but hardly enough should all three guys pounce at once.

As I hobbled to the front door with cane in one hand and a brown lunch bag in the other, I glanced at the robbers in the van, and then at the guy with the latex gloves behind the dumpster. I expected them to charge any second.

Fortunately for me, they didn't. We later learned that when the robbers saw my car pull into the lot, one of them remarked, "That's either an employee or a cop." He said that because the car I was driving had tinted windows.

When they saw me get out with the cane, both robbers burst out laughing. Then one of them said, "I guess he ain't no cop."

Natasha and I entered the bank and went through the opening procedures we had learned. The two robbers sat in their van watching our every move. The guy in the latex gloves didn't seem interested. We found out later that he was employed at a nearby cement factory and was taking an unauthorized smoke break.

The next day we repeated the same protocol. This time as I wobbled across the parking lot, the van with the two bank robbers passed within five feet of me. I shot the guy in the passenger seat a neighborly smile. He smirked back.

I remember thinking: *Smirk now, motherfucker. Your time is coming.*

This game of cat and mouse between the robbers and us continued another week during which we observed them purchasing a pellet gun, ski masks, fake beards, and other disguises. They ended up being arrested as they approached another bank in full disguise.

Earlier this year, I completed my final UCO. The subject this time was a knucklehead who had smashed a sleeping roommate in the head with a hammer, twice, and when he didn't die, stabbed him with a knife two more times. He then fled from Massachusetts to Brazil. After securing a UFAP (Unlawful Flight to Avoid Prosecution) warrant, we found him, and during the UCO, lured him out of Brazil into Panama where we could arrest him on an

Interpol warrant and extradite him back to the United States. He now sits in jail awaiting trial.

It was my last FBI arrest. My first took place in 1987. A neat, exciting, and rewarding thirty years!

As I get ready to retire this summer, I can't help looking back at all the fun, anxiety, nervous jitters, exhaustion, laughter, and exultation. Two things stand out: love of my job and my total admiration for certain colleagues. I'm talking about people like my mentors Jarhead, Chris Brady, and WFO (Washington Field Office) Mark D; contemporaries including Mike Sullivan, Stork, BPD Eddie; NDURE brothers Gonzo, Patricio, Ron, Steph, EJ, and Atlanta Mike; and my protégés Tanner and Liquita. All are dedicated civil servants who represent the best our country has to offer and have risked their lives to defend and protect people like you and me. They did so (and some continue to serve) not for the accolades or the money, which isn't going to get anyone rich, but out of duty and pride.

As I write this, Tanner is currently deep undercover on a very dangerous assignment. Liquita, El Viejo's Florida girlfriend, recently completed a UCO in which she played a female drug baron in a Mexican cartel. That UCO, dubbed "Rural Scarface" by the media, resulted in the conviction of fourteen corrupt police officers on the East Coast. The beat goes on.

Certain of my colleagues, especially Brady, taught me how to become a successful UCA by leading by example and correcting me before I made a fatal mistake. I hope I've paid their wisdom and knowledge forward.

Speaking of learning to become a successful UCA, I should point out the process is a whole lot different than it was when I started out. No longer are untrained FBI recruits sent into Italian Mob social clubs and told to "find shit out." In today's FBI, an

Agent must be certified to work undercover and pass three separate phases of training, which include a brutal two-week undercover school from which only about 50 percent of Agents pass.

In Boston, I take it a step further, assigning any newly certified UCA to partner with a more experienced UCA, so they can learn firsthand to operate in that difficult environment without having the pressure and responsibility of being a primary UCA.

I've trained some great new UCAs myself. Upon hearing about my upcoming retirement, one young female Agent I mentored as a UCA wrote the following:

> The FBI is losing its best. You have [been] and continue to be my inspiration to do this job well. Thank you so much for everything you've taught me. You have no idea how often (daily) I refer back to the lessons and insights you provided me.

A senior male Agent said in an email:

> Wilford. . . . [He calls me Wilford because I resemble the TV actor and pitchman Wilford Brimley.] You will always be one of the very few people on this job that I truly respect, admire, and have tried to emulate. One of the greatest things you taught me was not to give a shit what anyone else thinks, if you know what you are doing is the right thing.

Words like that from colleagues I respect mean more to me than any awards. In 2007, my Division selected me as the recipient of their highest award. It was special, because it was given to me by my peers—fellow Agents who worked beside me every day. The SAC who presented it described me as an Agent who "continually goes into the belly of the beast . . . against the worst of the worst."

I stood at the podium and addressed my fellow Agents with

my wife and daughter in the audience, (my oldest son was over-seas with the Marines, and my youngest son was away in college), and said:

> I work in a specialty area within the FBI, which by its very nature is secretive and whose success is recognized by the ability to remain unrecognized as an FBI Agent. I'm not comfortable being recognized. I much prefer to remain a ghost—a shadow hiding in the background.
>
> In closing, I want to acknowledge the only things in my life more important than the FBI: my family. My wife and three children are the ones deserving of an award for putting up with my sorry ass. To my oldest son, proudly serving his country as a second lieutenant in the United States Marine Corps; to my other son away in college and spending every last dime we have ever made and having a helluva time doing it; to my sweet daughter whose first reaction to being invited was a massive shopping spree . . . ; and most of all to my wife . . . from the bottom of my heart, thank you for letting me play cops and robbers for the last twenty-five years, while you took care of everything else, and all the important stuff, you are incredible, thank you!

Finally to the FBI, and all my FBI friends for the opportunity to do what I believe is the greatest job on earth. It's been an honor. Godspeed.

ACKNOWLEDGMENTS

Writing a book, like FBI undercover work, is hard, especially your first time out of the chute. Like novice FBI undercovers, you must rely on seasoned professionals who have been there before to teach and show you the way.

Thanks to the pros at WME, including Eric Lupfer and Mel Berger on the book side, Erin Conroy and Jill Gillett on the TV/film side, and Lisa Reiter at WME's Speakers Bureau. Thank you, Eric, for giving me my first shot, and thank you, Jill, and Erin, for trying to make sense of the entertainment world, a world far stranger and more bizarre than my FBI world.

Thanks to St. Martin's Press Executive Editor Marc Resnick for making this book a reality, and for understanding what I am trying to do and how best to express it. Remember always that I love straight shooters.

Thanks to my coauthor and now good friend, Ralph Pezzullo, for the experienced and sound advice along the way. Your "grain of salt" theory has been my guiding light as I wrestle my way through this interesting journey. If nothing else, I can expect a few chuckles during our frequent phone calls. All the best.

Thanks to Lt. Detective Emmet B. Helrich (Ret. of the Burlington, Vermont, Police Department) for teaching me the right way to be a good cop, and for being a true friend and my blue mentor.

Thanks to Tom Suddath, a brilliant attorney but more importantly, thank you for your years of friendship since the days of improper use of the FBI car's loud speakers. We have been together throughout professional good and bad times, and we always came out a little banged up but no worse for wear. Thank you for the introduction to Michael.

Special thanks to attorney Michael Sherman for whom, without a doubt, none of this would have happened. I cannot thank you enough for your sage guidance, steady hand, and your crystal ball of all things Hollywood. Thank you for your quiet and relentless work ethic on my behalf. Thank you for always putting me in the best position to succeed, even if I didn't recognize it until much later. You are the consummate legal pro, with sharp elbows when needed and the no-nonsense truth when predators are lurking. I am forever in your professional debt.

A huge thank you to the FBI and all FBI Agents, especially street Agents past, present, and future, for letting me play cops and robbers alongside you for thirty-plus years. It was the professional ride of a lifetime, with so many crazy experiences and cases, but most of all, the crazy laughs. I miss it and all of you every day. Be safe. Godspeed.

Lastly, and most importantly, the biggest and most special thank you to my family for putting up with my sorry ass, while I ran around doing all this insane stuff . . . not knowing when I would be home or even where I was. To Rachel, thank you for being there every second of every day of every year. We done good.

To James, Shane, Devon, Sam, and Lainey, thank you for reminding me of what matters most in life. Time for a new mystery ride.

From Ralph: Thank you Mike for granting me the honor of sharing his amazing and inspiring story with the public. The world needs more brave, dedicated people like you, my friend! My great appreciation also goes out to our agents, Eric Lupfer and Mel Berger; Marc Resnick and the talented professionals at St. Martin's Press; and especially my wife, Jessica, and my children—John, Michael, Francesca, and Alessandra—for their love and support.